ARCHAIC MODERNISM

"Few filmmakers challenge us as Pier Palolo Pasolini does. His films contain deep contradictions and Pasolini refuses to resolve them for us. Daniel Humphrey's *Archaic Modernism* grapples with these contradictions to great effect, offering elegant, lucid, and compelling explanations for why Pasolini matters so persistently in his engagements with cinema, politics, sexuality, and history."
—Matthew Tinkcom, professor and director of communication, culture, and technology, Georgetown University

"Pier Paolo Pasolini has often presented a stumbling block for critics and audiences alike, given his controversial film theory, his eccentric formal practices, his troubled relationship to the Italian Left, and his unapologetic homosexuality. In this fascinating and ambitious study, Daniel Humphrey is able to show the necessary—indeed, structural—relationship between those things. Humphrey's analyses of three lesser-studied works of Pasolini pay nuanced attention to the transgressive formal systems of the films, in the process making important contributions to current debates about queer futurity, queer spectatorship, postcolonial filmmaking, and the ethnographic impulse in the art cinema of the 1960s."
—Angelo Restivo, professor of moving image studies in the School of Film, Media & Theatre, Georgia State University

ARCHAIC MODERNISM

Queer Poetics in the Cinema of Pier Paolo Pasolini

Daniel Humphrey

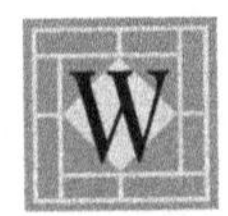

Wayne State University Press
Detroit

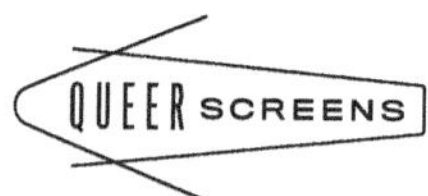

ISBN 978-0-8143-4310-4 (paperback); ISBN 978-0-8143-4606-8 (case); ISBN 978-0-8143-4311-1 (ebook)

Library of Congress Control Number: 2020938184

Wayne State University Press
Leonard N. Simons Building
4809 Woodward Avenue
Detroit, Michigan 48201-1309

Visit us online at wsupress.wayne.edu

CONTENTS

ACKNOWLEDGMENTS

A project as long gestating as this one has a significant honor roll of people who deserve my most sincere appreciation.

I've always been extremely fortunate and, indeed, privileged to work with and around a number of brilliant and generous people. Looking at the names of so many friends and colleagues as I craft this acknowledgments page is a compelling reminder of that. At Texas A&M University (yes, we do queer theory here), I've benefited enormously from my engagements with members of the sadly now defunct Film Studies Working Group and the Queer Studies Working Group that include Kris May, Harriette Andreadis, Caitlin Brenner, Richard Curry, Desirae Embree, Stefanie Harris, Jun Lei, Manuela Marchesini, Rebecca Schloss, and Teresa Vilaros. Other members of our small but passionate Film Studies Program who have shared ideas with me and who have constantly inspired me include Juan A. Alonzo, Robin Means Coleman, Daniel Conway, Lisa Ellis, John Lenihan, Cain Miller, Anne Morey, Michelle Simms, and David McWhirter.

I have also had the joy of being a core faculty member of the Women's and Gender Studies Program at A&M and have shared many invigorating conversations with a number of profoundly intelligent scholars in that community, including Nandini Bhattacharya, Cynthia A. Bouton, Adrienne Carter-Sowell, George Cunningham, Tasha Dubriwny, Marian Eide (who deserves a special shout-out), Melanie Hawthorne, Sonia Hernandez, Joseph O. Jewell, Claire Elise Katz, Chaitanya Lakkimsetti, Teresa Morris, Claudia Nelson, Mary Ann O'Farrell, Kristan Poirot, Rumya Putcha, Srivi Ramasubramanian, Vanita Reddy, Sally Robinson, Jane Sell, Jyotsna Vaid, Nancy Plankey-Videla, Cara Wallis, Cynthia Werner, and, alphabetically last but certainly not least, the passionate, inspiring Joan B. Wolf.

Mindy Bergman, my office-suite neighbor and director of the Interdisciplinary Critical Studies Program (overseeing both Film Studies and Women's and Gender Studies) deserves special thanks for her intellectual, emotional, and practical support. She has been both a beneficent scholar and a friend. Pam Matthews, our Dean of Liberal Arts enthusiastically supported this project and, more importantly, my career;

I am fortunate this book came to fruition during her helm at our college. My good friend Antonio La Pastina in the Department of Communication gave me a copy of Enzo Siciliano's biography of Pasolini not long before I was asked to write this book for the Queer Screens series. I've often felt that his gift represented something of a sign to move ahead *and* to move outside of my comfort zone. Other individuals at A&M quickly came to the rescue when I worked through questions on Ancient Greece, Jacques Derrida, and Leo Bersani. For these and other intellectual engagements I am grateful to Steven M. Oberhelman, Adam R. Rosenthal, and Mikko Tuhkanen (who I believe knows more about Leo Bersani than anybody except, well, Leo Bersani). Other lifesavers include Agostino Buono, Francesco De Dilectis, Samanta Dell'Acqua, Francisco Castro Videla, and Michaela Russo.

A good deal of my theoretical inspiration came about because of my extremely bright queer-theory students who met on a weekly basis. My thanks to Na Young Ahn, David Anderson, Megan Buck, Jed Chalupa, Kyle Colglazier, Jake Donohue, Manuela Jimenez, Gunok Kim, Shelby Landmark, Ryan Rigda, Justin Rogers, Landon Sadler, Peter Scaramuzzo, Dana Sycamor, David Yagüe Gonzalez, Sijin Yan, Mehri Yavari, and Zhuwen Zhang.

Beyond College Station, Texas, a number of wonderful individuals have been instrumental for my thinking and writing about Pasolini, including Joe McElhaney (who is part of the Queer Screens series in which I'm proud to release this monograph); Hamish Ford, Naomi Greene (whose study on Pasolini is critical to my decision to pursue a life of scholarship rather than filmmaking); John David Rhodes, another sharp reader of and elegant writer about Pasolini, raised the stakes on the work completed in this volume. I was also assisted by my favorite contemporary queer artist-scholar, William E. Jones, and the gifted filmmaker Lára Martin.

While studying for and preparing this book, we lost two great scholars and friends who positively influenced my work in many ways: film archivist and curator David Pendleton and scholar/critic Douglas Crimp. Crimp, one of the few Pasolini partisans with whom I studied for my doctoral degree at the University of Rochester, shared endless discussions about the director and his films. His love for Pasolini and, indeed, all things queer are unmatched. I miss him but I am deeply privileged to have enjoyed his friendship and wisdom. I once told Douglas that my Rochester housemates, T'ai Smith and Norman Vorono, and I were thinking of throwing a Pasolini costume party. When I asked him if he would come, he instantly said yes, as "Medea, of course!" The memory of that moment comforts me enormously now that he is gone. I'm only sad that I can't give him a copy of the book now and tell him how much he has always inspired me.

I thank Amy Sloper at the Harvard Film Archive in Cambridge, whose quick turnaround of frame enlargements from their 35mm print of *Il fiore delle mille e una notte* rescued me (and this book) from poor DVD screenshot reproductions of that film. Tiziana Appetito, Sabina Ambrogi, and their colleagues at Archivio Enrico Appetito in Rome similarly provided the necessary cover illustration for this book.

It has been a pleasure to work with the triumphant staff of Wayne State University Press: Editor-in-Chief Annie Martin, Acquisitions Editor Marie Sweetman (who, with great effort, got us the rights to the amazing photograph for the book cover), Editorial, Design, and Production Manager Kristin Harpster, Marketing and Sales Manager Emily Nowak, and Promotions Manager Kristina Stonehill. Andrew Katz, my copyeditor, deserves special thanks for his keen eye and his thorough review of hundreds of Italian names in the filmography and bibliography.

I wish to conclude by thanking four people. My dear friend Mark Terry, has gotten me through more tough spots than I think he knows, and Raul F. Medina, whose love of Pasolini, right here in the heart of Texas, sustained me from my very first months upon my arrival at A&M. Just when I thought nobody within a hundred miles would be interested in watching any of these films with me socially, Raul enthusiastically participated in my cinephiliac adventures. Steven Gurr brilliant proofreader, writing guru, and author, is also my oldest, closest friend who continually improves my taste in, well, just about everything. Finally, and when I had my own doubts, David A. Gerstner, the editor of the Queer Screens series, believed in my scholarly abilities to tackle a project on this most complex figure in queer and film cultures. His support for my work nourished this project from its beginnings to these final notes.

Roger Palomino's love and devotion not only kept this book on track but guided me during several turbulent years. I simply cannot thank him enough. It is to him I dedicate this book.

INTRODUCTION
Archaic Modernism

In journal entries that Pier Paolo Pasolini wrote as he was making *Uccellacci e uccellini* (*The Hawks and the Sparrows*, 1966), and eventually published with that film's screenplay, the director discusses the development of his cinematic style. As he puts it, the aesthetic style on his first feature was, essentially, a simple, "per la strada" (on the street) form of no-frills realism.[1] He explained that, "con *Accattone* (1961), inesperto di cinema, io avevo semplificato al massimo tale oggettiva semplicità" (with *Accattone*, inexperienced as I was in cinema, I had simplified to the maximum this objective simplicity; 44). In other words, for that painfully bleak film about a violent, brutish character, Pasolini aspired, cinematically, to little more than recording the re-creation of reality that his actors were performing. The outcome, however, was unexpected: "Il risultato mi pareve essere—e in parte, lo era—quello della sacralità: una *sacralità tecnica* che poi investiva nel profondo paesaggi e personaggi" (The result seemed to me to be—and in part it was—sacredness: a *technical sacredness* that would then wash over landscapes and characters alike; 44, emphasis in original). Thus, through an expressed humility and naked simplicity, Pasolini realized that he made a profane world seem sacred. A couple of years later, however, when he brought the same approach to *Il vangelo secondo Matteo* (*The Gospel According to St. Matthew*, 1964), he felt that the simple style and the sacred text canceled each other out: the images became, in Pasolini's terms, "pura enfasi: una riproduzione" (pure emphasis: a replica; 46). Therefore, days into the production period, Pasolini decided to adopt the opposite approach. He began filming with both an extremely long telephoto lens (300 mm) and a short, wide-angle lens (25 mm), each of which noticeably distorted the image but in very different, even contrasting, ways. However, by now betraying the sense of realism with which he began his filmmaking career, Pasolini was led, once again, remarkably enough, to sacredness (46–47).

Reading these notes, Pasolini's spectators might well be surprised to encounter a filmmaker who quickly came to understand how focal lengths and, by extension, other formalistic cinematic features function in complex and oftentimes counterintuitive ways. Regarding his change in strategy on *Il vangelo*, for example, the director references that film's scene in Gethsemane, expressing regret at the relatively subtle stylistic mismatches that most viewers would overlook: "Che poi ho potuto solo in parte rigirare e che quindi porta indelebile il segno di quel mio primo errore: quando ora, quella scena passa sullo schermo—per quanto corretta e accomodata in montaggio—me ne vergogno selvaggiamente" (I could only partially reshoot it later, and now it carries the indelible sign of my error: when that scene comes up on the screen, albeit adjusted and patched up in editing, I am wildly ashamed of it; "Confessioni tecniche," 46). As someone who would regularly be accused of sloppy, even careless filmmaking by the mainstream critical, if not academic, establishment (as we shall see through a sampling of popular reviews later in this study), Pasolini indicates here that he was anything but thoughtless or ignorant in his aesthetic choices. Ultimately, in retrospect, Pasolini saw that the "[cross] contamination between [his] point of view and that of an ideal believer" in *Il vangelo* resulted in a "magmatica" (literally "magmatic" but figuratively "chaotic" or "jumbled") technique that was, essentially, an example of what the filmmaker-theorist would soon define as a cinema of poetry (52).

In a conference presentation a year after *Il vangelo*'s release, Pasolini offered his controversial but ultimately celebrated paper on a "cinema of poetry." In the decades after its much-derided presentation at the inaugural Mostra Internazionale del Nuovo Cinema in Pesaro, Italy, the essay gained wide circulation under the title "The 'Cinema of Poetry.'" Initially presented under the title "La mimesi dello sguardo" (The mimesis of the glance),[2] it has indeed become a central, if somewhat ill-fitting, text within the canon of film theory. And film scholars, taking their cues from Pasolini's protean interests, have negotiated many different critical pathways in their reading of the essay's multivalent theoretical turns. Indeed, Pasolini's numerous sequels and appendices to his initial essay, most of which are collected in a celebrated anthology of his work, *Heretical Empiricism*, created further divergent, critical engagement.

Hence, "The 'Cinema of Poetry'" has been discussed in terms of feminism and psychoanalysis, auteurism, the art-cinema genre or "mode of production," and, not unexpectedly, the field that was first so scandalized by its presentation, semiotics. In 2014, two substantial monographs appeared that adopted its title into their own—Joseph Luzzi's *A Cinema of Poetry: Aesthetics of the Italian Art Film* and P. Adams Sitney's *The Cinema of Poetry*. Both writers engage with the filmmaker's famously messy (in Pasolini's own words, his "extravagantly interdisciplinary") intervention in the world of critical theory to address a broad range of European and American films, from those of Roberto Rossellini and Ingmar Bergman to those of Stan Brakhage and Gregory J. Markopoulos.[3] Both studies are essential reading for the Pasolini scholar. Among other things, this book aims to employ "The 'Cinema of Poetry'" in the service of illuminating Pasolini's own filmmaking. In that regard, I have found myself face-to-face with the profound queerness of a filmmaking enterprise that predictably emerged out of that most personal practice of narrative feature filmmaking: crafting cinema poetically.

"The 'Cinema of Poetry'" and Pasolini's subsequent essays on the topic have not been employed as much as one might expect in the service of illuminating the director's own filmmaking, certainly not in book-length studies that use the essay as its starting point.[4] Among other things, my book means to do precisely that. In doing so, I will argue that Pasolini's cinematic style, one that operates according to the insights laid out in the filmmaker-theorist's writings, is, in the final analysis, a thoroughly queer style—in some ways queerer than commonplace understandings of the word might be able to suggest. That queer style is, put simply, archaic modernism.

Archaic Forms/Destructive Modernism: Pasolini's Bitter Poetry

Following Pasolini's aesthetic breakthrough during the production of *Il vangelo secondo Matteo*, the filmmaker found himself shifting more or less permanently from the "cinema of prose" to the "cinema of poetry." The first feature film project he created under these new theoretical auspices was *Uccellacci e uccellini*. Pasolini ultimately completed this aesthetic turn, however, for a vastly different set of reasons than he originally intended, reasons that cast a particular, often overlooked, illumination on his concept of a cinema of poetry. When he initially conceived of *Uccellacci e uccellini*, a Marxist parable of life in Italy in the aftermath of the death of Palmiro Togliatti, Pasolini held the silent comedy of Buster Keaton and Charles Chaplin foremost in his mind. With it, he wanted it to express "things and men through the cheerful and carefree eyes of forgiveness" after the passing of the beloved Italian Communist leader.[5] As he was shooting, however, a deep sense of melancholy and bitterness arose, and a "cinema of poetry" as it finally manifested itself in this film became the ideal form through which Pasolini could express his "atrocious bitterness" (atroce amarezza; "Confessioni tecniche," 51–53). This bitter poetry would reach its apotheosis in the majority of Pasolini's subsequent feature films. These films balance, troublingly and vitally, the archaic and the modern while manifesting the malleable ways Pasolini approached the "cinema of poetry."

Virtually all Pasolini's films are, in Ian Aitken's simple and elegant summary, "centrally concerned with the opposition between archaic forms of consciousness and the destructive impact of modernity."[6] This formulation could serve as an epigraph for any number of rich studies on the writer-director, and while Aitken's thesis might be true of some Pasolini films more than others, it seems fair to say that the opposition, juxtaposition, or, really, *collision* of the archaic with the modern is not merely fundamental to our understanding of the life and work of Italy's most complex queer filmmaker;[7] the collision, as such, is also essential to the appeal that Pasolini and his work have for us in the first place—certainly for those of us who consider ourselves queer spectators. Pasolini's popularity within the international art-film circuits of his time resulted, at least in significant part, from a sense of his work's unsteady balance between the rudimentary and the sophisticated, the bluntly primitive and the sharply cutting-edge. If Aitken draws us toward a consideration of both the "archaic *forms* of consciousness" in Pasolini's films and the "destructive *impact* of modernity" envisioned within them, I want to focus on the filmmaker and his films not simply as *formed by* a sense of the archaic and *critical of* the era of modernity but as a disfigured imbrication of both. This, of course, requires accounting for both the self-destructive qualities and effects inherent in modernity and its unstable impact on Pasolini's archaic spirit.

In this study, I use "archaic" in two different ways, firstly as it generally defines a culture's, or, as many psychoanalysts would argue, even an individual's, earliest phase. For instance, one can speak of the period from approximately 8000 to 2000 BCE as Archaic Mesoamerica, just as a one could mention a subject's pre-Oedipal sexuality as archaic. Secondly, and more often, I employ the word the way it has been regularly used to reference the emergence of Western culture in Greece between, roughly, 700 and 480 BCE.[8] In both the wide and the narrow sense, the word is well suited to define a core component of Pasolini's late-1960s work. With regard to the broader definition of "archaic," Pasolini's films can, of course, often be read as exploring the beginnings of a society: Christianity, literally, in *Il vangelo secondo Matteo* and, metaphorically, in *Teorema* (*Theorem*, 1968); Renaissance Europe in the "archaic" half of *Porcile* (*Pigsty/Pigpen*, 1969); Renaissance Italy in *Il Decameron* (*The Decameron*, 1971); and Renaissance England in *I racconti di Canterbury* (*The Canterbury Tales*, 1972).[9]

With regard to the second, more specific definition, Archaic Greece began with the rise of tyrannical rule in the seventh century BCE and ended, following "an age of continuing social, economic, and political upheaval," with the "cataclysmic" Persian War of the early fifth century BCE. As Brian M. Lavelle summarizes, although the Greeks managed ultimately to expel the Persians from their homeland, by the time they did, "much of mainland Greece was destroyed . . . , including Athens. The invaders respected neither man nor god during their invasion, razing temples as readily as houses, stealing what they could, destroying what they could not steal."[10] None of the texts Pasolini chose to adapt actually date from the Greek Archaic Era. Indeed, the oldest of Pasolini's source materials, Aeschylus's *Oresteia*, comes from Greece's, more recent, Classical Era. On the other hand, the legends on which those tragedies were based come from long before Greece's Archaic period, essentially from the prehistory of Greece. All told, the Archaic Era—which did manage to vividly convey the myths of Orestes, Jason and Medea, and Oedipus from Greece's Dark Age to the Classical period, when they would be captured for the ages by Aeschylus, Sophocles, and Euripides—serves as a crucial metaphor for Pasolini. It is the beginning that contains both the promises of an ultimately betrayed civilization and the seeds of its eventual end.

Pasolini's adaptations of classical Greek tragedy utilize many of the same narrative choices, as well as, in some cases, the precise wording (translated into Italian) of the originals. Nevertheless, they beckon back to an earlier era even than that in which they were produced, not just in their precise historical settings (of course, even in the fifth century BCE, these were presented as stories of the mythic past) but in the seemingly primitive ways in which Pasolini chooses to adapt them. Much later, as the nineteenth century transitioned into the twentieth, early-modern artists incorporated tribal and prehistoric art forms from Africa, the South Pacific, and even Europe into their work. Indeed, few art historians would argue with Sieglinde Lemke's claim that "there is no modernism without primitivism."[11] And yet, while this tendency within modernism waned before Pasolini's birth, the central place of so-called primitive art in modernism's own beginnings (its own archaic phase) bespeaks a fundamental connection between the West's formative stage and, for Pasolini, its final stage. One of Pasolini's vital insights during this period of his career, just as modernism was prematurely giving way to the cultural decimations of postmodernism, was that one can only fully grapple with the end of an era by maintaining a sharp concentration on how that era began.[12]

But if, in a dialectical move, Pasolini embraced the archaic as a way to chart the end of his civilization, he did so within the broad tradition of modernism, a form he clearly associated with disastrous culmination, if not the apocalyptic. This is made apparent by the artwork on the walls of the villa in *Salò o le 120 giornate di Sodoma* (*Salò, or the 120 Days of Sodom*, 1975) and, perhaps somewhat more subtly, by the images of Francis Bacon seen as the bourgeois son, Pietro (Andrés José Cruz Soublette), and Terence Stamp's mysterious visitor thumb through an art book before disaster strikes in *Teorema*. Pasolini was hardly alone in thinking of modernism as a sign of end times. The art critic Clement Greenberg, while stressing modernism's continuation of previous artistic traditions, allowed that it "may mean a devolution, an unravelling."[13] Less pessimistically, modernism simply signaled the era in which it was born, one characterized by rapid industrialization and urbanization, as well as fin-de-siècle anxiety. The modernism of Pasolini's cinema is consistent with that of postwar art cinema generally as described by David Bordwell: "Stylistic devices . . . gain prominence with respect to

classical norms—an unusual angle, a stressed bit of cutting, a striking camera movement, an unrealistic shift in lighting or setting, a disjunction on the sound track, or
any other breakdown of objective realism which is not motivated as subjectivity. . . .
There may be little or no exposition of prior fabula events, and even what is occurring
at the moment may require subsequent rethinking. . . . Odd ("arty") camera angles
or camera movements independent of the action can register the presence of self-
conscious narration."[14] Of course, the last of these all but defines Pasolini's project of
a cinema of poetry, as we shall discover.

Together, archaic energies and modern concerns, as well as archaic concerns and
modernist energies, circulate within Pasolini's oeuvre—certainly that part of it created
in the mid- to late 1960s and early 1970s. They constitute its world-shattering power.
Like queerness itself—historically perceived to be both animalistic *and* unnatural,
antisocial *and* decadent—I consider *archaic modernism* a compelling and, in some necessary ways, destructive paradox. In Pasolini's cinema, a celebration of a sexual desire
uncorrupted by capitalism (if one often violent, murderous, and beholden to the death
drive) coexists with a hyperintellectualized political and social perspective that seems
both self-serving and, troublingly enough, ethical. The films' desire to brutally abolish
meaning and the civilized legacies of consciousness never quite outruns their urge to
attenuate this brutality through recourse to exceedingly *civilized*, with all the problematic baggage that term implies, mediations on the discursive. This contradictory
state, I argue, is key to the films' sense of queer contestation and its ultimate power as
a manifestation of deep, if ambivalent, negativity.

In a Word, Queer

Debates over the word "queer," particularly as it functions according to what Michel
Foucault calls a "reverse discourse," have been legion since the early 1990s.[15] In a very
short period of time, this new discourse developed through the emergence of the word
in the name of the activist group Queer Nation, the practice of queer theory, and
the New Queer Cinema.[16] Nearly thirty years later, however, the erstwhile buzzword
seems almost antiquated, a once-trendy signifier from a both romanticized and, at
least for some people, nearly forgotten era of radical social commitment and sexualized
contestation. Since it is, however, the antiquated to which I am drawn in my study
of Pasolini's queer style, the "archaic," paradoxically, promises to introduce fresh turns
on "queer."

In arguing for the continued political relevance of "queer," a reexamination of its
etymology, tracing it in reverse chronological order, is in order. As a colloquial adjective marking a person who engages in same-sex sexual activities (e.g., "he's queer"), the

word dates back to at least 1914. Near the end of the nineteenth century, a full twenty years prior to that, it had emerged as a noun denoting the same (e.g., "he's *a* queer"). The word, of course, had hardly been newly coined then, either; rather, it came to define that which was previously described as the "sodomite" in a metonymical relationship to earlier, broader definitions of the term. In 1846, "queer" first appeared as a verb meaning "to interfere with or spoil the business of a street vendor or performer; (later more generally) to interfere with or spoil the business in hand; similarly, to queer a person's pitch." Continuing to move backward through time, one finds the word used as a verb meaning "to cause (a person) to feel queer; to disconcert, perturb, unsettle" (1845), to "put out of order, to spoil" (1818), to "puzzle, flummox, confound, baffle" (sometime after 1781), as an adjective synonymous with one who is "out of sorts; unwell; faint, giddy" (1749), an adjective meaning "bad; contemptible, worthless; untrustworthy; disreputable" (1564), and, in its earliest adjectival form, as marking the "strange, odd, peculiar, eccentric. Also: of questionable character; suspicious, dubious" (approx. 1513). Finally, in its earliest known appearance in English, in 1390, it emerged to mean "to ask, inquire; to question." To trace it back further, the *Oxford English Dictionary Online* points the reader to French (*quere*) and Latin (*quaerere*).

So many of these usages have applicability to what, almost exactly six hundred years after the word's introduction into English, would be defined as queer theory.[17] What I wish to point to here are the ways in which asking, inquiring, and questioning—certainly not the exclusive prevue of *queer* theorists—in this specific discourse continue to carry the promise, or the *threat*, of odd, peculiar, eccentric understandings, understandings that make one feel out of sorts, unwell, faint, and giddy.[18] If, as the eighteenth century transitioned into the nineteenth, the practice of inquiring, or, perhaps, ultimately in*queer*ing, served to puzzle, flummox, confound, baffle, and spoil dominant/dominating understandings of cultural ideology, by the twenty-first century queer theory emerged as a deconstructive, abolitionist challenge to the constructs of phallogocentrism, heteronormativity, and, finally, homonormativity. At the same time, the very concept wrestles with its place in the hypercommodification of creative and academic institutions that shaped the contours of twentieth-century capitalism. In short, queer itself is nothing less than archaic modernism *tout court*. Pasolini was all too aware of this kind of theoretical-political impasse in his own time. Thus, one might well conclude that his work is more valuable at this stage in the evolution of queer theory than ever before.[19] To come to terms with the paradoxical and queer nature of Pasolini's work, therefore, we must begin with a survey of the filmmaker's specific ideas that are informed by—aesthetically, theoretically, ideologically—the violent thrusts of modernity.

Reality Contaminated

In order to understand what Pasolini meant by a cinema of poetry, or, as I contend, his formulation of a *queer cinematic style*, one must attend to what is *left out of*, or rather *repressed* in, what Pasolini poses as the *opposite* of the cinema of poetry, the *cinema of prose*. What is left out of the cinema of (*straight*forward) *narrative* prose—exemplified by both classical Hollywood cinema and tradition-of-quality art cinema—is, according to Pasolini, "the fundamentally irrational nature of cinema . . . , all its irrational, oneiric elementary and barbaric elements [which have been] forced below the level of consciousness."[20] A cinema of poetry, which Pasolini defines as a post–World War II phenomenon, must therefore avoid any false promise of documentary objectivity in two simultaneous and interlocking ways. First, the cinema of poetry is characterized by what Pasolini refers to as the "free indirect point-of-view shot." Second, it is "completely and freely expressive" of something personal to the filmmaker him- or herself ("Cinema of Poetry," 182).

Pasolini's employment of the former, free indirect point-of-view shots, derives from the literary concept of "free indirect" discourse, in which an author drifts into the mind of his or her character to the point that the author's words and the character's words converge. In applying "free indirect" discourse to the cinema, Pasolini argues that this idea is, "simply, the immersion of the filmmaker in the mind of his character and then the adoption on the part of the filmmaker not only of the psychology of his character but also his language" ("Cinema of Poetry," 175).

Regarding the consideration of a cinematic style "completely and freely expressive" of the filmmaker's perspective, it can be said, although Pasolini never quite says it, to combine with free indirect discourse through actual or virtual point-of-view shots. This conveys a relationship between text and subject, filmmaker and character, that is a sign of both love and betrayal. In a cinema of poetry, we sense a love of, or at least an empathy for, human subjects by a filmmaker who is acknowledging his or her irreconcilably *attenuated place* in relation to those subjects while still attempting to *speak for* the subjects. This is accomplished primarily, though not exclusively, through, in Pasolini's example, "that phenomenon that is normally and banally defined by persons in the business as 'allowing the camera to be felt'" ("Cinema of Poetry," 183). And if this poetic relationship constitutes a betrayal, one in which the selfhood of the auteur cannot help but emerge as eclipsing her or his subject, it is, arguably, an *ethical* betrayal in that it serves as testament that the filmmaker recognizes and takes responsibility for his or her own intertwined and self-destructive relationship to the subject.

It is revealing that two primary examples Pasolini rehearses in his description of the cinema of poetry involve male filmmakers who cross the gender divide in order to situate themselves within the subjectivities of "neurotic" female characters. The first is Giuliana (Monica Vitti), the "neurotic protagonist" portrayed in Michelangelo Antonioni's *Il deserto rosso* (*Red Desert*, 1964); the second is Gina (Adriana Asti), the protagonist's "young neurotic aunt" in Bernardo Bertolucci's *Prima della rivoluzione* (*Before the Revolution*, 1964) ("Cinema of Poetry," 179–80). Regarding the cinema of Antonioni, Pasolini posits that that filmmaker's earlier work had simply super-imposed the director's own "formalistic vision" onto the "content" of the film (content that inevitably dealt with, as Pasolini put it, "the problem of neuroses caused by alienation"; 179). With *Il deserto rosso*, however, Antonioni "looks at the world by immersing himself in his neurotic protagonist, reanimating the facts through his eyes," yielding "a wholesale substitution which is justified by the possible analogy of the two views" (179–80).

While one may anticipate the objections of post-1968 feminist film critics who, not unreasonably, critique male auteurs for ventriloquizing their male subjectivity through female characters, Pasolini posits something altogether more complex, some-thing queer in the way this speaking-through-the-other questions the then taken-for-granted nature of essentialized subjectivity: "It is clear that the [use of the] 'free indirect point-of-view shot' [in *Il deserto rosso*] is a pretext, and Antonioni took advantage of it, possibly arbitrarily, to allow himself the greatest poetic freedom, a freedom which approaches—and for this it is intoxicating—the arbitrary" ("Cinema of Poetry," 180).

One could offer an entire study arguing for the ultimately queer appeal of the "arbi-trary" status of gender through a reading of Antonioni's earlier trilogy (*L'avventura* [*The Adventure*, 1960], *La notte* [*The Night*, 1961], *L'eclisse* [*The Eclipse*, 1962]) along with *Il deserto rosso*, as these four films are unique in their stylistic commingling of female and male subjectivity. More significant for our queer understanding of the cinema of poetry, however, is Pasolini's reading of the cinema of Bernardo Bertolucci. Bertolucci's cinema, in many ways, will prove far queerer than Antonioni's. Consider the deeply ambivalent but trenchant and florid critique of homosexual repression in *Il conformista* (*The Conformist*, 1970), the all-but-consummated homoerotic bond between Olmo (Gérard Depardieu) and Alfredo (Robert De Niro) in *Novecento* (*1900*, 1976), the unsettling, and autobiographical, queer coming of age in *La luna* (*Luna*, 1979). To be sure, as Pasolini presents it, "while in Antonioni we find the wholesale substitution of the filmmaker's vision of feverish formalism for the view of the neurotic woman, in Bertolucci such a wholesale substitution has not taken place. Rather, we have a mutual contamination of the worldviews of the neurotic woman and of the author. These views, being inevitably similar, are not readily distinguishable—they shade into each other; they require the same style" ("Cinema of Poetry," 180).[21]

In *Allegories of Contamination*, Patrick Rumble offers an insightful and fecund reading of Pasolini's work focusing on the processes and effects we might glean from a style of formal and aesthetic concerns that reflects larger dynamics of transcultural and transhistorical contaminations. These are precisely the critical signposts Pasolini references in regard to Bertolucci. Rightly seeing this narrower process of contamination as a core component to Pasolini's aesthetic theory, Rumble argues that the "pluralization of perspective" encouraged by the filmmaker-theorist is connected to "the cinema of poetry['s] attempts to release its spectators from the confinement of the rational structures they inhabit."[22] This point will bear heavily on Pasolini's relationship to the spectator in the films studied here. In the context of 1960s academic debates about the cinema in which revolutionary ideas were prominent, Pasolini's attempts to transcend rational structures were nonetheless seen as reactionary, and indeed, they essentially were—thus the protestations of his progressive colleagues. Pasolini's thinking on the rational betrayed the newly formed, often dazzlingly radical theories of semiotics that raised the stakes on the mimetic in structural terms. In doing so, semiotics "collaps[ed]," as Giuliana Bruno puts it, "the notion of reality onto cinema and reintroduce[ed] a neo-Bazinian reverence for reality."[23]

Those who occupied center stage as advocates for scientifically grounded theories dedicated to cinema semiotics and were, to put it mildly, displeased with Pasolini's treatises included Stephen Heath, Umberto Eco, and Christian Metz. For Heath, Pasolini's intervention "could only lead to the denial of cinema as semiotic system."[24] For Eco, who seemed even more incensed, Pasolini's theories contradicted "the most elementary principles of semiology which hold that facts of nature become cultural phenomena, and do not reduce cultural facts to natural phenomena."[25] Metz, who pursued a more sympathetic and respectful engagement with Pasolini's ideas, nevertheless considered his central concept of a "codified, or at least codifiable, language" of images to be "dubious, burdensome" and his entire approach to semiotics to be, in a largely negative sense, "hypothetical and adventurous."[26]

Although Pasolini's reconfiguration of the concept of reality was central to the debates around the filmmaker-theorist's larger arguments in the 1960s and 1970s, that discussion is not the only important aspect to consider when grappling with his theories of a cinema of poetry and is not central to this study.[27] If Pasolini found himself in the crosshairs of the strongly asserted and championed concepts of semiotics held by highly regarded men, it is an Anglophone feminist to whom we must turn to disrupt the purportedly rational arguments hoisted on Pasolini's work.

Toward a Deconstructively Queer Spectator

A year after the appearance of "The 'Cinema of Poetry,'" Pasolini made yet another scandalous claim in his follow-up essay. In "The Written Language of Reality" (1966), Pasolini asserted that *reality is, in the final analysis, nothing more than cinema in nature*."[28] In the context of that historical moment, in which claims for the realism of the sign held court, Pasolini seems to have deliberately worded his assertion to engender maximum outrage. Indeed, it did just that. But the assertion is hardly mere provocation. As Teresa de Lauretis explains, Pasolini pointed out, among other things, that words on a page already hasten the realization that language—written and spoken—is nothing more than a construct, an attempt to express meaning. In other words, language is not simply a natural emanation of an essentialized consciousness. Likewise, the cinema, certainly a modernist, poetic cinema, similarly reveals itself as a text, performing an equally fundamental intervention in reality. In fact, the cinema does something more: it encourages us to recognize reality's previously unnoticed *readability*—readability in the most profound and precise sense of the term. Because cinema serves "as the recorded, stored, 'written' moment of a 'natural and total language, which is our action in the real,'" we are finally witness to "written language *instituted* [as] *a cultural consciousness of thought as representation*."[29] In other words, cinema performs as the unconscious.[30]

In Pasolini's dense, difficult 1966 essay, therefore, he struggles to demonstrate that the cinema registers the world of thought and action as operating according to a functional grammar and that this is most effectively analyzed according to the tools and terminology of semiology. His argument in this regard may not seem as politically urgent as it did in the mid-1960s. But in the essay's concluding remarks, Pasolini offers observations that have not received the attention they deserve. Retrospectively, these thoughts cast a strong and sharp light on ideology and the audiovisual and are as much of a concern to us today as they were fifty years ago: "Audiovisual techniques are in large measure already a part of our world, that is, of the world of technical neocapitalism, which moves ahead, and whose tendency it is to deprive its techniques of ideology or to make them ontological; to make them silent and unrelated; to make them habits; to make them religious forms. We . . . must therefore fight to demystify the 'innocence of technique' to the last drop of blood."[31]

Keeping in mind, then, that both reality-as-language and "thought as representation" are indeed the linguistic reality or thought-representations enabled by neocapitalist ideology, the ultimate question for New Left filmmakers of the 1960s and early 1970s remains crucially prescient: To what extent can cinematic "technique" reposition, even "disconcert, perturb, unsettle" the situated spectator in relationship to neocapitalism?

The goal of this study is, therefore, to show how Pasolini's cinematic technique—*his thinking cinematically*—elucidates a deep negativity that informs a "positive" cinema, or that which is understood as the sign of the real.

Crumbling Violent Hierarchies

When considering the juxtaposed sets at the core of Pasolini's argument—speaking/writing and reality/cinema—it is useful to draw on what Jacques Derrida has called "violent hierarchies." Reflecting on the first of these (speaking/writing), Derrida's most provocative, and central, insight comes to mind: "The priority," in the Greek and European philosophical traditions, "of spoken language over written or silent language stems from the fact that when words are spoken the speaker and the listener are supposed to be simultaneously present to one another; they are supposed to be the same, pure unmediated presence. . . . Writing, on the other hand, is considered subversive in so far as it creates a spatial and temporal distance between the author and the audience; writing presupposes the absence of the author and so we can never be sure exactly what is meant by a written text; it can have many different meanings as opposed to a single unifying one."[32]

Although Derrida's and Pasolini's writings coincide, I have found no evidence that either engaged with the other's work. Yet the paradigms under which both drew their theoretical concepts cross-pollinated the volumes of material they read and reflected. It is not irrelevant, then, to consider Pasolini's conception of cinema in relation to Derrida's claims that "language is a possibility founded on the general possibility of writing," particularly considering that, according to Derrida also, cinematography (along with "choreography, but also pictorial, musical, and sculptural" inscription) represents a form of *écriture*, that which "gives rise to inscription in general, whether it is literal or not and even if what it distributes in space is alien to the order of the voice."[33] Given that both writing and cinema are engaged in the complexities of language—broadly speaking—and given that both concern themselves with violent hierarchies that drive the impulses of language, Derridean *écriture* serves well the filmmaker's critique of "originary" language that purportedly defines a cinematic real.[34]

Furthermore, if we interrogate another Derridean concept, *phonocentrism* (Derrida's term for the West's privileging of speech over the written word) and develop it through Lee Edelman's conceptualization of sexuality and language, or more specifically male homosexuality and inscription, we discover a particular form of *queer écriture* that is specific to Pasolini's cinema. Hence, in forging the understandings of Derrida, Edelman, and de Lauretis, I argue that Pasolini's cinematic form challenges the grounds on which heteronormative neocapitalism *writes* (in all senses of the term) itself into culture and that Pasolini's cinema disrupts claims that ideology as such is natural. Pasolini's "writerly" cinematic technique is a practice that holds the promise to undermine these ideological structures with the very tools used to create them.

Écriturexuality

Rather than concentrating on the overrehearsed theories of Michel Foucault to "examine social regulation and ideological power, " Edelman's *Homographesis* instead employs the "rhetorically based textual practices of Jacques Derrida and Paul de Man."[35] By drawing on Edelman's use of Derridean *écriture* as an avenue to unite queer theory and cinema studies, I intend to expand this interdisciplinary project through Pasolini's heretical semiotics and film theories so as to offer a perverse challenge to the heteronormative bases that undergird neocapitalist ideology. Approached in this way, Pasolini's filmmaking-as-writing reveals itself to be "queer theory" *avant la lettre* and on the screen. His critique of capitalism and its attendant aesthetic forms of realism do not remain invested in a vulgar Marxism beholden to class and imperialism. Rather, Pasolini's concerns with class and imperialism overlap with concerns about what we can call heteroreproducibility. For Pasolini, representations that reaffirm ideals supporting class structures and imperialism can most effectively be dismantled through perverse homosexuality and its manifold challenges to the logics of capitalist ideology. It is in this regard that Edelman's understanding of Derrida illuminates my reading of Pasolini's cinema.

As an example of *écriture*, male homosexuality has been employed as a sign. First, as Edelman has argued, gay-male sexuality manifests itself as a perverse sexuality; it is seen, second, as the negative that proves heterosexuality as such; and, third, it is the sign of sexuality *as a whole*. In short, establishing its part within sexuality as a whole, homosexuality confirms the ideology of heteronormativity. "Gay male sexuality," according to Edelman, "will be seen to occupy a position much like that of 'writing' in the Western philosophical tradition—a tradition that enshrines, as Derrida has argued, a metaphysics of presence bespeaking its phonocentric orientation. Like writing, gay male sexuality comes to occupy the place of the material prop, the excessive element of representation: *the superfluous and arbitrary thing* that must be ignored, repressed, or violently disavowed in order to represent representation itself as natural and unmediated."[36] For Edelman, then, the sign as such is critical to homosexuality's dangerously subversive power precisely insofar as the place it occupies serves as the negative in a binary sign system. Queer negation, represented by the homosexual, is nothing less than the guarantee of meaning that portends the collapse of the veracity of the sign as such.

In effect, Edelman's turn to *écriture* identifies the homosexual body as a text. In marking the homosexual less as a categorized body (à la Foucault) and more as an unsettling site of writing, Edelman calls "attention to the formation of a category of homosexual person whose very condition of possibility is his relation to writing or textuality, his articulation, in particular, of a 'sexual' difference internal to male identity that generates the necessity of *reading certain bodies* as visibly homosexual."[37] Significantly, homographesis suggests that *to write* is *to activate* queer bodies and desire. Pasolini, for his part, pushes things further than what Edelman describes. Again and again, in his cinema, the bodies of the male characters and the actors who play them are inscribed as queer—Ettore (in *Mamma Roma* [1962]), Jesus, Oedipus, Jason, Orestes—precisely through Pasolini's cinematic *écriture*.[38] But if Edelman's queer negation makes heterocentric ideology uneasy, Pasolini's queer cinematic *écriture* brings all sexual desire to the point of failure precisely because, in his films, male sexual desire finds itself at a loss; not ensconced in historically situated heterosexual or homosexual terms, male sexuality disintegrates as do the ideological terms for its very existence.

Difference and desire, and finally a different sort of desire, are written onto the bodies of the individuals on Pasolini's screen. Unavoidably, they are presented in troubling ways, through representations that have occasioned charges of racial objectification and gendered essentialism and, in his "Third World" projects, Orientalism.[39] And yet Pasolini's queer *écriture* also deconstructs both the difference and the *discursive construction of* those ideological subjects of myth and history along with those objects of desire that appear before the camera's gaze. For instance, Oedipus is both the active ur-heterosexual hero and the passive sign of queer desire in Pasolini's adaptation; so, too, are his Jason and Orestes. If sexual desire is revealed as ideologically and historically contained in Pasolini's cinema, Western colonialism is ultimately unveiled as the most violent and disconcerting aspect of history. Yet, presented through the terms of a cinema of poetry, Pasolini's camera lens, when foisted onto the colonized Other, in effect demands Western viewers confront their own complicity in this history of violence. This mode of autocritique in Pasolini's cinema might well be called *queer Orientalism*.

Furthermore, Pasolini's cinema has one of the strongest senses of an epic worldview in film history while palpably constraining itself within the primitive limitations of what often seems to be a handmade or amateur cinema. This engagement with commonly understood reality, written on two very different fronts, offers a strategic resistance to the "regulatory" representation of reality by queerly reinscribing it. In other words, Pasolini's written reality is palpable despite, or really *because of*, strategies that highlight the differently constructed nature of the historical world and material culture. Examples include his films' detailed and nuanced re-creations of classical paintings juxtaposed with other shots embodying the simplest of presentational styles; their strategic use of major Italian and international stars (from Anna Magnani and Terence Stamp to Totò and Orson Welles) who are mixed with unskilled nonprofessionals, crooked teeth, acne, an inability to offer a verisimilar performance and all; and, finally, their surfeit of anachronisms and cinema-grammar "mistakes," along with crude special effects in jarring contrast to dazzling period costumes, cinematography, and location shooting. As with the work of his queer progeny Derek Jarman (some of which can best be thought of as intimate and felt records of a collaborative artistic production), Pasolini's films can productively be considered documentary accounts of their own making, accounts of the endless remaking of discursive reality through reworkings of master texts, imitations for which there are no, true, originals.

Pasolini's Future

Over the past two decades or so, a split in queer theory surfaced, dividing its practitioners into two separate camps. One represents the "negative turn" in the discourse and is characterized by its purported embrace of "antirelationality," while the other argues for "queer" as an aesthetic and theoretical turn toward *futurity*, a queer utopia. The latter perspective can be traced back to Ernst Bloch's work and had, as its initial proponent, the late José Esteban Muñoz.[40] It is, as Mari Ruti summarizes, "invested in understanding the ways in which *context-specific* negativity—marginalization, dispossession, exclusion, and abjection—is unevenly distributed across the collective field (the ways that life works less for some subjects than others)."[41] The negative/antirelational school is epitomized by Lee Edelman's *No Future* (2004) and ignores, again in Ruti's words, "trauma's circumstantial modalities in favor of the *foundational* negativity of human life (the way that life, inherently, 'doesn't work')."[42] If my current and recent graduate students can be taken into evidence, it seems like the "utopian school" has more emerging adherents at the moment than the negative camp does. However, for reasons that will become clear throughout this study, the antirelational perspective seems much closer to what emerges in Pasolini's own cinema.

Edelman's work builds somewhat rhetorically and pessimistically on broader philosophical understandings of the value of negativity in development since Hegel introduced his theory of dialectical thought in the nineteenth century. However, the positions underpinning queer negativity within the discourses of queer theory may be traced to the 1995 monograph *Homos*, in which Leo Bersani posits "a revolutionary inaptitude for heteroized sociality" or "sociality as we know it" within "gay desire."[43] These foundational ideas in Bersani's thought actually appear earlier and fortuitously, in 1980, in a study of *Salò* that Bersani coauthored with Ulysse Dutoit. Bersani and Dutoit articulate an argument that "the most intense . . . sexuality depends on symmetry." This is a concept derived from Sade's book *Les 120 journées de Sodome* (1785), in which "sexual excitement" is generated by same-sexed bodies (and transferred faithfully by Pasolini into his film adaptation) and is "the representation of an alienated commotion."[44] Homosexuality, as inherently unconsummatable desire, thus comes into focus as a privileged exemplar of *desire-as-violence*. Bersani and Dutoit thus argue that same-sex encounters are "not an exchange of intensities between individuals but rather a condition of broken negotiations with the world."[45]

This formation of the antisocial thesis is then further elucidated in *Homos*, in which Bersani writes, "the most politically disruptive aspect of the homo-ness . . . in gay desire is a redefinition of sociality so radical that it may appear to require" of queer subjects "a provisional withdrawal from relationality itself."[46] This represents a radical eschewal not just of the progressive ideals of cultural inclusivity and liberal tolerance but of the value, writ large, of the multitude of heterogeneous associations that make up cooperative societies—in short, sociality itself. Edelman develops Bersani's position in *No Future*, arguing that queerness, in "its stubborn denial of teleology, its resistance to the determinations of meaning . . . , and, above all, its rejection of spiritualization through marriage to reproductive futurism," embodies a particular manifestation of the death drive, *jouissance*.[47] Here, queerness is envisaged as "*sintho*mosexuality."

A play on Jacques Lacan's concept of the "sinthome," Edelman, in his second major monograph of queer theory, fuses Derrida's concept of *écriture* and Edelman's own extension of it as homographesis into the Lacanian register. If the sinthome is, for Edelman, an "old way of *writing* what was written later as 'symptom,'" *sintho*mosexuality thus "scorns . . . belief in a final signifier, reducing *every* signifier to the status of the letter and insisting on access to *jouissance* in place of access to sense, on identification with one's sinthome instead of belief in its meaning."[48] Edelman does not simply replace homographesis with a sinthomosexual process. Instead, he broadens his scope to elucidate a darker universe of nonmeaning beyond the localized practice of queer *écriture*. As a result, "fantasy [is] turned inside out, the seams of its costume exposing reality's seamlessness as mere seeming, the fraying knots that hold each sequin in place now usurping that place."[49] Seen in this way, Pasolini's films exemplify cinema as writing. His cinema of poetry is "fantasy turned inside out" in that his work shows the seams of "reality," the "fraying knots" that invariably hold it together. As such, Pasolini's filmography invites the acknowledgment of queer reality. It is a constructed, cinematic reality inseparable from but making palpable the symbolic order and the machinations of the discursive regime as a whole.[50]

A Trilogy of Myth

In this short, modestly intended book, I focus on three undercelebrated films by Paso-lini that I posit constitute a "Trilogy of Myth."[51] To me, these films serve as ideal examples of Pasolini's aesthetic practice as it draws on a cinema of poetry. In addition to *Medea*, the "Trilogy of Myth" includes *Edipo re* (*Oedipus Rex*, 1967) and *Appunti per un'Orestiade africana* (*Notes for an African Orestes*, 1970/1973/1975). As I see it, the films present an unofficial and most likely not consciously constructed trilogy that immediately precedes Pasolini's fully recognized *Trilogy of Life* (*Il Decameron*, *I racconti di Canterbury*, and *Il fiore delle mille e una notte* [*Arabian Nights*, 1974]). I choose this focus because these three films merit more scholarly scrutiny than they have thus far received, although, to be sure, none of Pasolini's productions and writings have exhausted the possibilities of critical appraisal. Furthermore, because of their particular cinematic techniques and theoretical inquiries, they signify the complex dynamic that fuses the archaic and the modern in ways that speak both to the time of their produc-tion and to their director's larger queer project. Based on classic myths and told in an invigoratingly rich cinema verité style, they expose the false dichotomy between textuality and reality. The films, in short, simultaneously signify the birth of a civiliza-tion and its apocalypse or, again, the seemingly paradoxical imbrication of the archaic and the modern. Not incidentally, they are filled with both a youthful energy and a darkly compelling *jouissance* that speaks to the terminal. Following the conclusion of this triptych for Pasolini was a penultimate work that garnered the director his greatest popular and financial success, the *Trilogy of Life*, and, had I been asked by the editor of the Queer Screens series for a book of twice the length of this study, I most likely would have moved on to those three films as they represent a continuing unfolding of Pasolini's archaic modernism. Of course, the *Trilogy of Life* was in turn followed by the scandalous *Salò o le 120 giornate di Sodoma* in 1975, a cinematic masterwork that concluded the director's career with a stunning sense of irredeemability and finality.

The three films I focus on, therefore, mark the beginning of the end of Pasolini's project dedicated to the "cinema of poetry." They prove invaluable in understanding all that his oeuvre came to signify. Moreover, I wish to connect this unofficial triptych to the theoretical prescriptions found in Pasolini's mid- to late-1960s writings since the "cinema of poetry" elucidates a theoretical project inseparable from recognizing queer subjectivity, and these films are among its purest manifestations. With this in mind, in my attempt to shed light on these still-enigmatic works, I review the films through the lens of what is now a canonical body of Anglophone queer theory. This body of work has fruitfully been applied to a number of filmmakers, from Rainer Werner Fassbinder to Alfred Hitchcock. Curiously, Pasolini's work finds itself largely appraised through an Italianist context in which the work of Antonio Gramsci, Alberto Moravia, and Umberto Eco is more likely to be referenced. Although this trenchant Pasolini scholarship is considerable and vastly illuminating, I am interested in drawing lines between Pasolini's cinematic language—*the cinema of poetry*—as it merges with theoretical concepts we now identify as queer.

As a non-Italianist, one trained to study film through a tradition of Anglo-American film theory and queer theory, I offer, first, an analysis that concerns itself with Pasolini's queer theory *avant la lettre*—this is to say, not just queer theory before queer theory but queer theory before it was written in words. I am interested in Pasolini's "queer theory" as it is written through the *language of cinema*. In this way, and given Pasolini's own emphasis on the shortcomings of language *tout court* (dialect and so forth), *Archaic Modernism* demonstrates an exploration of a filmmaker intent on making meaning cinematically. Second, I am especially concerned with cross-cultural spectatorship and the connections between "foreignness" (or, more broadly, Otherness) and "queerness."[52] To my mind, these connections occasion a theoretical approach very much at the heart of Pasolini's work. Given that a large percentage of queer spectators who view Pasolini's work do not speak Italian, I find that a unique form of alienation, or distanciation, occurs precisely because of the "lack" that takes place between an English-speaking queer and a Pasolini film. The loss—in the Lacanian sense—only amplifies a queer energy for a queer audience.

Pasolini recognized that he produced films for a global audience. He designed them with that broad audience in mind. His films function profoundly, even outside a specifically Italian-language context. Indeed, the fact that many of these films have struck such a chord internationally suggests the different yet remarkable ways that they operate for the spectator beyond linguistic and strictly cultural constraints. Finally, projects participating in the realms of interdisciplinarity and queer theory challenge the strict policing of academic inquiry. Scholarly cross-fertilization encourages new connections and fresh perspectives. Herein, therefore, we discover the very paradoxes associated with "archaic modernism" that illustrate the contours of Pasolini's work. In the spirit of the cinema of poetry, *Archaic Modernism* delights in the complex and illuminating—if vexed—texts that Pasolini invites us to engage.

QUEER OEDIPUS

Oedipus Rex (1967)

A haunting tale is presented near the end of *Il fiore delle mille e una notte*, Pasolini's penultimate film, based on part of the "Tale of the Third Dervish" from the *Tales of 1001 Nights*. It follows young Prince Yunan (Salvatore Sapienza), who washes ashore on a remote island containing an underground chamber. Within its confines, an even younger prince, whose fifteenth birthday it is, is hidden by his father to protect him from being murdered that day according to a prophesy. Perhaps four or five years older, the gentle and beautiful Yunan promises to protect the youth from harm, thus earning his trust. The unnamed boy (portrayed by an uncredited actor) quickly lets down his guard and eventually allows Yunan into his bed to sleep. Soon, however, Yunan is overtaken by a trance in which he is compelled to leave the bed, return with a knife, and kill his slumbering host by thrusting the knife into the boy's lower backside. This sequence can certainly discomfort a contemporary spectator conditioned by twenty-first-century mores associated with eroticism, sexuality, and teenaged bodies.

In an excellent short essay on *Salò*, John David Rhodes addresses a curious response by spectators to that scandalous film, one disavowing any erotic enjoyment it might occasion, due not so much to the violence and coprophagia the film eventually presents but to the age of its very literal sex objects. As Rhodes puts it, "The film's deadly serious play with the vicissitudes of arousal depends on bodies of precisely this age. These are bodies that may in fact be legal fair game, but whose proximity to a just-vanishing childhood . . . makes the film's presentation of their nakedness to us as discomfiting or embarrassing as it is potentially arousing."[1] Implicit in Rhodes's discussion of Pasolini's pubescent bodies and the thematic of agency/exploitation they occasion is a disturbing ambiguity signified by these bodies at the tipping point between child and adult. This biological and legally defined tipping point stands, in much of the late work of Pasolini, in allegorical relation to the moment innocent bodies are corrupted by late capitalism. The legend of Oedipus also has a number of "tipping points"—between innocence and knowledge, to mention only one—and these have rough corollaries in the transitions outlined in Freud's Oedipus complex. More importantly, however, for my purposes at this moment, the two male characters' fateful encounter in the "Tale of the Third Dervish" presents a darkly homoerotic example of *situational irony*. It beautifully illustrates Pasolini's rich, disturbing tendency to connect fate with queer desire. And although this is seen at its most thrillingly distilled in *Il fiore delle mille e una notte*, it is most effectively elaborated in *Edipo re*.[2] The concept of fateful queer desire is inseparable from the filmmaker's broad formulation of queer irony, a rarely discussed component of the artist's work and one that has provocative ramifications for queer theory. A comparison of Pasolini's adaptation of the "Tale of the Third Dervish" with the centuries-old original brings these concepts into focus and sets the stage for the way I will approach the director's earlier adaptation of *Oedipus Rex*.

Rhetoricians have defined many different types of irony, such as philosophical irony, rhetorical irony, practical irony, dramatic irony, comic irony, and self-irony.[3] Two of the earliest forms, identified in the work of the classical Greeks, are dramatic and situational irony.[4] Dramatic irony occurs when "characters are unaware of important circumstances about which the audience is fully informed."[5] Situational irony is more crucial to Pasolini's cinema. It is best understood not as a mode of rhetoric but as the outcome of events, specifically as an incongruity between one's behavior and the results of it as they ultimately unfold in a narrative. It involves, as Joana Garmendia puts it, a "lack of intentionality as a clear distinguishing feature." Interestingly for our purposes, the first example Garmendia offers is a comically queer one: "When the Turkish police created a rainbow with their water cannons in their attempt to stop [a] gay parade," she writes, we witnessed a "clear example of situational irony."[6] More regularly, however, situational irony has been employed to illustrate the unavoidability of fate: you can exercise for health but might well die of a heart attack at the gym (hence, the irony of the "situation"). This form of irony is disturbing in that it chillingly suggests the ultimate futility of human action. It is precisely the overlap between situational and dramatic irony—and, as in the real-world Turkish example, the emergence of an unexpectedly queer outcome from machinations of patriarchal control—found in *Edipo re* that links it to Pasolini's cinematic version of the "Tale of the Third Dervish." Pasolini's adaptations of *Oedipus Rex* and the *Tales of 1001 Nights* are ultimately both testaments to the filmmaker-theorist's manifested vision of sinthomosexuality, as defined by Lee Edelman and detailed in the introduction. This is to say, they articulate sexuality in terms of homosexual desire, and homosexual desire in terms of *jouissance*.

As for the cinematic adaptation of "Tale of the Third Dervish," it is important to keep in mind that, while the many translations of the story vary in their level of homosexual connotation,[7] Pasolini's adaptation practically exemplifies a (pederastic) male homoerotic sensibility, one spun through with ironic force. For instance, rather than reconstructing the stone staircase in the underground chamber as described in

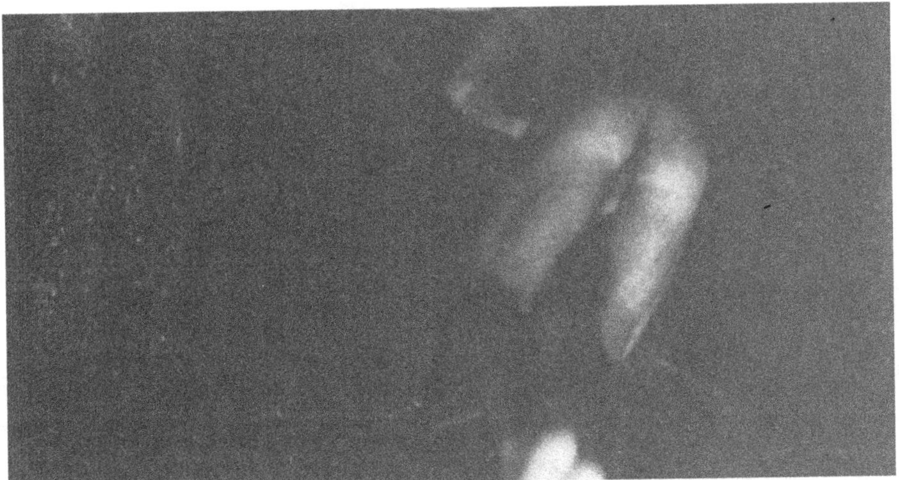

FIGURE 1. A naked Yunan climbs down the rope ladder.

every translation of the original tale that I have consulted, Pasolini's film gives us a rope ladder for Yunan to climb down. Filmed from below, his naked body, with his genitals and anal cleft central in the frame, descends closer and closer toward the spectator (see figure 1). Once inside the chamber, the sensitive Yunan weeps over its occupant's initial, fear-based rejection of him—like a rejected would-be lover might respond. But Yunan quickly earns the boy's trust, and the two then joyfully embrace. The original tale also describes the older male giving his new friend a bath, "rubbing him down and bringing him a change of clothes."[8] Pasolini, however, takes things further. In the film, we see the two bathing together naked, embracing each other again while playfully splashing about in the water. Furthermore, while the earlier version never describes the older man in the younger man's bed, the two do sleep together on the same *maṭ raḥ* in the film. Although Pasolini biographer Barth David Schwartz contends that the film's image of the two men sleeping side by side offers "no hint of sexual relations,"[9] the fatal conclusion of the scene, moments later, strongly alludes to sexuality, if not actual sex—and, as we come to expect with Pasolini's cinema, in the most violently provocative way.

In the original story, the boy's death occurs while the two are awake. Yunan takes hold of a knife to cut a melon, only to slip and fall on top of the youth, penetrating his heart with the blade.[10] In Pasolini's version, the assassination resembles anal copulation *a tergo* so strongly as to make a sexual allegory of the tale almost unavoidable. As both slumber, Yunan gets out of the bed and sleepwalks to the wall, where he takes the lethal dagger from the shelf. Returning to the bed, he climbs in and straddles the boy,

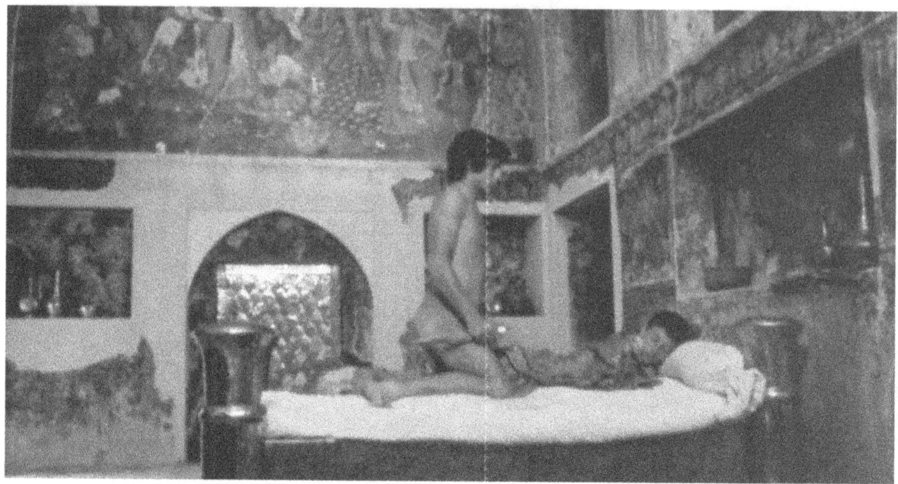

who is sleeping on his stomach (see figure 2). Pulling the boy's blanket down around his legs so that his buttocks are exposed, the somnambulist raises his knife, and, from the position he would have to assume to penetrate the youth's anus with his penis, he plunges the dagger into the boy's back.[11] In this way, Pasolini rewrites the "Tale of the Third Dervish" to change an absurdly comic fulfillment of prophecy in waking life— killing someone by slipping with a knife meant to cut a melon—into an erotically unsettling encounter set in the land of the nocturnal unconscious.

Beyond those just addressed, there are a great many differences between the original work and the cinematic adaptation—indeed, too many to note here. The crucial element shared by both, however, revolves around the boy's prophesied death on his fifteenth birthday, a fateful anniversary repeatedly posited as "the limit between childhood and manhood" in the Islamic tradition.[12] As Leo Bersani points out, in the ancient world (whether Grecian, Roman, or Muslim), the role of the *penetratee* in male homosexual relations is exceedingly problematic. It is a position certainly not approved of for adult citizens, let alone for polis leaders.[13] Indeed, according to Michel Foucault, in ancient Greece, male citizens—even in adulthood—found their leadership curtailed if they were proven to have been "the passive partners in [sexual] activity" when they were boys.[14] As a result, the fifteen-year-old prince's penetration by another male invalidates his ability to assume his ordained role as king.[15] In effect, the literal killing of the boy stands for the metaphorical death associated with male homosexuality. It thus connects desire and death in an uncanny way, one that haunts Pasolini's cinema.

Rather than Pasolini retrospectively criticizing or praising the morals or ethics of the "Tale of the Third Dervish" in his adaptation, he is more interested in the poetic possibilities of Eros and Thanatos that the relationship between Yunan and the young boy evokes. This is to say, the stakes for pleasure are high since, in Pasolini's take on the ancient tale, pleasure is marked at the unconscious site where homosexual penetration merges with the death drive. Furthermore, as an account of two ancient royals' intergenerational desire leading to a patriarchal linage's destruction, the "Tale of the Third Dervish" queerly echoes an only somewhat less homoerotic account of regal filicide, albeit one disguised as patricide, previously dramatized in Pasolini's oeuvre. The filmmaker's visions of the "Tale of the Third Dervish" and, as we shall see, *Oedipus Rex* show how as the death of a lineage, filicide (virtual or real) is simultaneously patricide, since the killing of one's only royal son is the killing of one's family line and one's own patriarchal subjectivity. When sexualized, this expresses how the Oedipal family harbors an inherently self-destructive queer energy that is both its negation and its apotheosis. It is with this in mind that I have been drawn to the rich metaphor found toward the end of *Il fiore delle mille e una notte*. Through it, Pasolini demonstrates how, vertiginously enough, homosexual sodomy is at once destructive and seminal to the cultural imperatives that ultimately define bourgeois heteronormativity.

Unlike Pasolini's filmed version of the all-male "Tale of the Third Dervish," I argue that his earlier *Edipo re* illustrates a paradigmatic instance of heterosexual relations only operative *within the deconstructive forces of homosexual desire*. In this way, Pasolini's queer turn on the Oedipal complex is one that offers the family romance as the metaphorical death for culture itself. This is, in the context of a civilization founded on the values illustrated by Greek texts like *Oedipus Rex*, a supreme irony. Like the homophobic water canons at that gay pride event in Turkey, the force of heterocentric law finally manifests itself to be ultimate midwife to an intangible queer actualization.

Blindness as Insight

A critical detail that Pasolini brings to his adaptation of the "Tale of the Third Dervish," not found in the original, is revealed when the younger prince tells Yunan that the prophecy that led him to the underground chamber specified that his own death would occur at the hands of a man with *no eyes*. It is in this way that Pasolini's "Tale of the Third Dervish" is best understood in relationship to *Edipo re*. The fact that Yunan cannot *see* while he sleepwalks with dagger in hand toward the naked boy is a crucial allusion to the queer negativity more subtly articulated in *Edipo re*. Oedipus, in the film Pasolini made five years before *Il fiore delle mille e una notte*, has full access to the literal sense of sight when he fulfills the prophecy to kill his father. Yet, like

Yunan, Oedipus blindly, if metaphorically so, destroys. But rather than a brother/son/ lover figure, Oedipus kills his father, the patriarch. Ultimately, there is no difference between the two impulses. A son, brother, or male lover is always already an embodiment of the patriarch.

By bringing these two texts into play with each other, one from Arabia and one from ancient Greece, a form of queerness emerges that is central to Pasolini's larger, career-long project in which myths of all kinds fold and refold into one another. This is to say that an archaic modernism emerges through Pasolini's queer cinematics. It reveals itself in the homoerotic, exotic, historical, and mythic that is visible through the filmmaker's cinema of poetry. Significantly, his archaic modernism, this cinema of poetry, also makes perceptible that which is unseen yet ever present: the vital workings of sinthomosexuality within ideology.

On the one hand, *Oedipus Rex* is a near-perfect text for illustrating archaic modernism, in that the story, as originally dramatized by Sophocles, lends itself to Pasolini's interest in the ideological relations between the archaic and the unstable maturation of a civilization. On the other hand, Oedipus, as a primary figure in Freud's narrative of complex human subjectivity, exemplifies the maturation of a form of consciousness to which modernity responds. Oedipus also relates to modernity through irony, itself a trope of significance at least as great for the modernist mind as it was for a classical consciousness. The turn of events in *Oedipus Rex*, in which the protagonist's parents endeavor to thwart a bloody, incestuous, dynasty-destroying destiny, only to assure its realization, is a particularly clear, even paradigmatic instance of situational irony. As there can hardly be a soul who does not know the outcome of the tale before witnessing a production, it is, arguably, a paradigmatic instance of dramatic irony as well.

In order to make the strongest case for the deep situational irony of the Oedipus myth, Pasolini dramatizes on-screen a backstory that is only described in dialogue in Sophocles's theatrical version of 429 BCE (all that happens in Thebes prior to the plague, which descends on the land under Oedipus's rule). In the filmmaker's reconstruction of the Sophoclean text, virtually every potential manifestation of this particular form of irony is highlighted at the level of dramatic incident rather than through direct dialogue. For instance, in the now foregrounded backstory, the infant Oedipus is denied a quick death by a compassionate slave. Rather than killing the child in the desert, the slave abandons him on the ground, where the child would seem to face a much crueler death by exposure to the elements.[16] And in yet another ironic twist, while the child is saved, he is nonetheless fated to an even greater level of suffering due to his foreordained patricide and incestuous union. When a Delphic oracle eventually warns Oedipus, "You will kill your father and make love to your mother," the young man, as a precaution, chooses to stay away forever from Corinth and thus his (adopted) parents.[17] He flees in the opposite direction in order to put the greatest distance possible between him and the mother and father he thinks he is fated to destroy; he thus unknowingly, and oh-so-ironically, moves *toward* his biological parents. As Pasolini crafts his adaptation, each turn of events and its cruel outcome is assured by the very actions Oedipus takes to avoid tragedy.

The crucial question thus comes into focus: How does Pasolini queerly rearticulate the tragic irony that permeates the male body, both incestuously prone and exogamously driven, both homoerotically celebrated and heterosexually ordained, on dramatic display in his narrative film? Indeed, in order to cinematically render the ironic sense of tragedy the Oedipal narrative rehearses in modern terms, it is precisely filmic technique and narrative structure to which Pasolini turns to demonstrate the fate that the vexed and vexing family romance holds.

Oedipus Introductus: A Close Analysis

The first and second shots in *Edipo re* are shakily handheld, unsettled, and faltering. In distinct contrast, the third and fourth shots are balanced, studied, and still. The first shot, recorded with a handheld camera and set in ancient Greece, shows a road sign carved in stone pointing toward Thebes. In the second shot, one encounters equally wobbly camera work; but at this point, and without warning, we have leapt westward, geographically, and forward in time, to a provincial Italian town sometime during the early twentieth century.[18] The modern town we see is foregrounded by a lush field of green corn.

Subsequent to these two spatiotemporally disparate but stylistically similar shots are two more shots that sharply contrast them. In the distinction among the shots, we are taken toward the main action of the film's prologue, the birth of a modern-day Oedipus. It is here, as well, that we encounter the first intimations of conflict with his father and his relationship with his mother. In these more conventionally presented and logically connected tableaux, we see a house in which a twentieth-century Jocasta (Silvana Mangano) will give birth to her accursed son. The structure is made visible, first, in long and, then, in medium-long shot. Unlike the previous unsteady images, both shots of the house are as studied and formal, as complete unto themselves, as one would find in images in films crafted by Ozu or Kubrick. If these mannered "home" shots indicate that the film is now developing in a more classical, more "professional" manner, the spectator is soon jarred by a fifth shot that immediately dislodges the classical-cinema moorings. In this shot, the camera's tripod is suddenly removed. It again clearly rests on the shoulder of an awkwardly mobile cinematographer.

Nonetheless, we remain looking through the house window. Now voyeuristically, the handheld camera conveys a very-present witnessing of the moments following Oedipus's birth. The newborn's unusually large genitals, clearly visible through the window from outside the house, momentarily hold center screen; they are on full display for the scopophilic spectator.

All told, this introductory five-shot sequence constitutes a very short prologue *to* the prologue. In it, the spectator experiences the filmmaker's deliriously perverse aesthetic in distilled form as a rough cinematographic style is countered with one that demonstrates a balanced, classical worldview. But just as one assumes the filmmaker has settled into a classical style and begins to anticipate a "prestigious" adaptation of a classical text, Pasolini disrupts what is indeed a *bourgeois expectation*. In choosing to mix both unsteady and formalistically rigorous shots within a single scene, the filmmaker embarks on an unsynthesized, unbalanced concatenation of oppositions. This disturbed cinematic formalism in effect bespeaks the unresolved conflicts between modernity and classicism that will inform this "Trilogy of Myth" and are a crucial part of Pasolini's worldview. It is a queer worldview in the most complex and disturbing sense. Conceptualized as potentially unlimited and unstable differential equations, queerness all but scrambles the binaries of sex and gender while never fully abjuring the underlying logics of either. As a result, Pasolini destabilizes cinema by evoking queer desire, which ultimately transfigures gender identification, morality, and the ideological and psychoanalytic ground on which desire is inextricably linked to the anticipation of death.[19]

Edipo re re-presents a tale that purportedly exemplifies heterosexual desire that, in Pasolini's hands, ultimately elucidates a logic of desire that deconstructs heteronormativity. *Oedipus Rex*, together with Pasolini's adaptation of the classic text, is both the master narrative of sexual maturation and proof of a still-present archaic universe, that fundamental instability that is sexual desire. Irony indeed! Pasolini's film reminds the spectator of the queer hauntings drawn from the archaic that at once enable yet fracture the modernist terms for heteronormativity, terms ideologically manufactured as "the real."

Homosexual Desire

To be sure, Sigmund Freud contends that, centuries after Greece's decline and fall, the Oedipus tale remains fixed at the heart of human sexuality and deeply intertwined with the patriarchy. It is worth, therefore, a short review of the way Freud incorporates *Oedipus Rex* into his psychoanalytic theories since his reading plays a significant role in Pasolini's cinematic return to the classic narrative. According to Freud, the male child's psychic journey to assume the place of the father and find an adequate sexual substitute for the mother is the very process of the construction of masculine human sexuality and, in an androcentric order, gender itself. Moreover, the "father of psychoanalysis" posits that the original "Oedipal journey" is the structuring prologue that prepares the stage for patriarchal society as a whole. But Freud effectively deconstructs his theory as he elucidates it. This is to say, he offers innumerable, sometimes contradictory variations of the Oedipus narrative that provocatively interconnect with his also-protean theories of bisexuality and homosexuality.

Kenneth Lewes spotlights Freud's shifting theoretical terrain where homosexuality and Oedipus encounter each other. According to Lewes, Freud's theories centered on male homosexuality may be divided into four basic variants. In the first, as elucidated in a study of Leonardo da Vinci, the male child's castration anxiety dissolves the boy's "erotic bond with the mother," leading him to afford himself a compromise in the sexual object, "a 'woman with a penis,' a boy with a feminine appearance."[20] The second theory, articulated most clearly in Freud's *Three Essays on the Theory of Sexuality*, involves a boy so erotically attracted to his mother that, once forced to separate from her, he unconsciously comes to identify with her and with her sexual desire for men. Put another way, he comes to adopt his mother's desire for his father as his own desire, through the process of incorporation. The third theory of homosexuality in Lewes's review is that which gives the "negative" Oedipus complex its definition and is considered the most common among the four types. It references men who are largely heterosexual in practice but whose innate bisexuality may produce homosexual desires. The male child's "libidinal position" in this formulation has become a "female" and "passive" one as a result of a disrupted or lacking identification with the father. The complex that undergirds this form of homosexuality is thus an inverse of the basic Oedipus story; here, the male child sees its mother as a threat and finds himself attracted to the father. The fourth theory (introduced relatively late in Freud's career) involves a violent and intense love for the mother by the son, in which his desire for her is demonstrated by ferocious jealousy toward competing family members.[21] The resulting "reaction formation," or the adoption of a completely oppositional position from one's original strong feelings of hatred for the father, ultimately becomes an ironic attraction to the father.[22]

There is, of course, at least as much in the Greek tradition that speaks to queer sexual impulses as there is in Freud's psychoanalysis. *Edipo re* embraces these narrative pulsations, in often-unexpected ways. The ancient myth of Oedipus has itself functioned to elucidate the Möbius strip–like way in which heterosexual and homosexual desire circulates according to heteronormative understandings of masculinity/femininity and activity/passivity. Transgenerationally, the myth has clearly served to secure hetero ideals. Yet the incest allegory makes ironically perverse the seminal mythological tapestry it purportedly reaffirms. Pasolini is remarkably honest when he asserts his personal sexual investment in the queer variations that give shape to the Oedipus complex: "If anything, I have dreamt . . . of making love to my father (against the chest of drawers in the wretched little bedroom my brother and I shared) and perhaps to my brother as well."[23] In claiming, shortly after the release of *Edipo re* in 1967, that he has "emerged from the wilderness of the Freudian and Marxist dogma" associated with the Oedipus myth, the filmmaker declares, "instead of projecting the myth on to psycho-analysis, I have re-projected psycho-analysis on the myth."[24] In this regard, Pasolini engages in the same project as many twentieth-century intellectuals, psychoanalysts among them, who launch their theoretical enterprise through long-standing myths consistently appropriated for the modern era.

One of the more provocative scholars to think along these lines, and who came on the scene midcentury, was Georges Devereux. Devereux brought together a number of classical sources that survived antiquity and now serve well the work of more recent scholars who seek to illuminate *Oedipus Rex*'s homosexual underpinnings.[25] As he reminds us, King Laïus, long before his son, Oedipus, was conceived, had forcibly taken the boy Chrysippus, son of King Pelops, as his lover. Laïus's initial abduction and rape of Chrysippus is considered particularly gratuitous in the logic of its era since, as Devereux points out, Pelops most likely would have given his son to Laïus willingly.[26] Pelops, therefore, places his curse on Laïus as part of a linked genealogy of violent homosocial and homosexual relationships.

But if homosexual rape triggers Oedipus's miserable destiny, it is not merely a starting point. Homosexual desire permeates Oedipus's familial relations. In surveying the literature, Devereux argues that Oedipus's feelings toward his father were nothing less than incestuous as well; more than that, in earlier versions of the myth, Oedipus, like his father, was in love with Chrysippus. As Freud's colleague Otto Rank points out, "Oedipus himself was considered to have been homosexual in his youth, as shown by the fragments of Praxilla, a woman poet of the fifth century B.C. In her story, he was in love with the same youth (Chrysippus) as his unrecognized father [Laïus]; according to Euripides, Laïus is killed out of jealousy over Chrysippus, or in a fight over the youth—the complete opposite of jealousy over the mother."[27]

Pasolini's film does not allude directly to Chrysippus or King Pelops; but the scenes that feature Laïus with Oedipus are rife with homoerotic tension, including the encounters between the Laïus figure and his infant son in the prologue and, later, in the flashbacks to ancient Greece when Laïus dies at Oedipus's hands. And, as we shall see, two Chrysippus figures eventually appear in the film as well.

The first interaction between Oedipus and Laïus, or really their twentieth-century equivalents, witnessed by the spectator occurs minutes into the film. Chronologically, however, the event takes place a few months after the baby's birth. Suddenly and without transitional signposts, the child has transformed from a nearly bald baby to a young boy sporting a full head of dark hair. In the meantime, the twentieth-century Jocasta along with a nursemaid takes the baby into the courtyard of the local military barracks, wheeling him in a black stroller that disconcertingly matches the black fascist flag that was only seconds earlier seen in the hands of a group of children. Presently, the new mother stops to talk to a group of men and women, one of whom is a soldier—a young lieutenant (Luciano Bartoli) in full uniform. At this point, the mother does not acknowledge him, talking instead to men and women in civilian clothes who have approached her and are complimenting her on her appearance. Nevertheless, Pasolini favors the handsome officer with a close-up as the soldier looks into the infant's carriage; he maintains a piercing but ambivalent expression. The mother, along with the rest of the villagers, leaves the baby with the soldier for a few moments so as to engage in some business in the nearby barracks. The intense look of the man as framed by Pasolini offers our first indication that the handsome officer may, in fact, be the child's father. And to confirm this supposition, we are made privy to the soldier's fatherly thoughts, which are not presented in voice-over; instead, we enter the father's world through words typed on a page, a mode of *écriture* in which the fonts on the typewritten page mimic the film's opening credits. Pasolini's cinematic text folds into the weaves of the paper; the modern medium folds into the archaic one.

This distinctive authorial choice that juxtaposes the soldier's close-up with the haptic quality of the inscriptions on the page effectively materializes the soldier's thoughts as representation. We read, "Tu sei qui per prendere il mio posto nel mondo, ricacciarmi nel nulla e rubarmi tutto quello che ho" (You are here to take my place in the world, send me back into the void and rob me of all I have). In Pasolini's original screenplay, the child's reaction to his father is provocatively described: "The child looks at him, his limpid little eyes devoid of expression: perhaps he is already *pretending* indifference."[28] But what is this false "indifference" the child hides? Jealousy? Fear? Love? In the film itself, the child betrays some emotion on his face, which can best be described as a kind of joy at seeing the father. Yet it is immediately followed by apprehensiveness and then, in a final turn, an intimation of hopefulness through what appears as the beginnings

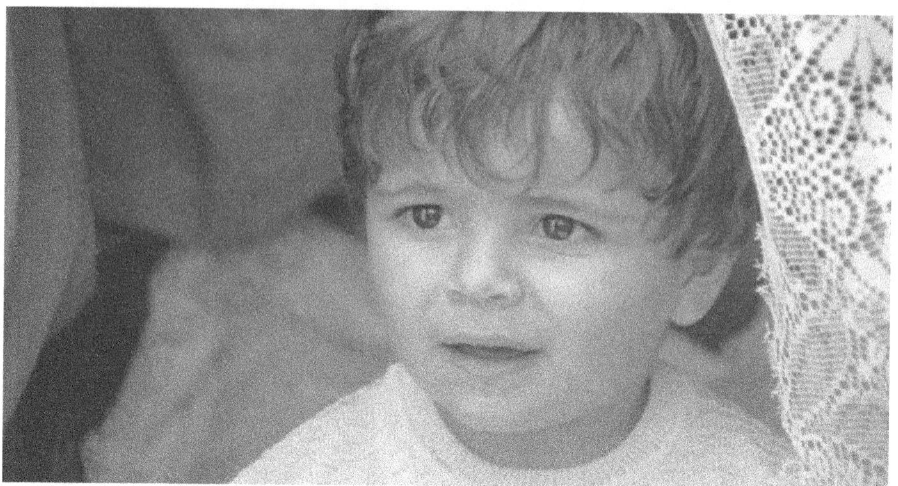

FIGURE 3. The child betrays some emotion on his face.

of an ambivalent smile (see figure 3). The father's cold stare, however (see figure 4), has the effect of shaming the child, who covers his face with his hand, as if about to burst into tears (see figure 5).[29]

Shortly thereafter, following an instance of lovemaking between father and mother, a critical moment takes place between father and son. The officer rises from his bed and walks to the baby's crib. Here, just before this modern-day prologue comes to its end, the soldier/father grabs the child by his feet. At that moment, we hear the shrill, plaintive sounds of a primitive flute.

Roadside Encounters

Oedipus's feet are a key element both in the original myth and in Sophocles's tragedy, as well as in Pasolini's film. "Oedipus" has two literal meanings, most famously "swollen feet" but also "knowing feet." The name "Oedipus" is said to have been given to the child by his adoptive parents when they noticed that his extremities were engorged, a result of his ankles being pierced and tightly bound together by his would-be killers. The ways in which the penetration of a male child's body leads to both engorgement and knowledge, all brought together in the tragic hero's name, suggests, at the narrative's outset, an understanding of the queer nature of human desire.[30]

In effect, the moment the father grabs the child's feet marks Pasolini's cinematic bridge between the Modern and Classical Eras. Furthermore, the shot of the Italian soldier/father grabbing his child's feet juxtaposed with a shot of the Greek infant, feet (and arms) bound and carried by a slave to the hills where he will be left to die, suggests a will to knowledge, a reckoning with sexual desire and power relations at their most extreme. Pasolini's cut, in which homosexual, incestuous, and murderous inferences between father and son are seen from the perspective of a father penetrating, piercing, and binding his child to the extent that the boy's extremities swell, evokes a concept already anticipated by Georges Devereux.[31] Devereux argues that when the adult Oedipus killed Laïus in an emasculating and sexually evocative way, he "turned the tables" on the father "by castrating . . . and feminizing him . . . as he himself had once been castrated and feminized . . . by Laïus."[32] The less-recognized yet extant tale of father-son homosexual incest in the Oedipus narrative is suggestively reintroduced by Pasolini. In this way, the film thrusts a wedge into the foundational assumption

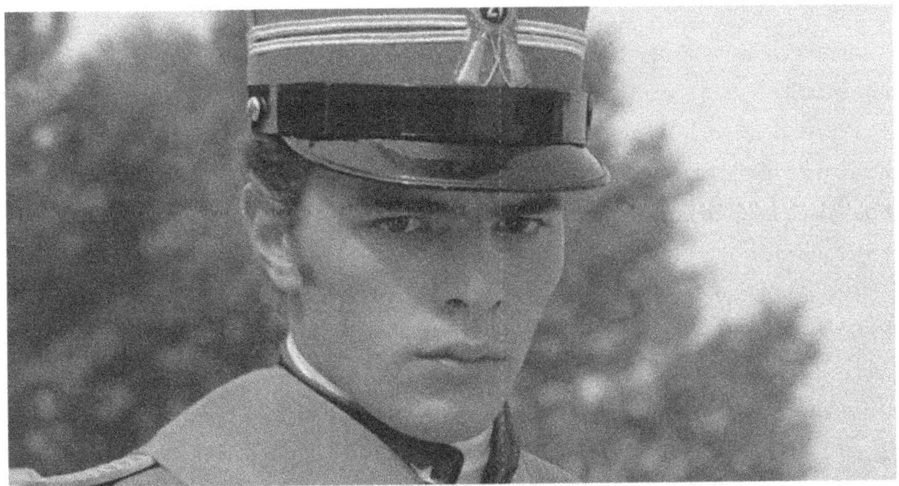

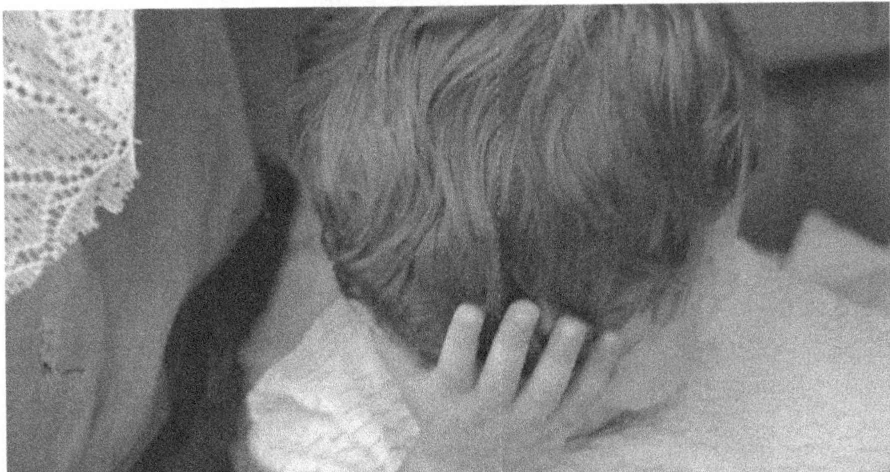

FIGURES 4 AND 5. The father stares coldly; the child covers his face with his hand.

driven through academic interpretations and psychoanalysis that reiterate the Oedipus narrative as presumptively heterosexual.

With the homo-incestuous dynamic unveiled, Pasolini re-creates the legendary patricide, most perversely, in what is one of the film's tour-de-force sequences. Tellingly, the eroticized violence here begins with Oedipus throwing a rock at one of the solders only to have it fall just short of its target and land, violently enough, on the man's foot, suggesting an act of outward aggression that also reflects violence done to the self. As elsewhere, the filmmaker utilizes an admixture of elements that are variously cinematically sophisticated/controlled and filmically ungrammatical/tremulous, including a number of awkward jump cuts. Pasolini uses handheld cameras as the adult Oedipus (Franco Citti) variously runs both toward and away from Laïus's four soldier guardians. Thus, the frenetic energy of the camera heightens Oedipus's series of desperate advances and retreats. At the same time, Pasolini also employs static images that display his characters momentarily stalled, beleaguered by exhaustion or physical incapacitation. Additionally, the sequence dramatically contrasts frantic, sometimes disorienting point-of-view images with authoritative, well-composed medium-long shots that dynamically follow or pull back from the characters. As in the prologue to the prologue, a queer juxtaposition of styles both evokes and undercuts normative cinematic form.

Throughout the patricide sequence, Pasolini's style also returns us to the dialectic of blindness and sight. Through complex, if rough-hewn, cinematic form meant to invoke the twin poles of the seen and the unseen that occupy the narrative, Pasolini, in short, *reveals*. Cinematically, and most memorably, we experience this when the second and third soldiers are killed. Here, the camera first points directly at the sun, recording its blinding rays, which effectively burn the center of the image to a state of bright nothingness (see figure 6). But then, in those moments when Oedipus's torso moves slightly within the frame so as to directly *block* the blinding sun, we are unexpectedly able to see, with shocking clarity, the fateful, violent killing (see figure 7). The positioning of the actors in these variously seen/unseen killings is markedly sexualized, with, in one instance, Oedipus astride a soldier in a position identical to that assumed by a man atop another engaged in anal intercourse. Before being killed at the end of this long, harrowing sequence, Laïus (played by Luciano Bartoli, who portrayed the prologue's father figure) tries to intimidate his assailant with a broad show of patriarchal authority by putting on his phallic crown (see figure 8); Oedipus merely laughs at Laïus's naked but futile attempt to assert patriarchal dominance. The father is finally killed when the son administers two decisive thrusts of his penis-shaped sword (particularly obvious when compared to the triangular-shaped swords of the soldiers) into the ruler's abdomen (see figure 9).

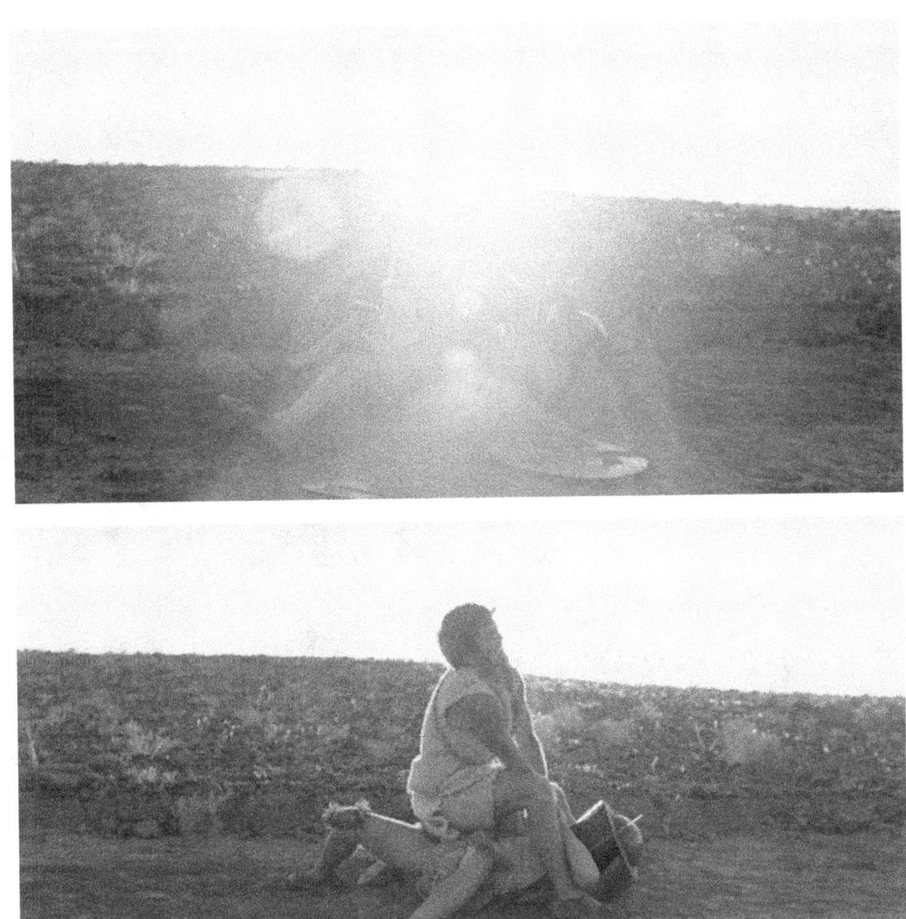

At the end of this nine-minute sequence is one final, significant, act of violence. The first person wounded in the deadly crossroads massacre is the last to be killed. Oedipus began the fight by throwing a rock, which landed at the feet of one of the young soldiers, a figure who remains alive after his three comrades and Laïus have been killed. Oedipus returns to him and, as he did with his father, lethally thrusts his sword into the body. The soldier's helmet then falls off, and we see a close-up of the young man's face. Even dead, he strikes one as, arguably, the most attractive man yet seen in the film, rivaled only by Laïus himself (see figure 10).[33] If there are evocations of the Chrysippus figure in the film, this young man is surely one of them. In following

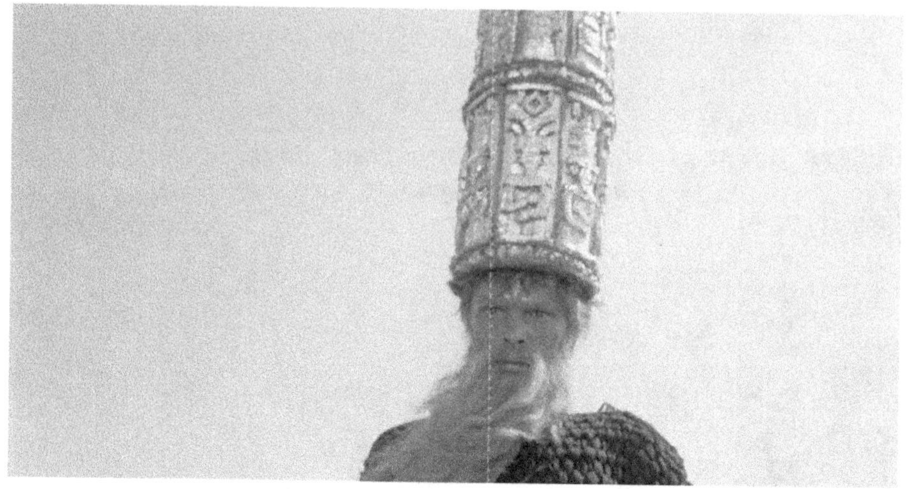

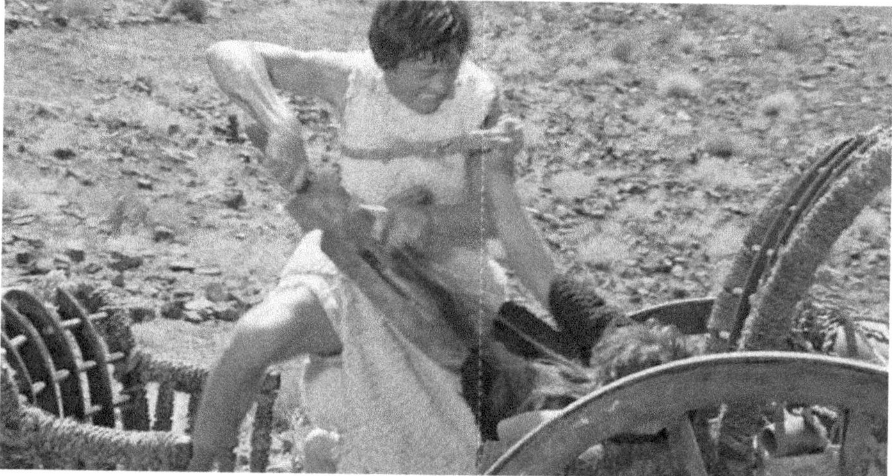

FIGURES 8 AND 9. Laïus's phallic crown; the father is ultimately killed by the son.

conventional ideas of beauty as well as Pasolini's own, Oedipus has killed the two most attractive males in the film in an obviously sexualized manner: an adult man, the father figure (Laïus), and a boy/surrogate son who is intimately, sexually associated with that man/father figure (his slave/soldier).

Oedipus is now on his way to fulfill his destiny, to sleep with his mother. Lest one think this is a journey away from homosexual desire and toward the heterosexual variant, it must be remembered that Oedipus is destined to penetrate with his penis the vagina that once hosted his father's sex. By fucking the space of his own origin, Oedipus's body incestuously intermingles, once again, with that of the father who also inseminated the mother. This virtual homosexual incest is unthinkable as such, since, as Rey Chow reminds us, "the taboo against incest . . . has primarily been based on a heterosexual conception of sexual and family relations."[34] Yet, in Pasolini's formulation of Oedipus, heterosexuality is always already inflected with queer desire. Oedipus thus transforms not merely into his mother's husband but moreover, and more perversely, *into and as* his own father through the sexual act. And by entering the site of his own emergence, previously made fertile with the father's ejaculate, he joins with the father whose formative sexual desire for his son was displaced onto the slave/soldier. By killing his same-generation rival along with the father, Oedipus sets the stage to enter the mother in order to be one not simply with her but finally also with the father. Bersani quotes Freud's "A Special Type of Choice of Object Made by Men" to argue this truth at the heart of the Oedipus complex: "All [the child's] instincts, those of tenderness, gratitude, lustfulness, defiance and independence, find satisfaction in the single wish to be his own father." Bersani continues: "The mother is the vessel, the necessary but perhaps incidental instrument for this extraordinary working out of a fantasy of self-creation. . . . This pushes further than the son's fantasy of identification with the father. The latter has become the creation of the former. In a dizzying conflation of being, the self-fathered son is also that son's father. And why not continue this multigenerational oneness?"[35] Therefore, Oedipus merges with his father, thus moving closer to a phantasmatic bond with Laïus's now-dead boy-lover, also longed for by Oedipus himself. Bersani summarizes the final results of this logic: "Except for the nearly dismissible (if, obviously, indispensable) woman through whom all these self-replicas must pass,

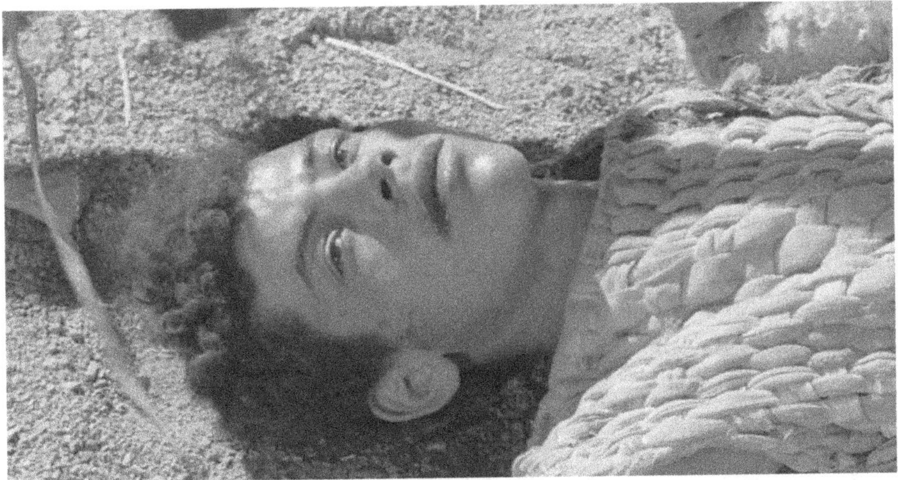

FIGURE 10. A close-up of the soldier's face.

the psychic logic of this very special type of object-choice culminates in a fantastical multiplication of sameness."[36]

With all this in mind, Oedipus's final encounter before returning to Thebes to face his destiny is hardly surprising; it involves him sharing a scene with two additional and decisive figures that mark Pasolini's queer cinematics. The first is a young messenger, played by Pasolini's lover Ninetto Davoli, who will eventually become the film's other Chrysippus figure; and the other, Tiresias, the blind poet and prophet, is played by the American actor and director Julian Beck. Beck's portrayal of Tiresias is the kind of creative casting choice that distinguishes many of Pasolini's midcareer films. The thin, effete, and balding performer might seem a counterintuitive choice for a ferocious prophet, but he was well known in artistic circles as "the bisexual lead of the resolutely experimental Living Theater."[37] His status as a queer interpreter of artistic texts with the renowned theater group underlines Pasolini's own perspective on the Oedipus myth and tragedy that we have thus far explored. Furthermore, in a film constructed with rough-hewn filmmaking technique, the scene that introduces Beck/Tiresias stands out because it features some of the most ill-connecting and disorienting shots in Pasolini's cinematic mosaic. Hence, Beck/Tiresias signals a conceptual choice on the director's part that challenges conventional heterosexual/cinematic vision. For Pasolini, perverse cinematic bodies must necessarily join forces with perverse cinematic technique.

Beyond mirroring Oedipus's ultimate inability "to see," the blindness of the prophet Tiresias functions as fulcrum in Sophocles's dialectic of (in)sight/blindness. Pasolini's adaptation incorporates the presence of the legendary figure, who has an outsized role in Greek mythology as a particularly queer character, to provocative effect. Greek mythology tells us that Tiresias was transformed from a man into a woman, long before his fateful encounter with Oedipus's family, after stumbling upon wounded snakes in the act of mating. Seven years hence, he would return to the same spot, see the same snakes mating again, and be transformed back into a man. Tiresias's experience living as a member of both sexes becomes instrumental in his ultimate prophetic blindness.

According to one version of his story, Tiresias is asked by Zeus and Hera to settle an argument: Which of the two sexes experiences greater sexual pleasure? In agreeing with Zeus that women experience greater erotic pleasure, Hera vengefully robs Tiresias of his sight. To compensate Tiresias for that loss, Zeus then grants him the gift of prophecy and longevity. In other words, his prophetic abilities result precisely from his blindness, which in turn resulted from asserting that a (presumably penetrated) woman enjoyed more sexual pleasure than a (almost certainly a penetrative) man. By standing before Zeus and Hera *as a man* and validating penetra*tion* over penetra*ting,*

Tiresias is implicitly breaking what Bersani calls "the moral taboo on 'passive' anal sex in ancient Athens . . . formulated as a hygienics of social power."[38] In doing so, again, according to the logic that Bersani charts, he has repudiated phallocentrism itself, which is "not primarily the denial of power to women . . . , but above all the denial of the value of powerlessness in both men and women."[39]

Finally, now, outside the politics of social power, Tiresias is both handicapped and transcendent. In his metaphorical blindness, he *sees* all. This is the state Oedipus will also, finally, attain. The ill-fitting building blocks of cinematic reality in Pasolini's film, nowhere more strikingly observed than in this sequence in which Oedipus encounters Tiresias, force spectators into a position in which they must validate and unify the signs that constitute a broadly written and laboriously performed reality. Spectators are therefore obligated to take responsibility for the film's completion and accept a position within something that is both constructed and authentic at the same time.

At the end of a long, fragmentary scene in which Davoli, ever the helpful messenger, takes Oedipus to Tiresias, a scene that has broken nearly every rule of continuity editing, framing, and cinematic space, we see the blind prophet, in close-up, through Oedipus's eyes. Tiresias, who has been playing his recorder, stares blankly forward, as if uncannily, gazing directly into the camera. Cutting back to Oedipus and the boy messenger, this sequence's penultimate shot is its most polished, most traditionally cinematic and thus a most radical departure from the style of the previous few minutes. Through a telephoto lens and a beautifully sustained circular pan, Pasolini smoothly captures the messenger quickly leading Oedipus away from Tiresias. At first, he shows the two men clearly and unobstructed. As they move, the action becomes more dynamic as their bodies move through out-of-focus corn stalks. Purposeful and calculated, the successfully executed dynamic shot is a thrillingly smooth conclusion to an otherwise roughly constructed and extended sequence. Ironically, the scene's ending, following the film's introduction to radical blindness, is a beautiful, highly stylized sight to behold.

Coming Home

After the uncanny—*unheimlich* to be sure—meeting with Tiresias, Oedipus, still accompanied by the young messenger, at long last approaches the outskirts of Thebes. Here he has his celebrated encounter with the Sphinx. As with many scenes in the film, the realized version is very different from the one Pasolini describes in his screenplay. The latter illustrates the creature, according to legend, as "a beast with a lion's head and a woman's body,"[40] but on-screen the almost amateurish costume worn by what is obviously a male performer offers a more abstract vision. The huge mask he

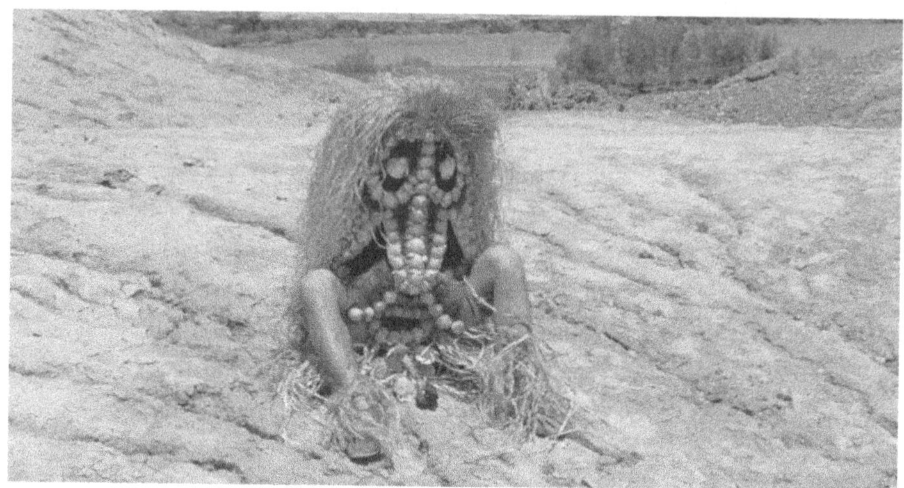

FIGURE 11. The mask of the Sphinx.

wears presents a crude image, with long ears, one on either side of two huge eyes, below which dangles a long nose. With so much of the film inviting sexualized interpretations, however, it is easy to imagine the mask as a representation of the male crotch, upon which hang a pair of testicles and a long penis. The straw hair above is readable then not as scalp hair but as pubic hair. As Pasolini frames and reframes the Sphinx, the mask takes on the quality of Wittgenstein's duck-rabbit, where what seems a human face in some shots becomes a human crotch in others: not only do the eyes become testicles and the nose a penis, but the mouth below can seem an anus, while the jowls appear as a pair of buttocks (see figure 11).

In the screenplay, the encounter between Oedipus and the Sphinx is presented from the perspective of Davoli's messenger, who has warned his new friend not to face the monster and who retreats to a safe distance, where he witnesses the unfolding events but can hear nothing. Almost immediately, the messenger becomes so frightened that he covers his eyes, only looking again after Oedipus has somehow killed the creature and just in time to see "Oedipus dragging the corpse of the Sphinx by the tail, dragging it laboriously down through the rocks. He has been victorious and the Sphinx is his trophy."[41] As thematically interesting (and fitting the rest of the film) as it may have been to have such an important plot point occur while its only witness has temporarily blinded himself to the horror, Pasolini made different choices when directing the film itself. Rather than remaining with the messenger, the spectator's point of view elides with that of Oedipus as he challenges the Sphinx. The Sphinx queries, "There is an enigma in your life. What is it?" Oedipus responds, "I don't know. I don't want to know." Unsheathing his sword, he charges the creature. The Sphinx stands and responds, "It is useless." Oedipus counters, "I don't want to see you. I don't want to see you. I don't want to hear you," verbalizing his hesitation over understanding his destiny, the true structure of his desire. "It is useless, is useless," the Sphinx utters just before Oedipus kills him. The monster's last words are, "The abyss where you're thrusting me is inside you." As in Oedipus's fateful coitus with his mother, which is soon to occur, the Sphinx reminds him that every thrust is a desperate desire for escape that ultimately only becomes a reunion with the self, an act of heterosexual penetration as imagined homosexual surrender. Crucially, we do not witness Oedipus throwing the Sphinx off the top of the hill to his death, giving the latter's final statement a more metaphorical meaning. Suddenly, though, the Sphinx is dead. The male creature that is supposed to be a female monster, the face that looks like a crotch or the crotch that looks like a face, the eyes that are also testicles and the nose (or tongue) that may also/instead be a penis, *all* this has been both *thrust away from* and *absorbed within* Oedipus. The Oedipus who did not want to see will soon have his eyes filled with the horrors of an imminent incestuous union.

Following the death of the Sphinx, the young messenger escorts the triumphant Oedipus into Thebes, allowing him to claim his reward: the queen/his mother as his bride (played, like the mother of the twentieth-century prologue, by Silvana Mangano). When the two first lay eyes on each other, the knowing looks of satisfaction they exchange may, for some viewers, suggest merely mutual desire. Perhaps Jocasta was worried that her ordained second husband would turn out to be unattractive. Perhaps Oedipus, likewise, was worried that his promised queen would be elderly and unappealing. It is only natural that the two would be happy to see their future spouses in the enticing forms that they have. But, as a manifestation of dramatic irony makes way for a queer alternative, one cannot quite escape the sense that both characters are thinking darker, perhaps even knowingly incestuous thoughts precisely because their expressions seem to betray an uncanny sense of destiny foretold. At any rate, Oedipus will now marry his biological mother and begin the heterosexual relationship with her that will also be a homosexual relationship with his dead father. Interestingly, although the camera enters the bridal chamber on the night of the queen and her new king's wedding, it stops short of recording, even discreetly, the first act of damnable incest.

Like many films from an era still beholden to state censorship or industrial self-censorship, *Edipo re* stops short of showing any sex on the wedding night, but unlike other films, which might cut from the marriage bed to something prosaic to imply the bliss of imminent sexual fulfillment, Pasolini presents a hard cut to a dead male body: the first on-screen victim of the plague that descends on Thebes as a result of King

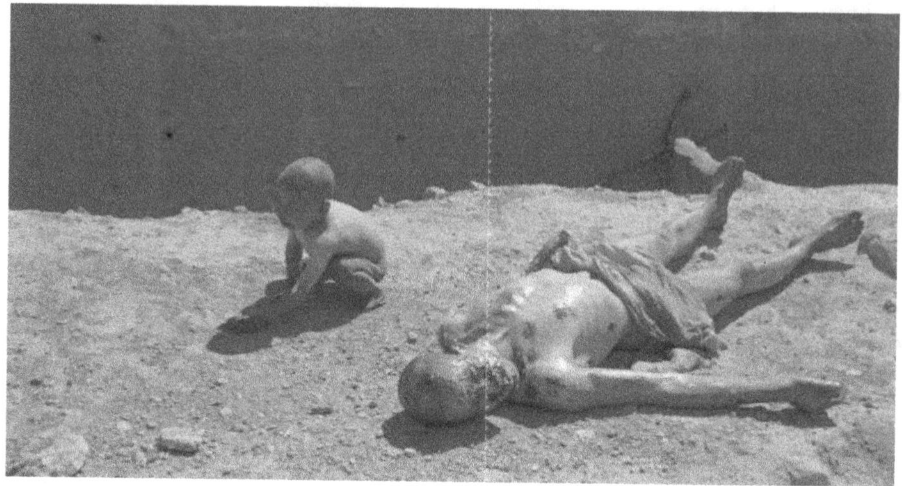

FIGURE 12. The dead is unsettlingly close to an erotic image.

Pelops's curse. This body, like the next five or six shown to us, is, despite its rotting face and otherwise sore-ravaged skin, uncannily, disquietingly sexually alluring. It is unclothed (but for a cloth over its genitals), young, with its legs spread just so far apart and with pronounced, youthful muscle tone in its extremities (see figure 12). Maurizio Viano rightly describes these images of the dead as "among Pasolini's most beautiful creations. . . . Sensuality and death, Eros and pathology mix as never before, forcing the viewer to see beauty in death, the sublime in horror."[42]

The connection between sexual desire and death in the Western imagination that Pasolini viscerally enacts here is hardly an original idea in this film. As an adaptation of the ur-text of Western sexuality, however, it is important to note that Pasolini startlingly emphasizes the connection and does so in such a way that it takes on a homoerotic cast—the several fit-but-plague-ridden corpses are almost all male casualties. Had Pasolini begun his narrative at the same point in the story that Sophocles does, these shots would have probably been the first in the film. The fact that they serve as something of a "money shot" for an unseen heterosexual wedding night darkly queers heterosexual coitus. The cut thus posits a deadly result for the homoeroticized male body in the shadow of a paradigmatic heterosexual union. With regard to traditional eroticism, only the last of the four sex scenes shown occurring or implied to soon occur between Jocasta and Oedipus is at all explicit. In it, Citti's buttocks are briefly, partially visible as he lies atop his out-of-view mother. As for Jocasta's attractive naked body, we will only see it after she is dead, through suicide from hanging, dangling from a rope tied to the ceiling. The moment after Oedipus pulls off her dress and looks up at her naked, lifeless form is, in fact, the moment he takes her dagger from her and punctures his eyes. In penetrating his eyeballs, Oedipus is frantically contesting (or, perhaps, the opposite: validating) the penetration of the image into his mind through his ocular organs. As Lacan teaches us, the gaze is not, originally, man gazing outward but a function of the world penetrating the subject's consciousness through the eyes. "That which is light looks at me," he describes, "and by means of that light in the depths of my eye, something is painted, . . . something that is an impression."[43]

Incest

For the final forty-eight minutes of the film, except for a five-minute modern-day epilogue that returns us to the Italy of the prologue, Pasolini follows Sophocles's text closely. Although not really known as an "actor's director" and often happy to present seemingly unprofessional performances, Pasolini here elicits surprisingly impressive, dramatically verisimilar work out of his largely unprofessional cast. One element only in Citti's and Mangano's performances seems inconsistent. Both actors repeatedly imply a sense of tragic horror at their unacknowledged incestuous status, as one would expect; on the other hand, here and there, they suggest a surprising acceptance of (even pleasure regarding) that possibility. This inconsistency also can be found in the delivery of the film's dialogue, much of which comes from Sophocles's original as mediated through Pasolini's written and published screenplay. For instance, Pasolini's Jocasta, replying to Oedipus's terror at the possibility of an incestuous relationship, says, "Why does the idea of making love to your mother hold such terror for you? Why? Think how many men must have made love to their mothers in their dreams! . . . Who has not dreamt of making love to his mother? And does he live in horror of his dream? Of course not, unless he wants to clutter his life with useless suffering."[44] Once the mere idea of incest is all but revealed to be reality, however, Jocasta responds differently: "It's much better, a thousand times better to know nothing of these things. . . . In the name of the god [*sic*], don't try to find out."[45] Sophocles's version of the first statement can be read as (and is usually performed as) a mere hypothetical based on the mistaken belief that Oedipus's adoptive mother in Corinth (played in the film by Alida Valli) is his biological mother. But Pasolini, having given both Citti and Mangano close-ups revealing a sense of uncanny recognition and a knowing complicity on their parts, makes her comments readable as a defense of her own semiconscious incest with her son / new husband. Furthermore, as Linda Belau puts it in her reading of the film, "most critics insist that [Oedipus and Jocasta] know who they are to each other" because of a later love scene in which Oedipus cries "'madre' during the prohibited act."[46]

Viano argues both that *Edipo re* is Pasolini's autobiography (an interpretation Pasolini explicitly invited)[47] and, as I do here, that the film explores the relationship of homosexuality to the Oedipus complex. As Viano puts it, "Pasolini chooses the Greek myth given primacy by Freud as the motor of human development because it is the myth which contains a 'scientific' explanation for his homosexuality. It all comes from an excessive love for the mother."[48] Certainly three of Freud's four variants identified by Lewes regarding the emergence of homosexuality in the adult male touch on an overweening desire for the mother. And Viano is right in positing that Pasolini's strong, determinative desire for Susanna Pasolini connects with the film's remarkable fixation on Silvana Mangano as Jocasta. But, as we have seen, the film's spectator is also made to be transfixed by Luciano Bartoli as the father, something that is unnecessary for the basic dramatological success of the story as it is conservatively understood, even one supposing a homosexual basis for a desire for the mother. This is not to say that Viano's thesis (roughly, that Oedipus loves men because he loves his mother) is wrong and that my alternative interpretation (roughly, that Oedipus loves his mother because he really loves men) is exclusively correct. However, in abolishing the "unity of time and space" that characterizes the play, in other words, by dramatizing the backstory and thus visualizing Laïus on screen and eventually having the adult Oedipus seen meeting the attractive actor Luciano Bartoli in the role of Laïus before he meets Jocasta, Pasolini creates a chronological narrative structure in which homoeroticism precedes heterosexual desire.

To the extent that any desired object in the film is traditionally gendered (and the attractive males are attractive *as* males, just as Jocasta is attractive *as* a woman), there can be no primary sexual object. Constitutional bisexuality, as divisible into a heterosexual/homosexual binary, does not presuppose any original sexual orientation. Indeed, the very definition of the term disallows that. Pasolini's worldview, however, at least as it is expressed cinematically, does not include any sense of sexual desire beyond gender, although Freud's does. Even the problematic attraction to pubescent boys that one registers in Pasolini's films is very much an attraction to sexed *males*. Nevertheless, Pasolini's gender-anchored queerness contributes to more radical notions of sexuality, including those forms defined as polysexual and pansexual, in its seminal instability. This is elucidated at the level of film form. One may think of Pasolini's verité aesthetic of handheld cameras and unbalanced framings, on the one hand, and his classical stylings, on the other, as corresponding to opposed binaries that, in their vibrant disequilibrium, support and vitiate each other. They thus, together, contribute to a queerly resonant critique of identities based on sexual-object choices, identities that are understood in terms of opposed binaries.

But if the desirability of the father is ultimately, inseparably connected to the desirability of the mother in the Oedipal drama, and not just in Pasolini's version, we must still come to a final accounting of what we might call the Chrysippus factor. In Oedipus's desiring his father's "other" boy, his queer longings for an exogenous brother figure who also loves the father pulls one both away from and toward an intragenerational incestuous object choice, even in, perhaps especially in, Pasolini's revision. Chrysippus both is and is not Oedipus's brother, just like Oedipus's love for him both is and is not a love for the father. This brings us to an accounting of the role of the messenger played by Ninetto Davoli, whose resemblance to Laïus's last-killed solder, the film's first Chrysippus figure, is notable. But if Chrysippus is dead on the roadside at Oedipus's hand (really as a result of the thrusting of his sword), and he resembles the Davoli who will appear as the messenger in the very next scene, what are we to then make of the messenger's relationship to Oedipus as the film reaches its conclusion?

As Viano helpfully points out without fully pursuing the implications, this messenger represents "Pasolini's most significant change from Sophocles's original." He is "the replacement of Antigone," Oedipus's daughter/sister, in the film.[49] In giving Antigone's role to a young, attractive male, particularly one played by Pasolini's own lover and resembling the attractive youth who had been protecting his father and who also stands in for Chrysippus, the filmmaker makes his homosexual/incestuous perspective clear: Pasolini (the ultimate referent here) desires a son/brother figure (who stands in for the daughter/sister Antigone), whom the ultimately sightless, deposed, and accursed king of Thebes does and does not recognize as linked to his father. That then returns the circular desire of the tragedy to Chrysippus, who reflects Oedipus himself—King Laïus's *other* boy. This finally is the narcissistic, knotted love of the self. In other words, *Edipo re* invites a reading of the relationship between sexuality and subjectivity akin to that outlined in *Homographesis* by Lee Edelman, when he identifies homophobic connections between popular (non-Freudian) conceptions of narcissism and homosexuality to be the heterosexual male subject's attempt at self-definition against a disavowed nondifferentiation represented by constitutional bisexuality and homosexuality. Indeed, as Lord Raglan reminds us, no less an authority than Plato argued that the edict against incest was, in part, to forestall the natural desire to (narcissistically) marry those who are most like us, our own relatives.[50]

For Edelman, building from theoretical interventions offered by Bersani, Michael Warner, and D. A. Miller, the (mis)understanding of narcissism represents a homophobic logic operating behind the formation of the straight subject, "a subject fantasmatically brought into being through an act of self-cohesion . . . that makes its foundational moment the primal scene of differentiation from what it reads as the torpor or passivity of its imaginary 'history,' the state of non-organization to which, as Freud argues in *Beyond the Pleasure Principle*, the death drive would have us return."[51] But if the logic of the Oedipus myth and the eponymous complex implies the non-existence of truly exogenous sexuality, in other words, if all sexuality is incestuous, then all sexuality is narcissistic. "Normal" heterosexuality, taboo-free and defined as a nonnarcissistic attraction to the other rather than the same/self, is a lie. Oedipus's paradigmatically heterosexual crime ultimately, ironically, proves his queer constitution insofar as it is a crime that dramatizes the imbricated dynamic between sexual desire and the death drive.

As the story comes to its preordained conclusion, Tiresias is forced to tell King Oedipus the bitter truth. Oedipus's wife/mother will then hang herself. Oedipus will then take a dagger (in the film, off his dead wife/mother's dress) and savagely blind himself, leaving the image of his mother the last thing he ever sees. Staggering out of the palace, the king then moans the immortal, infernal lines, "I should have hacked off my ears as well . . . to *imprison this unhappy body* all the more securely *within myself . . .* to no longer have to see or hear anything . . . anything at all."[52] Subjectivity and desire are both trapped within the self. Oedipus no longer wishes a return to the womb. Yet he desires something often mistaken for that, displaced onto that wish. He seeks a return to the state of radical nothingness, an existential place that predates sex, desire, and gender. His burden is the realization that such a return is not possible. He has taken a circular journey from the nothingness of complete ignorance to the nothingness of knowledge. In short, he grasps the implications of the death drive.

Pasolini's Epilogue

While Sophocles offers several extended paragraphs of summation before concluding his play in Thebes, Pasolini quickly returns us to twentieth-century Italy—although, to match the twenty-five years or so of Oedipus's life we have seen transpire on film, these final scenes take place much later than the prologue, in the mid-1960s. Oedipus is thus portrayed as a more modern-day prophet, really a modern-day Tiresias. Resembling Julian Beck's personification of the blind prophet, Franco Citti's final scenes show us a man unseeing but with intact eyeballs: a marked distinction from the previous images of his gouged-out sockets. Like a man whose castration is only virtual or metaphorical (whose testicles are present but not functional), this twentieth-century Oedipus represents a different order of blindness than Sophocles's character. Like Tiresias, he has been compensated for his inability to see with a different order of insight and vision. He also now plays a primitive recorder. As he travels from urban streets to the pastoral field where he first recognized his mother from the crib, he seems to know everything but is none the happier for it. Pasolini leaves us with an image of queer (in) sight that, pessimistically enough, offers a form of radical negativity. Like the queer male sexual penetratee, then, who has the organs to function as a male in a phallocentric order but does not choose to do so, this Oedipus, unlike Sophocles's, has had his eyes restored but still does not see. Or, rather, he "sees" something altogether different than a sighted individual does, something that transcends normal vision yet leaves him alone, irredeemable. This radical negativity is also the truly queer ironic paradox of the myth of Oedipus as a whole.

The film gives the modern Oedipus some final lines of dialogue, which suggest the return to childhood that often occurs before death, much as the mythology inspiring the film suggests that adult heterosexuality is simultaneously a journey to the well-springs from which life itself has emerged and a journey to the land of the dead: "May the light that I couldn't see anymore, and which once was mine," he says calmly, "illuminate me now for the last time. I have arrived. Life ends where it began." The screenplay, however, leaves us with a description, something that could not likely have been clearly expressed cinematically: "The slightest breath of an ancient and inexpressible wind gives life to this pastoral scene; over its image flows that same musical theme, at *once investing the surroundings with its own disturbing meaning*—a repetition, a return— an original immobility in the vain movement of time—the mysterious music of childhood days—the love song of the prophet—older and younger than destiny itself—the source of all things."[53] Pasolini reminds us how the wind, a signifier of that which is seen only indirectly, gives life to the material world itself. This wind is like the cinema, that which allows us to understand reality in all its "disturbing meanings." It distinguishes itself from, and thus allows us to understand, the written language of reality.

The "ancient and inexpressible wind" invisible to the sighted but perceptible to one attuned to other senses indeed flows in our era, insofar as the occulted construct of homosexuality gave birth to the back-formation of a hypervisible heterosexuality, seen, like tree branches, shaking in the woods. Likewise, heteronormative ideological investments (bifurcated genders, the patriarchal family) have created the context in which male homosexual desire, as it would eventually be understood (as governed by the logic of penetration-as-power as a precondition of masculinity), became possible. Pasolini's Oedipus, in finally refusing the logic of the incestuous wedding bed by symbolically castrating himself, says no to heterosexual desire. He refuses to disavow the death drive to which heterosexuality, by the deceit of reproduction, is blinded. All told, Pasolini's queerness is expressed in a cinema, his cinema, rich in aesthetic imagery in which the seen is on full display and the unseen is utterly palpable.

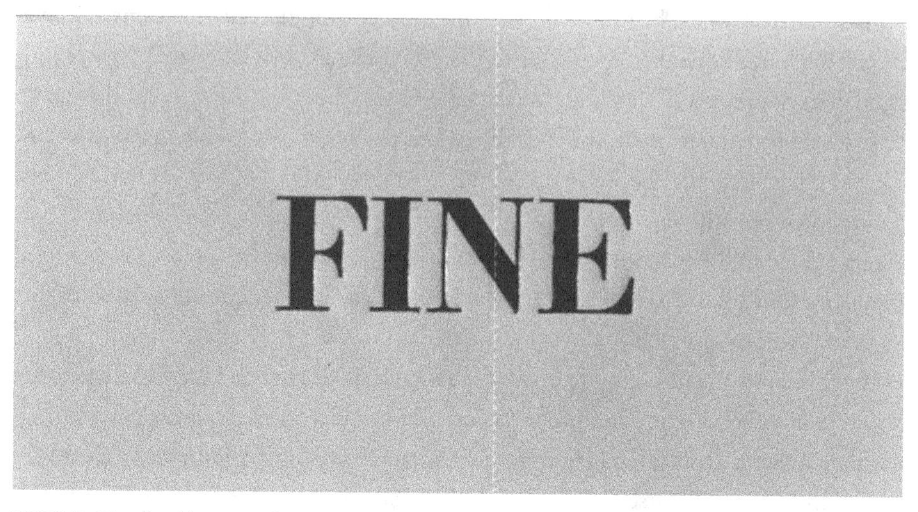

FIGURE 13. The final image of the indentation of the typewriter keys on the paper.

In the film's final moment, Citti actually closes his unseeing eyes just before Pasolini cuts to what would normally be considered a point-of-view shot from his character's perspective, looking up at the tall trees and sky above him—trees and sky that his infant self had also impossibly "seen" from the cradle decades before. Although Pasolini implies that Oedipus sees these trees at some level, he nonetheless asks Angelo where they are. "In a place with many trees in a row," Angelo replies, "and many little streams and a green, green field." Few viewers would begrudge Pasolini having Angelo accurately account for the trees and the field while also, oddly, mentioning "little streams" that the filmmaker might have expected to find and film but did not. Their absent presence only implies additional alternate visions beyond those of not only Oedipus but us as well.

Still, Oedipus *sees what he cannot see* and is returned to the plenitude of the love of and for the mother while also being comforted by the love of the son/Chrysippus (in the form of Davoli's Angelo). His blindness is and is not like the blindness of Yunan from *Il fiore delle mille e una notte*. It is the sign of Oedipus's queer vision but a vision, at this earlier, somewhat more optimistic stage in Pasolini's life and in his body of work, that does not portend negation and destruction pure and simple. Oedipus bathes in a love that his blindness allows him to feel. This is the same love that would be lost in its very articulation to Yunan in *Il fiore delle mille e una notte*'s womb-like underground chamber, after the sexual-murderous deed inflicted on his brother-son in a scene that is all but a prologue for *Salò*. For Pasolini, heterosexuality and homosexuality, as well as incestuous and exogamous desire, are fated to merge and collapse. What is left, however, and this is the film's supreme irony, is a new queer desire redolent of a profound, if ambivalent, negativity—an ironic formulation of desire in an irredeemable world. It is a negativity born of the erotically charged mourning of sexuality's unavoidability and impossibility. This is why Pasolini's work is uniquely interesting in one distinctly counterintuitive way: homosexual frisson is always at its most pronounced in circumstances psychically connected to heterosexual intimacy.

Viewers of the film are left with a final image. "Fine" (or "the end") is, like the words of the opening credits, presented literally as typed letters on a sheet of off-white paper. The letters have been pressed so powerfully on the paper, and the paper lit in such a way, from the side, that we see the violent indentation of the typewriter keys on the paper (see figure 13). It impresses language on a page as violently as the light of reality impresses itself on the celluloid in Pasolini's camera, as violently as the wind blows through the trees. There will be no Pasolini adaptations of Sophocles's *Oedipus at Colonus* or *Antigone* following *Edipo re*. Therefore, this really is the end of Oedipus's story in our time. But it is, like all endings, also a paradoxical beginning, the beginning of sexuality or, more precisely, of sinthomosexuality, of heterosexuality beholden to homosexuality, and homosexuality beholden to the death drive and/as *jouissance*. We are left to consider it as a form of queer *écriture* that will continue Pasolini's engagement with Greek tragedy and mythology as a way to elucidate a radically new form of homosexual desire.

A CINEMA OF (QUEER) POETRY
Medea (1969)

The Theater-Going Experience of Poetry

In "The 'Cinema of Poetry,'" Pasolini makes two things completely clear, even as he manages to make many others more complicated.[1] One, prior to cinema's being tamed through the vast arsenal of devices associated with both classical Hollywood film and the bourgeois art-film tradition, its essential nature is rough, archaic, and irrational. Two, Pasolini's newly identifiable cinema of poetry is, among other things, a form of filmmaking that, as it embraces this rough and archaic irrationality, makes itself perceptible as cinema itself. With the latter in mind, it seems fitting to address the contribution of the movie*going* experience—the all but vanished practice of seeing a film in a cinema with an audience of strangers—in relation to the cinema of poetry. As we shall see through a discussion of *Medea*, the experience of a certain way of, precisely, watching motion pictures in a theater seems built into Pasolini's most characteristic aesthetic choices in his mid- and late-career films. Through this development, the bitterness that developed for Pasolini in the late 1960s and that he spoke about in his reflections on *Uccellacci e uccellini* here becomes tempered by a certain positive sense of redirection of the part of the spectator/viewer.

As one approaches this concept, one might find oneself thinking of two of the most impressive if underrated art films of the past twenty years, Tsai Ming-liang's *Bu San* (*Good Bye, Dragon Inn*, 2003) and Julián Hernández's *Rabioso sol, rabioso cielo* (*Raging Sun, Raging Sky*, 2009). Each focuses, for a significant portion of its running time, on the intersection of cinematic spectatorship and homosexual desire—perhaps not coincidentally, both Hernández and Tsai have expressed a great artistic debt to Pasolini.[2] Furthermore, both filmmakers explore the homosexual subculture involved in cruising and public sex in urban movie theaters. In each of their films, we see spectators roughly divided into two groups: those who only occasionally take in a film's flickering images while negotiating sexual encounters with their fellow filmgoers and those who try to focus on the movie despite the disruptive activity around them.

Artists from Ingmar Bergman to James Baldwin have discussed the relationship between public cinemas and expressions of homosexual desire. On at least two occasions, Bergman notes his own formative experiences seeing films in an urban theater in the beneficent presence of an elderly, homosexual projectionist.[3] Baldwin begins *Another Country* (1962) with his protagonist, the bisexual African American artist Rufus Scott, dozing off watching an Italian film in a Times Square balcony only to be repeatedly awakened by the "caterpillar fingers" of other men "between his thighs."[4] The two recent films I reference offer more radical understandings of both the possibilities of sexuality and cinemagoing than do Bergman or Baldwin in their brief allusions to the topic. *Bu San*, for its part, offers several extended samplings of a King Hu martial arts epic, *Long men kezhan* (*Dragon Inn*, 1967), being screened in the run-down theater that is its primary location. *Rabioso sol, rabioso cielo*, on the other hand, offers only the briefest, largely out-of-focus glimpses of the film that its gay-male characters gaze on when not in pursuit of, or engaging in, anonymous sex. As something of an inside joke, the featured film is Hernández's own *Bramadero* (2007), which, as a twenty-one-minute short, would not, realistically, give queer spectators much time to make an erotic connection. Both features, however, ask us to reflect on the value of movies watched in such spaces and in such ways, suggesting that those values might diverge from the ones posited in the arguments of formalist or neoformalist critics.[5]

Each of these early-twenty-first century films alludes to a form of spectatorship that Roland Barthes described in "Leaving the Movie Theater." In that 1975 essay, Barthes claims that "there is another [radical] way of going to the movies" beyond that prescribed by leftist film culture at the time, which was simply being "armed" with "counter-ideological" theoretical perspectives. Barthes writes, "by letting oneself be fascinated *twice over*, by the image and by its surrounding—as if I had two bodies at the same time: a *narcissistic* body which gazes, lost, into the engulfing mirror, and a *perverse* body, ready to fetishize not the image but precisely what exceeds it: the texture of the sound, the hall, the darkness, the obscure mass of the other bodies, the rays of light, entering the theater, leaving the hall; in short, in order to distance, in order to 'take off,' I complicate a 'relation' by a 'situation.'"[6]

Here Barthes prescribes a practice of filmgoing in which the spectator both (narcissistically) revels in the cinematic illusion and remains (perversely) mindful of (indeed reveling in) various aspects of the apparatus that have often been unaccounted for (the materiality of the celluloid, the sound of the projector, audience members walking in and out, and most importantly the space of the theater auditorium itself). Interestingly, Barthes reframes the twinned desires he associates with cinematic pleasure (narcissism and perversity) by substituting the specific perversion most often associated with spectatorship, scopophilia, with fetishism, a perversion not regularly connected to either homosexuality or the cinema. In doing this, he is able to articulate a very different imbrication of the relation between private and public that facilitates queer desire. Ultimately, Barthes's rethinking of cinematic space to include the auditorium is suggestive for how one might best address spectatorship in light of Pasolini's cinema of poetry. He posits a different form of spectatorship that rethinks and centralizes the position of the queer spectator. In this light, and in the context of this book, the question is, How is the narcissistic relationship between spectator and screen complicated when the perverse promise of public sex intersects with the cinematic fantasy in a fetishistic way?

Hernández's and Tsai's films utilize metacinema not simply in the way they *illustrate* the Barthesian cinematic encounter. They also re-create, for a viewer watching these films anywhere, in any way, a queer spectatorial *experience*. The specific films-within-their-films are themselves palpable as necessary pretexts for structuring erotic reveries, reveries that require a cinematic text but are not centrally focused on them in ways familiar from classical spectatorship theory. They are, instead, cinema as queer aphrodisiac. Hernández essentially confirms his connection to Barthes's "situation"-based mind-set: "My narratives are intended to be disruptive, fragmented. . . . I try to free myself from the clarity of plot and invent a different structure in which I abandon the established grammar of film for a model of cinema as a state of mind."[7] Furthermore, the lengthy running time of Hernández's film (192 minutes), coupled with numerous early sequences and shots that repeat later in the film, albeit in revised form, creates a sense not of a single, discrete viewing experience but of spending the entire day at the movies. Kenneth Chan points out that Tsai has developed a veritable aesthetic of lingering in which "extremely long single-shot takes are part of [an] observational realist style, which has the effect of causing the audience to observe both visual and auditory details it would not otherwise be attentive to."[8]

Beyond Hernández's and Tsai's metacinematic endeavors, they have also, not incidentally, been categorized as practitioners of the late-twentieth/early-twenty-first century's iteration of the "slow cinema" ethos. Karl Schoonover and Rosalind Galt posit that recent slow cinema—which includes work by Kelly Reichardt, Béla Tarr, Abbas Kiarostami, and Apichatpong Weerasethakul and arguably emerged out of Italian neorealism—threatens dominant cinema with a "queer counterproductivity."[9] Indeed, in Schoonover and Galt's view, slow cinema even "performs an often unnoticed queering of time." "Like the willfully unproductive queer," they argue, "slow cinema refuses to labor along socially sanctioned narrative pathways."[10] Obviously, for those who are fortunate enough to see these slow films in theatrical exhibition, their deliberate, sometimes glacial pacing also has the effect of foregrounding the very environment (the leaking roof and sticky floor, the sounds and smells of the patrons as they shift in their chairs) to which the Barthesian spectator is attuned.

Ultimately, in simply "getting the gist" of Hernández's or Tsai's exemplary films, one can fully imagine the arena in which Barthes's differently engaged theatergoer finds a home. In experiencing *Bu San, Rabioso sol, rabioso cielo,* and, in a more direct way born of the design of the film itself, Pasolini's *Medea,* one not only delights in cinematic duration but experiences one's own body in erotic distraction. *Medea* does not fit any but the broadest definition of slow cinema, except in one or two sequences—which is certainly not to say that it has not been criticized in the popular press for being slow— and Pasolini's aesthetic, at a purely formal level, is very different from Hernández's or Tsai's. In effect, Hernández's and Tsai's films illustrate the link between what we will explore as Pasolini's "unconsumable" aesthetic of bitter poetry and the particularly queer dimensions of spectatorship that Barthes describes. But if slow cinema manages to alienate the viewer from narrative's hegemony through various scandalous disruptions, Pasolini's film puts its own longueurs into service with cinema verité camera work, narrative, and stylistic fragmentation in order to create something similarly, perhaps even more markedly, radical.

To begin my discussion of Pasolini's *Medea,* I wish to suggest, then, that its rough, fragmented visual and aural style and its unique and radical narrative construction offers an equivalent to the kind of experience Barthes explores in his essay, as well as to those we actually see in their contextual fullness in Tsai's and Hernández's films. *Edipo re* also offered a radically restructured version of its primary source material's narrative through a somewhat rough and fragmented style and with a production incorporating both location filming in the Third World (signifying authenticity) and repeated examples of artifice and alienation devices such as the bizarre costume designed for the Sphinx (signifying its constructed nature). And yet, despite the exceedingly disturbing cumulative effect it has, that film, in its narrative structure and aural and visual strategies, is not, finally, outside the norms established by art-cinema adaptations of classical texts in the long wake of neorealism. *Medea,* on the other hand, takes a quantum leap forward, or perhaps one should say backward, to a state of shocking archaic vitality and narrative and stylistic incoherence, one both constructed and deconstructed.

In short, with *Medea,* Pasolini effectively creates a film that constructs a kind of cruising-at-the-movies spectatorship position.[11] He directs his cinema of poetry toward hyperaroused spectators, simultaneously engaged in image and sound yet alienated from or, rather, differently related to the narrative. As we shall see at the end of this chapter, a spectatorship associated with the sociability of public sex proffers a new relational mode between filmgoer and film, analogous to the way cruising, in the formulation that Leo Bersani offers in his 2002 essay "Sociability and Cruising," proffers a new relational mode between individuals identified according to a self/other binary.[12] Furthermore, with one foot (barely) still in (heteronormative) cinema and another (firmly) in a foreboding queer landscape of fragmentary yet integrated pleasures, Pasolini now fully draws on an archaic, nearly "savage" form of consciousness to engender the perverse modernity of *Medea*. He will continue this project throughout his subsequent *Trilogy of Life*, only to abandon it with a jolt for his final theatrical film, *Salò*.

"Empty, Confusing, Passionless and Devoid of Humanity"

As was the case with many of Pasolini's later films, contemporaneous critics were largely unimpressed with *Medea*; indeed, some were angry and openly contemptuous at what they saw as directorial incompetence. The *San Bernardino Sun-Telegram*'s John Russell, to select a characteristic review from one US newspaper, decried *Medea* for a "lack of cohesiveness and some of the worst acting seen in any movie." Russell claimed that the violent tragedy "caused laughter instead of horror" when screened in Southern California.[13] The *Boston Globe*'s Kevin Kelly praised Maria Callas's performance as Medea but called the film "a completely incoherent version of the tragedy."[14] In Canada, Frank Daley wrote that "the film is empty, confusing, passionless and devoid of humanity" and ultimately "confuses even people who are familiar with Euripides's play"; more accurately, Daley points out that "the whole film seems to be focused slightly off to the left somewhere."[15] Perhaps the most caustic review of the era came, not surprisingly, from the prominent New York–based critic Rex Reed. *Medea*, he wrote, is "directed with typical confusion and pretentiousness by Pier Paolo Pasolini. . . . It is a movie of indescribable incompetence, directed with unrelenting hysteria and performed with unequalled amateurishness."[16]

Even the queer theorist and film scholar D. A. Miller, looking back at his college days in England in the early 1970s, remembers being perplexed. He believed that seeing the film would help him better understand the play, which he had coincidentally been assigned to study that week. As he reports in a recent, retrospective review, "The viewing was worse than a waste of time. Pasolini's film handled its narrative so strangely that far from refreshing my memory [about Euripides's drama] as desired, it obliged me, back in my rooms, to clear my head by rereading Euripides. . . . For long stretches, as every viewer recognizes, the film is bewildering, almost unfathomable, as if its director's cherished vision of a 'cinema of poetry' depended on spoiling the cinema of narrative after all."[17] Indeed. Miller is not inaccurate about Pasolini's "cherished vision."

The exasperation of many critics and audiences at the time was surely compounded by the fact that, more than any other Pasolini feature including *Il vangelo secondo*

Matteo, Medea was assumed to be a prestige picture. It was doubtlessly hoped that the film's splendid costumes by Piero Tosi (previously Oscar nominated for Luchino Visconti's *Il gattopardo* [*The Leopard*, 1963]), awe-inspiring location cinematography (in Anatolia, Syria, Pisa's Campo dei Miracoli, and the Grado lagoon near Venice), and a high-culture superstar at its center (the opera diva Maria Callas), would justify the reported million-dollar budget and deliver a middle-brow entertainment to establishment art-house audiences.[18] Furthermore, despite the queer warning signs, *Edipo re* had been just professional enough to suggest Pasolini might finally deliver the upscale, art-house goods with this production, which was his second in two years based on Greek myth.

This *Medea* did have its defenders. Vincent Canby filed a review that intelligently describes it as "an attempt to translate into film terms the sense of a prehistoric time, place and intelligence in which all myths and rituals were real experiences." Even he, however, criticized the film as "uneven" and declared it "not completely successful."[19] More cogently, *Newsweek*'s Paul D. Zimmerman approached the film in the same way many of Derek Jarman's sympathetic critics would later assess that queer filmmaker's adaptations of Shakespeare's *The Tempest* (1979) and Marlow's *Edward II* (1991). Zimmerman viewed *Medea*'s anachronisms ("cathedrals and potato dinners"), histrionic performances (a "covey of distressed widows . . . [screaming] like caged parrots in a parody of anguish") and prurient fascination with "the rituals of the pre-Christian period" as emblematic of "a winning lack of respect" for the cultivating influences of high art. Those who saw it at the screening he attended were, he reported, "hooting, laughing and cheering as though they were watching *The Maltese Falcon* [1941]." Without using the word, Zimmerman all but declared the film a candidate as a camp classic that would ultimately appeal to "movie-hip students . . . alive to Pasolini's purpose."[20]

Given the variously reactionary and insightful critiques of *Medea*, how do we approach this film, one that at once set high expectations for middle-brow sensibilities yet ultimately delivered an experience that "bewildered" even sympathetic traditional art-house audiences and critics? Despite the colorful costumes and "exotic" cultures on display, the film itself is hardly a shameless piece of kitsch along the lines of, say, Robert Siodmak's *Cobra Woman* (1944). Zimmerman admits, in fact, that the film is "slow and stately much of the time and were it not for . . . marvelous moments would remain . . . educational, respectable, boring."[21] All told, Zimmerman seems to be describing a film that queers the prestige picture, in much the same way cruising queers public space, specifically art-cinema space. In other words, Pasolini's film seems ready made for those who see the theatrical film experience as an opportunity for the building of a queer community, and Zimmerman senses that.[22]

"To queer" *Medea*, however, is to understand "queer" in another very particular and, indeed, unsettling way. As if in anticipation of the disapprobation, Pasolini announced *Medea*—not dissimilarly to the way he announced his other unloved "cinema of poetry" films, *Uccellacci e uccellini*, *Teorema*, and *Porcile*—as part of a group of his features he deliberately identified as "unconsumable." For Pasolini, "unconsumable" films admittedly may have sold some tickets; they were, however, unconsumed. "The consumers put them in their mouths," he said, "but then they spit them out or pass the night with a tummy ache."[23] This cycle of features, which would eventually be rechristened by Pasolini himself as "unpopular films," represents precisely the director's filmmaking that developed alongside his theory of the cinema.[24] Arguably, these films offer the most rigorous and advanced examples of the director's theoretical postulations within his oeuvre. They represent a turning away from the Gramscian "popular films" that Pasolini made in the early 1960s, such as *Accattone*, *Mamma Roma*, and *Il vangelo secondo Matteo*, in which, as Kriss Ravetto puts it, Pasolini "inscribes the sacred within a revolutionary political discourse, [drawing] . . . the subproletariat, the peasantry, and the third world from the periphery to the center to coagulate them as the locus of a revolutionary force."[25] In Pasolini's retrospective estimation, the earlier films fell short of his hopes for them in that by the mid-1960s there was no longer meaningful distinction between "the culture of the dominated class and that of the ruling class," an important insight on Pasolini's part because it confronts the reductive forces that lay claim to rote dialectics and vulgar Marxism.[26]

After the death of Palmiro Togliatti, the shift in political perspective Pasolini had while shooting *Uccellacci e uccellini*, and, consequently, the filmmaker's abandonment of the practice of working in a national popular spirit for a now-lost-to-revolutionary-passion lower class, the project of an unpopular, unconsumable cinema could be born.[27] By embracing his bitterness much as later queer filmmakers and theorists would embrace negativity, Pasolini now could create a form of high-art, formalist cinema that, beyond its appeal to a particular queer spectator, was designed both to appeal to and ultimately to confound an imperialist and sterile heteronormative bourgeois class, one cut off from its own history and the cultures of its emergence.[28] I will address a somewhat different reflection of this idea in Pasolini's work in chapter 3.

The body of work beyond Pasolini's more easily digestible cinema yielded, therefore, "an aristocratic cinema: an unconsumable one. Just like poetry, where each book is published in an edition with a limited number of copies, only a few thousand, because the readers are only a few thousand."[29] To my mind, these films are designed to offer at least incidental "low" pleasures such as nudity, violence, and melodramatic plot developments. Nonetheless, even an audience valuing such pleasures also would be likely to reject Pasolini's "forced aristocraticness" in much the same way as more bourgeois audiences would. Furthermore, there were seemingly countless other places to get those "low" pleasures in an increasingly liberated late-1960s/early-1970s cinematic landscape. In the final analysis, however, these "unconsumable" films operate according to a canny juxtaposition, offering, on the one hand, a style characteristic of the "aristocratic" perspective of the educated Western artist (Pasolini himself) and, on the other, a style (violent, awestruck, mystical, fragmentary) redolent of the savagery of the precivilized past. This is perhaps most obvious in *Porcile*, with its two stories, each told in radically different ways, but it occurs more subtly in all Pasolini's films of this period. In some sense, these films suggest that savagery and the aristocracy, despite the chasm that separates them, as class positions broadly understood, are not mutually exclusive.

In "The 'Cinema of Poetry,'" Pasolini asserts that "every linguistic reality is a totality of socially differentiated and differentiating languages, and the writer who uses 'free indirect discourse' must be aware of this above all—an awareness which in the final analysis is a form of class consciousness."[30] John David Rhodes cuts through a lot of the confusion surrounding this essay to fully connect cinematic style to class consciousness in film: "*Style*," he says, "*comes to stand in for class-consciousness that cannot otherwise appear in the cinema.*"[31] For Rhodes, then, "The 'Cinema of Poetry'" offers "a theorization of style as the very medium of the appearance of political consciousness in cinema."[32] But while Rhodes correctly points out that this consciousness is a consciousness, specifically, of the bourgeois subject, "The 'Cinema of Poetry'" also makes palpable Pasolini's own class-based but also queerly informed consciousness, one definable as a profoundly negative identity.

This consciousness, born of Pasolini's exceedingly perverse style and decadent aesthetics (in the tradition of Huysmanian Aestheticism), is employed throughout his unconsumable films in various milieus against which they inevitably clash: Western consciousness, Eastern iconography; modern political perspectives, ancient attitudes toward fate and tragedy. This process gives birth to a *savage* consciousness ultimately commenting on, but unbeholden to, bourgeois and heteronormative morality. The result is a hyperintellectual, hyper-self-reflexive experience grounded in its obscure and obscene beauty, fragmentary energy, and taboo-breaking content. It stands as a fitting cinematic accompaniment to Pasolini's own acted-on desires (surely, at some point in a movie theater) in which he masochistically serviced lower-class boys (putting their genitals in his mouth but never satisfactorily consuming them, i.e., satiating his desire).[33] In somewhat different terms, his "unconsumable" cinema is, finally, a cinema in which the relationships involved, implied and real—between spectator and screen, filmmaker and film character, cruiser and trick—are, perversely, relationships of nonreproducibility. It is a cinema of desire but one that refuses the illusion that desire may be satisfied with cinematic affect alone. In short, the "unconsumable cinema" blocks its spectators from full identification with, and a normative consumption of, the image, in the same way that the sexuality of cruising was and remains a radically nonpossessive form of sexuality. The participating spectator is forced to consider different registers of desire, registers shared with members of the surrounding audience, in the materialized theaters in which these films played. The stakes here are high. As Freud reminds us, to desire is to make one ill or uneasy, precisely because to act on desire is to reach simultaneously and endlessly for pleasure and death.[34]

The Martyrdom of the Artist

In the 1970 essay "The Unpopular Cinema," Pasolini develops a related if somewhat different idea. He reiterates a Freudian insight and acknowledges the artist's central role in the dynamic of unconsumability. Using the essay's original title, "The Freedom of the Author and the Liberation of the Spectators," as his springboard, Pasolini begins his discussion with a "metalinguistic" examination of the essay's four titular concepts: freedom, author, liberation, and spectator.

In regard to the first—*freedom*—Pasolini ominously posits an existential insight: "this mysterious word finally doesn't mean any more than 'freedom to choose death.'" He suggests that, since suicide is both a Christian sin ("thou shalt not kill") and a Communist taboo (one must live to fulfill one's duty to society), true freedom for the author (to die) is inherently scandalous. Pasolini argues that "nature" furnishes "us with the . . . instinct, that is, the desire to die." Our instincts, therefore, exist in opposition to the moral (ideological?) duty to live. And as a result, a "conflict . . . takes place in the depths of our spirit: in the unknowable depths, as is well known." The only artistic freedom for the poetic filmmaker, then, involves transgressing the "codes" of the dominant cinema, which is "an infraction of self-preservation." To resist the dominant mode of artistic creation, to actually say something new—really be an author rather than simply a regurgitator—results in the "wounds of martyrdom."[35]

For Pasolini, who was repeatedly prosecuted within the Italian legal system on charges of sacrilege and obscenity and was denounced by the Communist Party for heretical statements, "wounds of martyrdom" is hardly hyperbolic language on his part. All but citing Freud's *Beyond the Pleasure Principle* in discussing his second term, *author*, Pasolini writes, "In every author, in the act of invention, freedom presents itself as a masochistic loss"; in each expression of true authorship, "there is, in short, the 'pleasure' that one has in every fulfillment of the desire for pain and death." It is not surprising that an *author* is one who embraces masochistic freedom: a freedom that alienates the artist *profoundly* from his or her society. One asserts selfhood by violating the codes, but in doing so, the author's public turns on him or her. As a result, an author, for Pasolini, "can only be a foreigner in a hostile land."[36]

In his third critical term, *spectator*, Pasolini recognizes the intermingled, if often conflicted, relationship between artist and audience. From the position of the artist, Pasolini declares, "the spectator is merely another author." Rather than a relationship of subordination, then, Pasolini posits "a dramatic relationship between democratically equal individuals. . . . *Such a spectator is as scandalous as the author*: both [author and spectator] shatter the order of self-preservation which requires either silence or relationship in a common, average language."[37] At first glance, this seems surprisingly like a response to Barthes's "Death of the Author," published two years before Pasolini's essay, which ends with the provocative declaration of a "birth of the reader . . . at the cost of the death of the Author."[38] Pasolini seems to counter Barthes's death/birth binary with his own dual self-destruction metaphor (both the author and reader are killing themselves). More importantly for my purposes, Pasolini further complicates the concept of class consciousness he raised in "The 'Cinema of Poetry,'" in which filmmakers' class consciousness derives from their imperfect identification with the characters they create. Here he allows the spectator her or his own subjectivity, which imperfectly overlaps with the author's. In suggesting that the spectator shatters his or her "order of self-preservation" by refusing to call for or even respect an "average language" from or "a relationship in common" with the author, Pasolini makes a bold suggestion.[39] A (suicidally) liberated film spectator, much like a (suicidally) liberated film author, must eschew an adherence to limiting, objective forms of (respectful, traditionally spectatorial) engagement.

In a crucial insight, Pasolini finally introduces his fourth term, *liberation*: "Things being thus, one cannot speak of the 'liberation' of the spectator . . . because the REAL spectator is already FREE," already liberated. In other words, in an era in which freeing the spectator was considered a radical priority, Pasolini understood the fight to be elsewhere. Again, like the author, he argued, the spectator is free, precisely, to die. The spectator is free "to immolate himself on the mixture of the pleasure and pain in which the transgression against the self-preserving normality consists." But the spectator has a second kind of freedom unavailable to the artist. This "specific liberty of the spectator consists in ENJOYING THE FREEDOM OF OTHERS."[40] Pasolini destabilizes what is already a provocatively unsettling relationship by illuminating boundaries that are definitively drawn but also productively, sensually blurred. The spectator is invited to die along with the author, who is going down with his or her radically sabotaged cinema, or simply to stand back and watch the free author's self-immolation in a distanciated form of engagement. In the former case, the spectator, in her or his painful identification with the author, loses his or her own sense of objectifying autonomy, much as the modernist filmmaker in Pasolini's "Cinema of Poetry" blurs with a film's protagonist through privileged moments of identification across class (and gender, sexual, and, presumably, racial) structures. In the latter case, the "freedom of others" also implies a specific reference to those others whom the queer spectator finds in the "situation" of Barthes's cinema auditorium—fellow cinematic travelers. In either case, while the filmmaker breaks the codes of cinema, the spectator must, one way or another, to put it bluntly in the form of our controlling metaphor, break the codes of public space and fuck around in the theater. The surviving spectator, along with his or her other, enjoys the freedom granted by the artist who is prepared to martyr him- or herself for the spectator's pleasure. In two separate, ultimately similar ways, then, the traditional spectator (or reader) is surmounted and reconfigured.

Archaic Modernism

The story of *Medea* itself, if melodramatic, is not particularly complex, although the myths that it is based on and that exist in multiple versions certainly are. Portions of those myths have been narrativized in a number of films, from the Hollywood stop-motion animation adventure *Jason and the Argonauts* (1963) to Lars von Trier's seventy-five-minute 1988 television production, titled, like Pasolini's adaptation, *Medea*. Pasolini's iteration, however, as D. A. Miller and the many critics cited earlier point out, is most perversely difficult to follow. As if gleaning the director's claims for suicidal freedom, Miller argues, "Pasolini's decision to retell the Medea legend goes hand in hand with a refusal to tell it *well*."[41] More tellingly, in light of Pasolini's narrative concerns at this moment in his work, the film, as Naomi Greene puts it, "quickly passes over the familiar and lingers on invented sequences."[42] Indeed, Pasolini's recounting leaves large narrative holes. As one contemporaneous critic, with some exasperation, describes a moment in the film, "Suddenly it's 10 years later, Medea and Jason (Giuseppe Jentile) have two sons, and Jason wants to leave and marry the king's daughter."[43] Other sequences, particularly those of Pasolini's invention, are presented in ways such that on a first viewing they inevitably serve to puzzle and alienate; only in retrospect and with repeated viewings do they make sense. As a result, even those who know the source material intimately can become disoriented in short order. But it is precisely the insistence to be difficult that marks the film as archaically modern, arcane, and queer. As John David Rhodes puts it in a lovely short essay, "when we do not know quite what is happening in *Medea* but are arrested by the film's presentation of its happening, this is Pasolini's way of offering us a chance to experience what it might mean to feel the world's sacred unnaturalness."[44]

To address the archaic qualities first, I turn to Hayden White's studies that chart the various forms of historical narration. White compares "history proper" to its two primitive (or to what I refer to as its archaic) precursors: the annals and the chronicle. In White's summary, "the annals form . . . consists only of a[n incomplete] list of events ordered in chronological sequence. The chronicle, by contrast, often seems to wish to tell a story, aspires to narrativity, but typically fails to achieve it."[45] The list of well-known films operating in the annals mode is short. Andrei Tarkovsky's *Andrei Rublev* (1966) comes to mind, although a closer look at that film reveals a subtle narrative tracing the eponymous character's spiritual disillusionment and eventual return to the Christian faith. Films following the structure of the chronicle mode are, however, somewhat more common.

In White's formulation, if the annals form speaks a "world in which things *happen to* people," the chronicle brings to life a world "in which people *do* things." The former lacks "a notion of a social center by which to locate [events] with respect to one another and to charge them with ethical or moral significance"[46] A chronicle, however, may be seen to be reliant on a grounded social center. Structured as a chronicle, then, a straightforward (re)telling of *Medea* would have to reflect the grounding either of Medea's savage (but finally ethical) community or of Jason's classical society. While annals might not provide a story per se, chronicles do (thus Shakespeare's turn to *Holinshed's Chronicles* [1577] as the bases for a number of his fully narrativized historical dramas).

Teresa de Lauretis convincingly argues that *any* narrative construction lends itself to heteronormative and misogynist ideology. In a paraphrase of the work of the Soviet semiotician Jurij Lotman, de Lauretis reminds one of the stakes in securing even a loose, chronicle-like narrative structure: "In . . . mythical-textual mechanics . . . the hero must be male, regardless of the gender of the text image, because the obstacle, whatever its personification, is morphologically female and indeed, simply, the womb. The implication here is not inconsequential. For if the world of the mythical structuration is to establish distinctions, the primary distinction on which all others depend is not, say, life and death, but rather sexual difference."[47] In other words, a teleological and purportedly transparent narrative structure, even one undergirding mythological accounts, is predicated on sexual difference and therefore preserves heteronormative ideology. Strategically and critically destabilizing narrative structure arguably troubles sexual difference and, therefore, yields textual queerness.

One of the subtler but potentially dangerous features in Pasolini's *Medea* is the director's choice to chronologically juxtapose what are often considered two separate stories within a single film: Jason and the Argonauts in their attempt to claim the Golden Fleece and Medea exacting revenge on Jason for his marriage to Glauce. This is similar to the structure of *Edipo re*, in which the backstory is brought into the main narrative and becomes the film's first half. In *Edipo re*, however, one was, in both halves, virtually always experiencing events from the point of view of its eponymous character. The first half of *Medea*, on the other hand, might as well be called "Jason." Watching the 1969 feature, we are made to grapple with a narrative that commences with the story of Jason-the-(male)-hero through his point of view and, then, finally concludes with the tragic effects of that story as told from Medea-the-wronged-woman's perspective.

This has been a rare narrative strategy over the decades, one we have seen in just a handful of films, such as *Vertigo* (1958), in which we shift from Scottie's perspective to, more or less, Judy's for the final half hour. We have also seen it in Krzysztof Kieslowski's *Krótki film o milosci* (*A Short Film about Love*, 1988), in which the male lover's perspective suddenly gives way to the female's private experiences at the halfway point. More recently and more to the point, the American filmmaker Jonathan Wald's 1998 three-minute short *Just Out of Reach* suggests the potential queerness of this dynamic. It begins by focusing on a young trick who wakes to find he spent what was probably a drunken night in the arms of a significantly older man. Clearly embarrassed, he gathers his clothes as quietly as possible in order to escape the situation without waking his erstwhile sex partner. After the youth leaves, the older individual wakes, finds himself alone, and sadly realizes that his newfound lover has vanished without so much as saying good-bye, without leaving a note. In a question-and-answer session following a screening at the UCLA QGrad conference in 2000, Wald said that the shift in identification at roughly the halfway point of the film emerged as a result of his queer sensibility. Although he did not elaborate, Wald's canny observation points to the ways in which queer sexual mobility, from sexual top to sexual bottom (and back again), from being the younger sexual partner to being the older partner, and so on, might hasten a radically shifting kind of identification that can be expressed in narrative terms.

The consequences of joining the two mythic narratives (Jason's adventure and Medea's tragedy) together in Pasolini's telling are particularly significant with regard to the gender dynamics. If at first Medea is established as Jason's narrative obstacle with whom he successfully contends to acquire the Fleece, she later takes control of both her own and Jason's destiny and control of the film's narrative. As a result, Jason eventually loses his patriarchal birthright: his adopted kingdom, his new bride, and his sons. Medea, by destroying her children, annihilates her family's place in the future. She makes the supremely queer gesture of embracing the devaluation of family and future. Unlike Scrooge in Lee Edelman's incisive reading of Dickens's *A Christmas*

Carol (1843), who moves from the position of negative queerness to something, well, more "family friendly," Medea, after her temporary, disastrous dalliance with heterosexuality through her relationship with Jason, reembraces the archaic queerness of her people, right down to a return to the brutal sacrificing of the young.[48]

The traditional story of Medea, despite its archaic and mythic elements, involves actors exercising agency. They react in complex ways to fateful occurrences. But Pasolini's version does not present clear motivations for agency, and, unlike *Edipo re*, the film all but ignores modern psychological subjectivity, choosing instead to favor mythological understandings of character and agency. It also leaves many conclusive events unrealized. Throughout, *Medea* mimes the structure of a chronicle, as opposed to the annals on the one side or a historical narrative on the other. Nevertheless, the film *aspires to*, or more complexly offers the pretense of, a fully realized (hi)story. (Consider the majestic establishing shots, a goal-oriented journey-focused series of events and so on). Nevertheless, and as is characteristic of the chronicle, Pasolini's *Medea* fails to achieve coherence. The moral, thematic, and social meanings of "history proper" appear briefly and then vanish, lingering as unsatisfied possibilities. Indeed, at the bitter end, the film seems to just stop. No resolution to the "story" is to be had. The narrative registers as at once willfully archaic and vexingly modern; it is pulled in the direction of classical narrative but resistant. This artistic move challenges the social order and leads Medea to a queer—*unresolved, radically suspended*—conclusion. Critics can complain, "*That's* not the way this should be told," or ask, "Why is Pasolini going off onto that tangent and ignoring this *other* most important part of the story?" In doing so, they are not simply arguing for some sort of justifiable compromise version that would reflect the various canonical texts (Euripides, Herodotus, Seneca, etc.); they are in fact scolding a film for its unwillingness to conform to normative forms of narrative construction, themselves anchored to mythical archetypes, ones never far removed from long-held gender binaries that, in our era at least, propose notions of heteronormativity.

To Confuse / To Clarify

If Pasolini's radical retelling of a mythological narrative challenges standard versions of the moral and ethical tale, we must ask, What cinematic technique—within this cinema of poetry—is put into service to deliver the unconsumable product? The following analysis sets its sights on tracing both Pasolini's narrative choices and his challenging aesthetics that push the terms for queer cinema. Pasolini's filmmaking not only raises the stakes on what we might call queer cinema (shows it operating beyond narratives of homosexual desire, shows it as radically attached to negativity, failure, and (textual/structural) violence), but also dares the queer artist and spectator to cross hurdles he has set, hurdles that replace and renounce those structured into mythological narratives as Lotman and de Lauretis have described them.

Immediately after *Medea's* opening credit sequence, the spectator is confronted with an extended monologue in which the centaur, Chiron (Laurent Terzieff), apologizes to the very young Jason for the lies he previously told him. As such, from the beginning, the film both raises our skepticism about the stories we think we know and the deceptive storytellers who have told them and suggests that what we are about to experience will challenge our origin stories with new or revised ones that will change the way we think about ourselves. Here, Chiron offers a different and only ostensibly true account of the boy's family and how he has come to be in exile. But disconcertingly, Chiron does this in what quickly becomes a mind-numbing and lengthy monologue that confuses more than it clarifies—"Ino was the bride of Cadmus and second wife of King Orchomenus, who was called Athamas—Athamas, the son of Aeolus, who governs the winds, to whom Ino had also been married. . . . " The telling continues in just this way, and it is, in fact, completely unnecessary to our understanding of what subsequently unfolds in the film. Indeed, the two performers in the scene indicate that their characters are bored with the endless adumbration of names, relationships, and events: the centaur comes across as a well-meaning professor, slogging through a lecture on Greek mythology that even he seems to realize is probably too dense and detail driven for his students to absorb. At the same time, the unidentified child in the role of the five-years-old Jason, who initially sits naked and smiling on the floor, quickly falls asleep. As if spectators are being all but invited to tune out the monologue, more than a few of their minds will invariably drift to thoughts about the actors (that is a cute boy as Jason; that is a hot man as the centaur), the setting (a homey little hut on the banks of the Grado lagoon), or the general idea that there is a vast prehistory to the film's narrative (albeit one we may never really grasp). Still, spectators are engaged here (thinking about those alternative concerns) because they are productively *dis*engaged (from what is being said), and from this very first scene, spectators begin to mistrust the director's competence. Pasolini's freely embraced artistic self-martyrdom has begun.

Some of the knowledge revealed in this first sequence does prove helpful for spectators insofar as it allows us to anticipate the plot and themes Pasolini explores. We learn, for instance, of the Golden Fleece and the reason for Jason's exile. Significantly, as the film continues and we suddenly jump eight years into the future, the centaur elucidates for the now-thirteen-year-old Jason a major component of Pasolini's larger philosophical argument. On the shore, looking toward the sea and sky, the centaur acclaims, "All is sacred. All is sacred. All is sacred! There is nothing natural in nature, my boy." "Remember that," he continues, "the day nature seems natural to you, it means the end." To grasp the centaur's counterintuitive pronouncement, it is necessary to return to Pasolini's theories on cinematic aesthetics. According to Maurizio Viano, "nature" was, for Pasolini, something "to be scientifically studied and technologically mastered. In Pasolini's terms, the philosophy of the Enlightenment could be defined as reason severed from passion: pure reason." "Reason" is, in the final analysis, "rational activity deprived of any moral goal and transformed into a pure instrument of domination."[49] Read this way, the centaur echoes Pasolini, who in effect tells us, "There's nothing natural [or right] about empiricist ideology, my boy. . . . The day such a worldview seems natural to you is the day the end has arrived."

It is important to consider how this particular monologue is presented. As if to estrange the spectator from the narrative—and barely five minutes into the film—the dialogue's volume is unnaturally low. And yet, although the centaur is far away from where we are situated in the scene (to the extent that "we" are in the camera's position), we clearly hear his soft voice. The spatial and auditory discrepancy, in which what is little more than a whisper and has traveled through the air conquering a distance of over one hundred feet is so overwhelmingly obvious as to seem either uncanny or incompetently rendered or both. More disconcertingly for the spectator is that Jason, to whom the centaur is speaking, is even farther away from the camera position than the centaur is. Young Jason appears puzzled. It is not entirely clear if his bewilderment is a result of his literally not being able to *hear* the centaur, who is clearly talking to him, or not being able to fully *comprehend* him. The boy seems deep in thought, listening, perhaps trying to understand the centaur's paradoxical phrasing. Yet, along with spectators, Jason may very well be asking, "What is he saying, and why is he talking to me so softly from so far away?" By Jason's own actions, we are led to believe that he does indeed hear the monologue. When the centaur tells the boy, "Look behind you," he does so. Moments later, however, when the centaur directs Jason, "Look out there, that black streak on the sea," the boy instead looks down toward the ground, where he notices a crab—perhaps meant to be seen as one of the sacred creatures in a world that exceeds what the centaur calls the "apparition" known as nature. This, then, is a queering of both narrative and form. Spectators, discombobulated by questionable audio-spatial dynamics (the film's form), cling to a cause-and-effect logic (in the narrative) in which hearing is indicated by the responsiveness of the on-screen character. And yet this logic is suddenly placed into doubt by that character proceeding to act in a way that eventually diverges from the instructions spoken to him by the other diegetic character.

Ultimately, Pasolini's cinematic engagement of image and sound, sound and space, raises and problematizes the dualism between the physical ability to hear aural stimuli and the cognitive ability to understand the meaning of what one has heard (or thinks one has heard). Several important questions emerge here: How can one compare "I hear you" with "I understand you"? What are the implications for "understanding" without hearing someone "accurately"? How might *not* accurately hearing (or seeing, for that matter) actually hasten a more profound understanding? More broadly, Antonella C. Sisto argues that Pasolini's audiences "are asked to listen in complex and transformative ways. Pasolini methodically challenges their assumptions, forcing them to listen and actively make sense, or simply question his provocations, which entail a disruption of well-known textual and social structuration of meanings and values. He uses the soundtrack as counterpoint, to conflict, disorient and reorient, the images and narrative."[50] This sequence is a perfect example of that. It is also worth remembering that in the discourse of cruising that we see in *Bu san* and *Rabioso sol, rabioso cielo*, no verbal communication takes place between the men. They are essentially wordless creatures in silent films.[51]

This form of cinematic distraction is crucial for queer spectatorship. In other words, the filmmaker demands we think about the film—indeed, the cinematic experience in toto—not at the level of narrative; instead, Pasolini's presentation of the sound and image engages and, at the same time, distracts spectators. This cinema thus enables a particularly Barthesian function insofar as the movie-theater experience facilitates "a possible bliss of discretion [une jouissance de la *discrétion*]."[52] This is to say, as Barthes reminds us, discretion has long meant both "discernment, wisdom, sound judgment" and the "quality of being discreet."[53] Barthes punctuates the final remarks in his essay by evoking *jouissance*. He reminds us that "the pleasure of the text" is an integrated engagement between text and reader/spectator. [54] "Une jouissance de la discrétion" defines perfectly well the fully distracted queer spectator who cruises the disjointed scene of a Pasolini film.

Lost and Found in Colchis

As *Medea* continues from the sequence discussed in the preceding section, Jason suddenly appears fully grown. Chiron, now revealed to Jason not as a centaur but in a fully human form, continues his years-long monologue.[55] He instructs the robust young adult in the differences between ancient man and modern man.[56] He tells Jason to return to Iolcus, his ancestral home, in order to claim his birthright from his uncle. When what is ultimately an extended prologue ends and Pasolini cuts to a very different landscape (one that is drier and dramatically mountainous rather than marshy

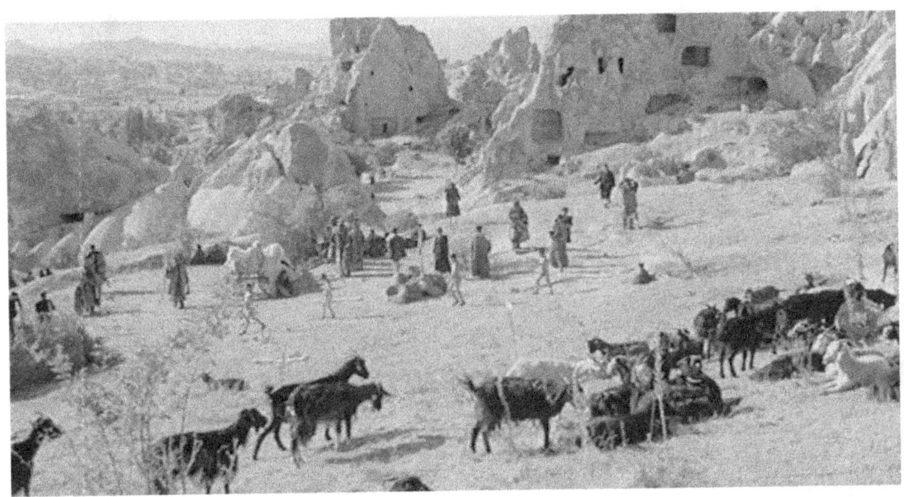

FIGURE 14. Nearly naked adolescents walking among robed shepherds, who are artfully arranged.

and flat), we believe, as narrative convention would have it, the location now to be Iolcus. Our logic would be confirmed with a film incorporating a traditional narrative structure since the centaur's instructions specifically tell Jason to confront his uncle there. Narrative, however, as we have discussed, is not central to Pasolini's cinema. Hence, the director takes us to *Colchis*, a locale that was only briefly noted by the centaur. Upon this unexpected arrival, we are introduced to Medea, her brother, Apsirto (Sergio Tramonti), and their parents, King Aeetes and his wife, Idyia, in what is immediately seen as an exotic and sublime land, particularly in comparison to the more bucolic landscape in which Jason was raised.[57]

The sudden shift in location not only disrupts spectators' spatial and temporal perspectives but quickly occasions an instance of the use of the "felt presence of the camera" or, more specifically, *felt presence of the camera and the (queer) camera operator*. The first camera movement in this passage is accompanied by a jump cut, which Pasolini describes as a technique in which one uses "the wrong editing for expressive reasons."[58] To begin, the sequence gives us a jerky, abortive pan/tilt as the camera points slightly downward on a gentle slope. Near the bottom of this hill, filled with goats and goatherds against a beautiful rocky background, we see a small group of nearly naked adolescent males wearing tan-colored loincloths (see figure 14). The jump cut that occurs during this sequence transports spectators a second or two into the future as seen through what is clearly the same camera setup at the same location. Now, however, the angle has changed slightly as if to signify Pasolini's intention to alter (or evade) space

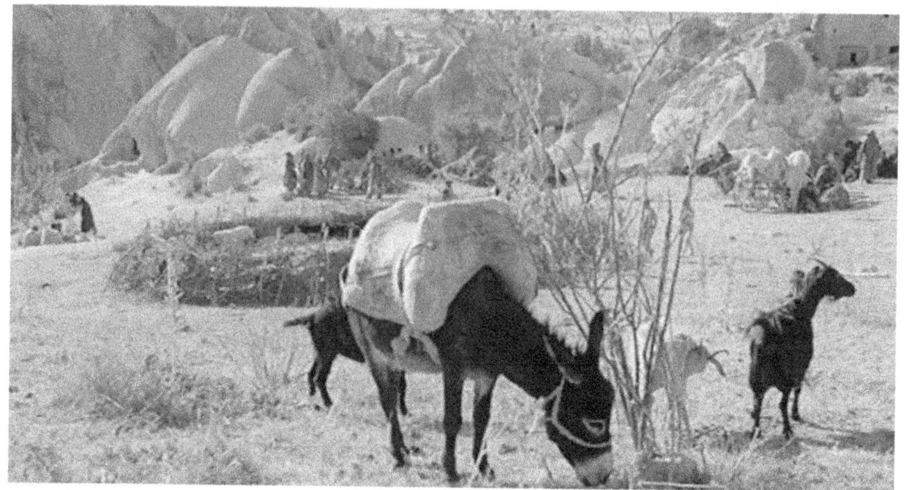

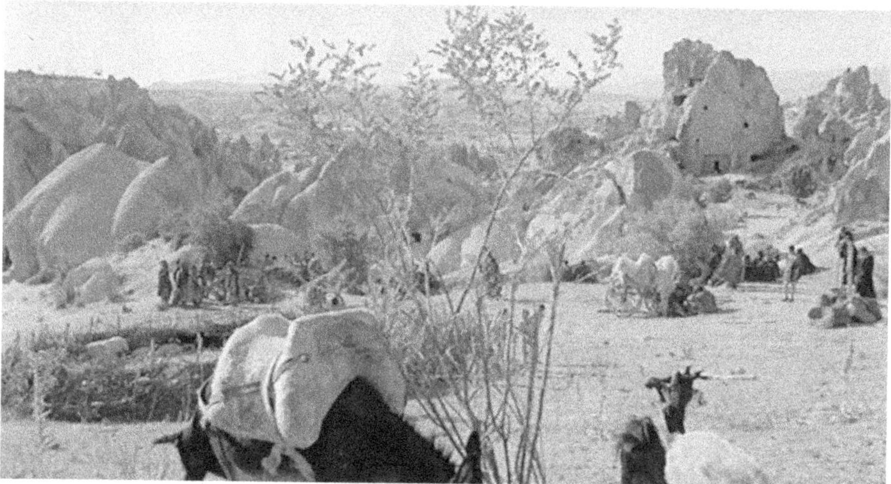

 The jump cut changes the camera angle slightly; the camera stops halfway through a pan back to the right.

and time. But the initial effect of the jump cut, made more obvious by occurring during a panning shot, is the disorientation of spectators (see figure 15).

The leap forward in time also robs us of our previously unobstructed view of the young male bodies. In the interstice of the cut, they have become obscured by the branches of a small shrub they have walked behind, and the disappointment that prurient queer spectators might feel is only slightly compensated by the now reasonably well-composed pastoral image of that tree, which is flanked by a mule and a goat. As if regretting the jump cut that robbed spectators of the nearly nude figures, the camera operator slightly but quickly pans back to the right in what appears to be a futile attempt to gain a better view of the unclothed youths. But spectators are disappointed given that the young men are now effectively veiled by the shrubbery. With the camera operator perhaps realizing that he has failed to effectively recapture the boys in his camera's gaze and as if shamefully rethinking what was obviously a tellingly salacious and prurient move on the filmmaker's part, the camera clumsily stops halfway through this "corrective" pan (see figure 16). The conclusion of this sequence is represented by an awkward angle. It is an image that is best described as halfway between two "good" previous angles. Sequences such as this, seemingly strange in what some people may view as cinematic ineptitude, give a sense of a palpably anxious, palpably maladroit organizing (or *dis*organizing) hand behind the camera. This felt cinematic presence shies away from allowing the filmmaker, or spectators, to openly ogle pubescent boys, but then it suggests that it wants to/wants us to ogle them after all. The filmmaker seems to have panicked and, ultimately regretfully, provides us with a purportedly more respectable and traditional pastoral image. The queer filmmaker plays a game of hide-and-seek, with the camera moving and removing veils and playfully revealing an erotic delight only to cover it again. The seen (the boys, the trees, the goats) and the unseen (camera, camera operator) are stridently made visible and interconnected through Pasolini's cinema of poetry. Ultimately, this characteristic moment from early in the film drives home Pasolini's embodiment of "wrong" cinematic technique. Yet this series of "mistakes" in cinematic form expresses, in part, an awkwardness that both announces and exemplifies queer desire.[59]

At this point, it has become clear that Pasolini's *Medea* is perverting genre and its conventional expectations. The film is, on the one hand, an erotically invested/erotically disavowed and roughly structured ethnographic film, of the kind that was particularly popular in the 1950s and 1960s.[60] At the same time, it is a stately but exotic epic, a genre also particularly popular during that period.[61] As a destabilizing hybrid, *Medea* achieves singular effects in its unorthodox patterns of editing in concert with strategic camera movements.

"An Infinitely Loved Object of Sacrifice"

In the final paragraph of Leo Bersani's landmark essay "Is the Rectum a Grave?," he defends "gay men's 'obsession' with sex, . . . not because of its communal virtues, not because of its subversive potential for parodies of machismo, not because it offers a model of genuine pluralism . . . , but rather because it never stops re-presenting the internalized phallic male as an infinitely loved object of sacrifice."[62] It is not surprising that, as Pasolini and Bersani have similar perspectives on male homosexuality, so many of the former's films feature homoerotically charged representations of male human sacrifice gesturing toward the latter's subsequent theories of the violence of desire. Perhaps *Medea's* most remarkable scene features just such an activity.

Here, the major Colchian characters appear—King Aeetes and his wife, Idyia (both played by uncredited performers), and their two adult children, Medea and Apsirto— but without the kind of introduction that would allow us to easily and quickly identify them in relation to each other or the narrative. We see a magnificently dressed woman who carries an affect of ultimate authority as she surveys the sacrifice. She remains unidentified until a full hour into the film, when we finally hear the three syllables of her name. Indeed, at this early point in the film, and given Maria Callas's performance, she might well be taken as the ruler of this foreboding kingdom, rather than the ruler's daughter. As for the king and queen, and unless one is an expert on ancient costumes or the staging of Greek dramas, their roles in the drama are initially unclear.

Once the sacrifice begins, both Aeetes and Idyia look suspiciously at Apsirto, who we glean is their son. As we shall see, however, Aeetes attitude toward his son seems every bit as libidinous as it is fatherly. Moreover, the king longingly gazes at the ado-lescent sacrificial victim as well, which in turn draws attention to a broader and ubiq-uitous homoerotic desire, especially since Apsirto, like his father, also appears to be desirous of the boy about to die.

The claim that this scene is "homoerotic" is not a new one. A number of scholars have described it this way, including Maurizio Viano, Kriss Ravetto, and D. A. Miller. Viano writes, for example, that Apsirto's "exchange of glances with the victim . . . contribute[s] to transforming the human sacrifice into an allegory of legalized vio-lence against socially designated victims such as homosexuals."[63] Ravetto notes the king's role in the homoerotic triad, adding that Pasolini "create[s] a sense of sexual ambivalence . . . by centering the gaze . . . of [Apsirto] and Aeetes on the chosen vic-tim in a series of shot reverse shots, linking the three characters in a circle of looks." Though Ravetto rightly points to the "sexual ambivalence" evoked in the scene, he does not accurately depict the cinematic design of the sequence.[64] To be precise, we first see Apsirto and Aeetes in a long panning shot, not a shot/reverse-shot sequence as Ravetto notes. And significantly, four characters are actually involved in the sequence, since we must finally include the mother, Idyia, which, in effect, introduces a female challenge to the male homoeroticism, foreshadowing Medea's role in the downfall of Jason. Furthermore, when we do see the relay of looks during a second round of close-ups in which the actors' looks are sutured one to another, they are not organized in classic shot/reverse-shot. In fact, we never see the victim directly from Apsirto's, Aeetes's, or Idyia's points of view, nor do we see the sacrificial boy looking in the

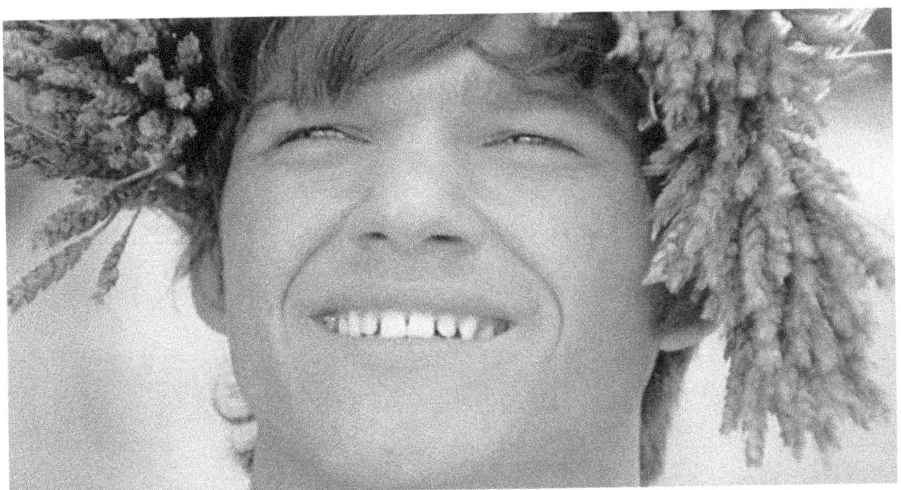

FIGURE 17. The sacrificial victim grins.

direction of the parents and their son. None of these images, properly speaking, are "point of view" shots. For Pasolini, something quite different is at stake. A more accurate and concise description of the sequence suggests the implications of Pasolini's cinematic technique.

The passage begins with a close-up of the victim, who grins and is obviously happy to be the center of attention for the tribe, if not the camera (see figure 17). With a quick, simultaneous pan left–zoom out, we see Apsirto smile, briefly, at the boy. The smile subtly changes, suggesting a more negative turn of events—fear, concern? As if with a shiver, Apsirto suddenly remembers why they are all there, and that the boy he desires is about to be killed and dismembered. Behind him, we see Aeetes and Idyia. They look on their son, obviously concerned with whatever queer thoughts he might be having at that moment. Pasolini conveys the range of these expressions in a single shot (see figure 18). But things are still more complicated than events occurring in unbroken time and space.

Immediately following the single long take, Pasolini repeats that same event—the circuitry of desire at play among a father, a mother, a son, and the son's beloved victim—but now through different cinematic means. In this alternative version, three close-ups are juxtaposed, one focused on the boy (see figure 19), one on Apsirto (see figure 20), and one on Aeetes (see figure 21). Framed thusly, same-sex desire commingles with patriarchal authority. That Idyia does not receive her own expected close-up in this brief concatenation of shots only confirms Pasolini's insistence on the family dynamic as one that is primarily homosocial/homoerotic and, to be sure, incestuous.[65]

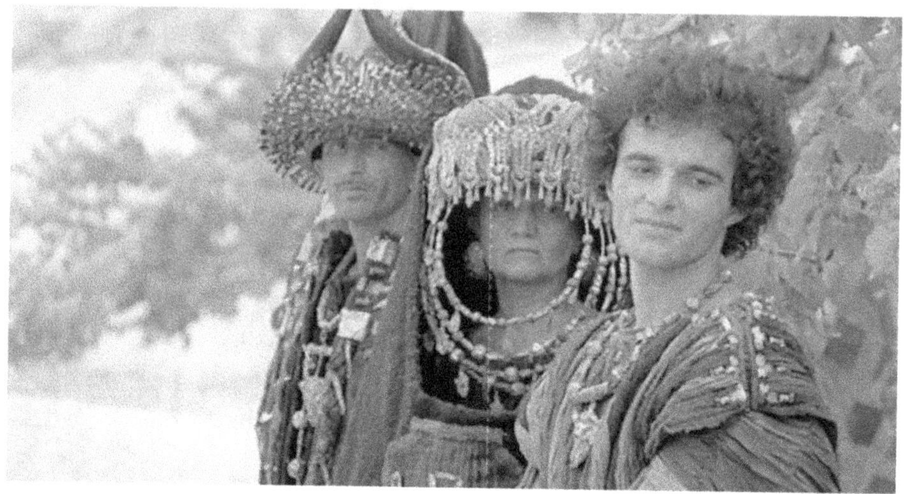

FIGURE 18. Pasolini conveys the range of the characters' expressions.

Although our interpretation of the motivations at play during the sacrifice may preliminarily anchor this point of the story to a traditionally patriarchal moral logic—a father pulls his son back from a too-profound homosexual infatuation so as to ensure his offspring's future through heterosexual marriage and thus the perpetuation of the royal lineage, and so on—another possibility is available. In reading the sequence closely and taking into consideration Pasolini's *re*-presentation of events in which desire is at once seen and unseen, we are made aware that the father is removing his queer competition in the form of the boy who is clearly about to secure, intentionally or not, his son's libidinous heart. In this way, Pasolini reminds us, as we have seen in a previous film, the Oedipus narrative derives its formulation through an original homosexual desire.[66]

In either case, Apsirto's willingness to follow Medea later in the film when she betrays her own people in the act of stealing the Golden Fleece may be seen as his revenge on the society that killed the boy he desired. It follows, then, that with his unauthorized love destroyed, Apsirto is motivated to help his sister honor her own unauthorized love for Jason. This is all the more erotically self-serving since Jason is one for whom Apsirto, like Medea, harbors desirous feeling, feelings that are perhaps reciprocated. As Viano remarks, "Medea's brother, whom the narrative had already singled out as a beautiful and effeminate man, . . . [will smile] at Jason when he first [meets] him."[67] Pasolini's family romance reproduces its forces of desire so as to destroy the family's existence.

That Apsirto is in love with the doomed boy is effectively confirmed when one remembers and then factors in a telling if odd moment from a scene prior to the boy's

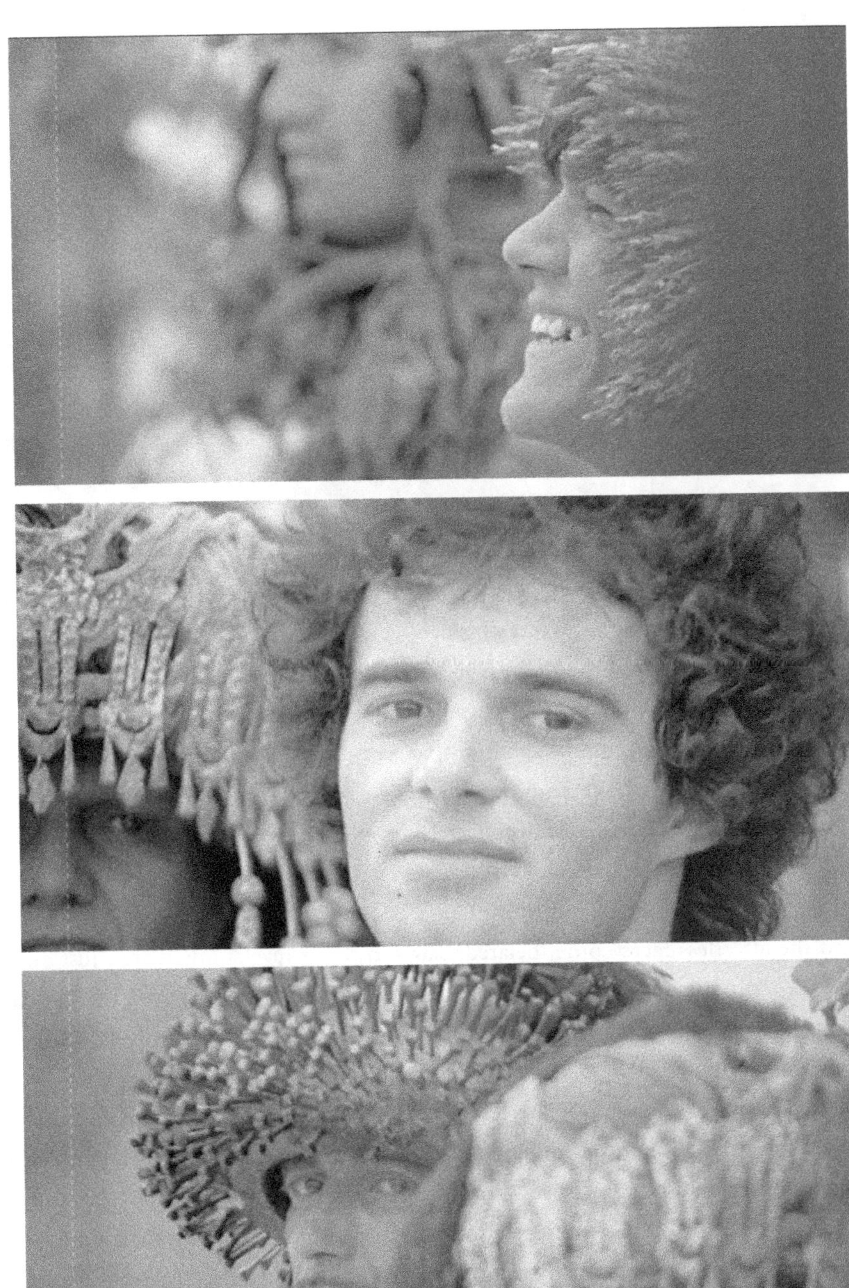

FIGURES 19-21. Three juxtaposed close-ups: one focused on the boy; a close-up of Apsirto; a close-up of Aeetes.

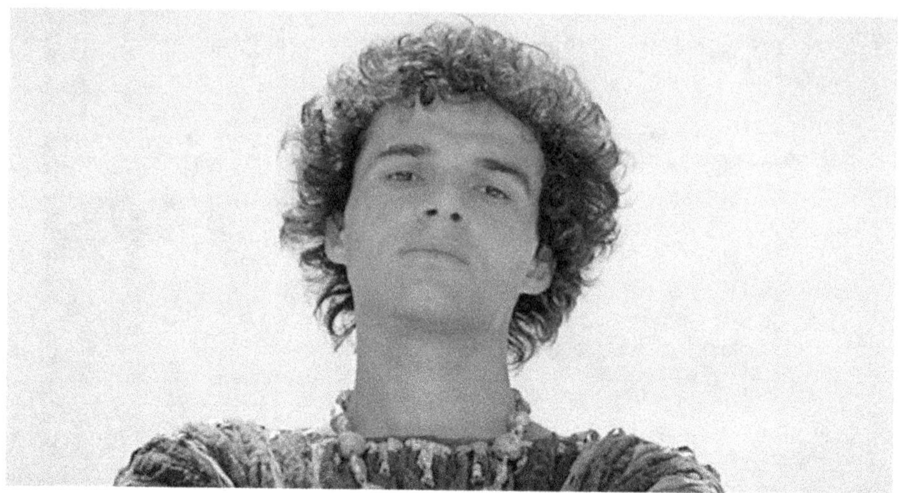

FIGURE 22. The deep sorrow on Apsirto's face.

murder. In it, Apsirto slips away from his people to sit in a secluded grove outside the city. He spends a moment there, deep in solitary thought, and his nearly blank yet perhaps slightly melancholy expression is punctuated, finally, by a barely perceptible sigh: it is as if he is mourning the sacrifice that he anticipates and that we will soon be witness to. Here, before the ceremony, with Apsirto anticipating the loss of his forbidden love, Pasolini puts into service an inverted form of the Kuleshov effect, as he often does, for his queer-world making. With all but blank faces on screen belatedly tied to emotions through subsequent developments, conformations of the queer thoughts behind the affectless faces come, belatedly, as surprising revelations. Later, just after the sacrifice, dismemberment, and burning of the remains of the beautiful boy, a final close-up of Apsirto looking down, again expressionless, at the ashes offers another, now clearer example of the Kuleshov effect. Here we project onto the actor's face the deep sorrow that a young man feels for his necessarily sacrificed object of desire (see figure 22). Pasolini creates an enigma early in the passage—what is blank-faced Apsirto thinking about in the grove?—that we eventually come to recognize as a queer romantic/erotic sorrow. This interpretation is eventually confirmed by the dramatized sacrifice of the boy and then finally *re*confirmed by a final blank-faced shot of Apsirto, reminding us of his earlier sadness in the grove. All told, we have been rewarded for suspecting queerness from the beginning. We are now primed to suspect that any blank-faced boy might be harboring hidden homosexual desires, to ultimately assume that any inexplicable image is destined to reveal subversive meaning.

Additionally, it is only at this point that, in a pair of impressive close-ups, we fully register the arresting corporeality of Maria Callas. But if her face, as John David Rhodes remarks, shows "signs of creeping middle age, . . . her body [has] material-ized some trace of Medea's chthonic feminine power."[68] Most obviously, Callas's neck, exhibiting both taut muscles and just-beginning-to-show wrinkles, signifies both physical strength and a vulnerability associated with maturity (and speaks to Callas's queer appeal as an aging opera diva whose talents only heighten as her body ages and disintegrates). In concert with the images of the fit young men, who, in their own dif-ferent way, are also often shown to be at the borderline of muscular and slack, Callas's body reflects a queer appreciation of the paradoxes of corporeality, often obscured by ideological understandings of gender division. This strong but aging goddess will be every bit the match for masculine but mortal men.

Already No Longer a Hero

Of all the many disorienting segues in the film, the one after the human sacrifice in Colchis is particularly disjointing. *Medea's* narrative now returns to the story of Jason, who has assembled his Argonauts and is ready to claim the city-state of Iolcus from his uncle, Pelias (Paul Jabara). Upon his arrival in Pelias's chambers, Jason markedly asserts a heterosexual identity, as befitting a male ruler in a patriarchal system, when he winks at a young maiden. If this undercuts the homoerotic undercurrents between Jason and his Argonauts in subsequent scenes, it does so only slightly. If anything, Jason's wink at the maiden suggests a cynical, utilitarian function for heterosexual seduction—Jason is trying to use sex as a form of underhanded diplomacy with his political foes' women—in contrast to the irrational manifestation of queer desire in Colchis.

In the meantime, and as the centaur had predicted, Pelias demands that Jason travel to Colchis to capture the Golden Fleece before he ascends to the throne. In an impres-sive cut from his discussion with Pelias, from a cramped interior to the vast blue sea at dusk, Jason and his Argonauts are suddenly at sea, traveling to the east. Just as suddenly, and after only a few notably homoerotic shots of the men in repose on the voyage, the crusaders are again on land, nearing Colchis. On their arrival, they capture horses and rob the inhabitants of their property. In other words, in setting down the evidence for Pasolini's political allegory, Jason and his troops disinvest the people of their natural resources. In effect, and before we can settle into a comfortable narra-tive logic in which masculine male heroes unproblematically claim for themselves the treasures of a remote part of the world, Pasolini introduces the disturbing resonances that colonialist exploitation laid bare.

As Susan O. Shapiro puts it in her reading of the film, "Pasolini departs from [a] heroic tradition. . . . His Argonauts are scruffy, rude adolescents, who break into the Colchians' primitive dwellings and take whatever they please. . . . [They] display a crass, self-centered attitude of privilege and entitlement."[69] According to Ivar Kvistad, "it is as if, like the centaur's opening confession about his lies [to Jason], the film is uncovering the shocking truth behind the celebrated mythological narratives of acquiring treasures from foreign lands."[70] Whatever frisson of innocent homoeroticism this community of half-naked, muscular men might have initially engendered in spectators is thus quickly problematized by the legacy of Western man's historical crimes against others; any sense of the savage Colchians as villains or Jason and his Argonauts as traditional heroes is thus quickly forestalled, if not necessarily brought to an end. Indeed, the queer male spectator is quickly aligned with Medea (and, as long as he remains alive, Apsirto). The queer male spectator, thus, sees that his quickly developing desire for Jason and his men is predicated precisely on that which betrays and oppresses him. Conversely, the queer spectator's sympathies for Medea and Apsirto create a tension in which he must chose a political alignment over a powerful erotic one. This tension is key to the film's complex queer ideological perspective.

As the Argonauts approach their destination, one is presented with more ethnographically crafted and prosaic footage of the Colchian people, tilling the soil, weaving, and preparing communal meals. While we see this bucolic landscape, we hear Koutev's "Draga est tombée malade," Bulgarian choral music that fuses folk song with Western-modern musical traditions, hardly, it would seem, a historically accurate sonic accompaniment to the era of the film. And yet, directly linking the archaic and the modern, this musical hybrid soundtrack of two cultural traditions is historically "accurate" to the extent that, although composed and recorded during the 1950s, it cannot be divorced from the very histories that inspire its contemporary existence.

Even more obviously disorienting and exotic (to the Western filmgoer) but anachronistic (for the time and place in which the film is set) is the ancient Japanese music that Pasolini employs once Jason, Medea, and the Argonauts journey back to Greece. It is the genre of music that one associates with the *Jidai-geki* films of Akira Kurosawa or Kenji Mizoguchi. Marianne McDonald, in her close reading of *Medea*, argues, "the Japanese music is suggestive of a refined civilization."[71] In other words, in the context of this film, ancient Japanese music serves to represent ancient Greek civilization qua civilization and, thus, in contrast to the visceral and confused traditions that Koutev's Bulgarian folk-music/modern-music hybrid suggests. And yet, all told, the film's vision of civilization and the uncivilized is, to say the least, broadly sketched. Indeed, with ersatz sensationalism, Pasolini's musical choices suggest that the very ideas of civilized/

uncivilized are unstable and relational. Seen this way, Pasolini's soundtrack also functions as an uncanny challenge to the purported authority of the image track, insofar as the use of music represents the purportedly *not*-Western world as a compositional hybrid that reflects the filmmaker's own archaic/modernist sensibility and informs his cinema of poetry. Ultimately, Pasolini's fast-and-loose practice of signification must be viewed as part of his career-long practice of autocritique. His filmmaking, in other words, deconstructs and further corrupts the already-corrupted signifiers that mark his cinematic world. As Kvistad puts it, "[*Medea*] would seem to be reiterating this symbolism [of "an imagined primitive or archaic culture"], not so much to reify or support it but to depict how it operates: it is precisely by deeming [some] cultures [as] primitive—that is by reducing them to a symbol—[and others not,] that European imperialists license their projects of domination."[72]

Arguably, the roughest passage in the film that exploits Pasolini's terms for authorial self-sacrifice may be seen when Medea, after laying eyes on Jason for the first time, decides to betray her people and steal the Fleece on his behalf. As confusing as this might be as a sudden plot development in even the most professional classical Hollywood version, it is even more so in Pasolini's presentation. With a storytelling strategy in which it is often unclear what motivates the characters, certainly according to modern psychological understandings of motivation rather than mythological or tragic understandings of motivation, or even *what the characters are physically doing moment to moment*, Pasolini does not simply vex narrative. More significantly, narrative is violated through cinematic form. Hence, when Medea wakes up in the early morning, she decides, for no obvious, psychologically plausible reason, to ascend to the holy temple high above the city in the cliffs. Once there, an awkward series of profile shots reveal her looking at the Fleece before finally being interrupted by Jason's unexpected appearance. This is the first time we see Jason within the primitive city, let alone right in the heart of it, in its holy temple. In one of the film's many confusing moments, Jason then wordlessly exits the temple. Following this, Pasolini offers an insert shot of a full moon, high over a mountain at night. In this way, what seems to be a continuous scene of Medea looking at the Fleece in a chamber flooded with midmorning sunlight is torn by unconnected images. Suddenly, as if overwhelmed by Jason's presence, Medea runs down to Apsirto and convinces him to help her steal the sacred object.[73] Considering that the theft of the Clochians' most valuable and holy possession signals a great betrayal against his own people, Apsirto remains nonchalant about his collusion.

With the theft accomplished, Medea and Apsirto's nonchalance is revealed, *in retrospect*, as self-serving, an attempt to satisfy their desire. Medea and her brother offer the Fleece *and* themselves to Jason, and myth-determined motivation is replaced, or problematized, by erotic/modern-psychological motivation. Kristi M. Wilson describes the queer resonance of this moment thusly: "Medea and Jason exchange desirous glances, as do Medea's brother and Jason, and Jason gazes victoriously at the golden fleece. This triangle of desire between Jason, Medea, and [Apsirto] is thus contaminated by Jason's parallel desire for the golden fleece."[74] As if to match Medea's newfound motivational clarity, the film adopts the basic forms of a classical cinema here, with cross-cutting between the fleeing of Medea, Apsirto, Jason, and the Argonauts and King Aeetes's pursuing army. A grippingly fast sense of pacing results from the kinesthetically inspired pans and camera movement during the chase. (Even here, though, out-of-focus or roughly composed shots predominate.)

And then, just as the film seems to be making sense through a cause-and-effect relay of gestures and actions, out of nowhere, Medea commits fratricide. She stabs and dismembers Apsirto so as to scatter his body parts along the road and thereby delay the encroaching Clochians. To put it mildly, this sequence utterly confuses and frustrates casual spectators. First, a series of disorienting close-ups show Medea's and Apsirto's heads. After Medea's fatal blow to her brother, however, and during the sequences in which his body is dismembered, we are suddenly surveying the scene in an obstructed long shot. Our desired view of Medea's violence is thwarted. Like Apsirto, Pasolini's spectator is positioned as a violently disregarded partner, made to feel at once disengaged (by the aesthetic) yet reengaged (by the diegetic violence). As part of the larger tapestry of the film, Apsirto's death scene punctuates a larger sequence—from Jason and Medea's meeting, through the chase, and up to the fratricide—that offers a stylistic chain and narrative chronicle. This is a structure in miniature that will play out broadly across the whole film. We move from archaic cinema to classical cinema (more or less) to a violent final resolution born of their incompatibility: archaic modernism via the cinema of poetry. And presumably, if spectators find that they have somehow missed important information, find that they are confused and bewildered again after finally thinking the film was beginning to "make sense," at least they are afforded the distractions that Barthes has shown to be so tantalizingly productive.

Toward an Archaic Ethnography

There are many ways to justify Pasolini's filmmaking strategies to those who would dismiss them as pretentiously incompetent—not only the Rex Reeds of the world but those less dilettantish spectators whose potential displeasure concerned supportive Pasolini scholars, such as Geoffrey Nowell-Smith, in the early years of the director's rising profile.[75] But how might we revisit Pasolini's rough-hewn cinema as a critical conceptual tool for coming to terms with a queer cinematic experience?

First, as I have previously suggested, Pasolini's aesthetic creates a sense of a theatrical experience that, no matter how closely and carefully one watches it, seems to exist for a spectator who is only half paying attention, whose mind is wandering, thinking about what other activities might be available in the theater. *Medea*'s narrative is often too confusing to follow, but it is also *too* visually dynamic and *too* aurally compelling to completely tune out or to stop watching. Second, one experiences *Medea* very much as one would experience the kind of ethnographic cinema that came of age in the 1950s and 1960s by the likes of Margaret Mead, Jean Rouch, and Robert Gardner, among others. Problematic as these films are, they attempt to present an experience of respectful, if radical, otherness for a Western filmgoing audience. They engage in documentary filmmaking that cannot readily control the reality it seeks to control. Such cinema is uneven, difficult to follow, and often disjointed. Third, despite the many anachronisms we see and hear, one gets the sense when watching *Medea* (and *Edipo re* and the *Trilogy of Life*) that one is watching a film that is not *just set in* the distant past but *made in* the distant past. In many ways, *Medea* appears to be made by filmmakers who did not have the luxury of rehearsing, blocking action and camera movement in advance, or reshooting unsuitable material. On the other hand, it is as if important material that must have been filmed and included in one or another version of the film has been lost as if over the centuries. Watching *Medea* is like watching surviving fragments or the remaining ruins of a film. Because of this, the film appears as old as the story embedded in it. But, as we have also seen, Pasolini's films of this period also clearly adopt mannerisms of the modern consciousness. They feature anachronisms and elements of Brechtian distanciation, and spectators can hardly have forgotten their knowledge of classical cinema and the modernist revolution of late nineteenth and early twentieth centuries. All of this has the effect of both historically situating and decentering the spectator in queer directions.

Ultimately, all of the different ways of seeing *Medea* help define it as a cousin of the so-called Archaic School of filmmaking that was developed by (often non-Russian) filmmakers within the Soviet Union in the late 1960s, such as Sergei Parajanov, Otar Ioseliani, Tengiz Abuladze, and Andrei Tarkovsky, and that connects with at least some of the Italian cinema of that era.[76] As Karla Oeler explains the term, "Films of this school often feature the folklore, costumes, decorative arts and music of particular ethnic groups." More importantly for Oeler, "The visual ethnography of the Archaic School is often realised through a poetic style, which emphasises not the accretion of narrative information, but rather the visual and metaphorical or symbolic qualities of a shot and the graphic 'rhymes' between shots."[77] It also might cross our minds that *Medea*'s near-total eschewal of the techniques of classical cinema—master shots and inserts, continuity editing, verisimilar acting, cause-and-effect narrative chains—suggests a different but equally radically "other" form of contemporaneous filmmaking, the kind that practitioners of Third Cinema, broadly defined, such as Glauber Rocha and Ousmane Sembene, created at that time. Such cinema, for self-consciously ideological reasons, eschewed the bourgeois refinements of the "well-made" movie as if doing so were an ethical imperative.[78]

If the rough-hewn filmmaking accompanying the murder of Apsirto mitigates the shock of violent betrayal and fratricide, the sequence in which the Colchians (including, touchingly enough, Apsirto's father) find the young man's dismembered body, gather it up, and take it home impacts the spectator more strongly. One does not receive the expected clear image of Apsirto's decapitated head, particularly surprising considering Pasolini had no qualms about showing a medium close-up of a decapitated head a year before in *Porcile*; the focus instead seems to be on the colorful and elaborate costumes of the Colchian soldiers as they slowly and mournfully return home. Remarkably, Pasolini does not craft the scene of their arrival back home so as to make it clear exactly when Idyia realizes what has happened to her son. There is no eye-line match cut from her face to Apsirto's dismembered body. Nevertheless, much like many of the other crucial plot developments in the film, the spectator can intellectually intuit that this mother's sudden cries of anguish come from the realization that her son has been murdered and that she has seen, even though we do not see her having seen, his body parts wrapped in the cloth being held by the soldiers. Idyia's hair-raising wailing, which spreads in a moment of sublime horror throughout the assembled people of the land, may be taken, primarily, as a lamentation over the loss of the mystical Golden Fleece—that is how I interpreted the scene the first time I saw the film—but as Shapiro points out, the actual loss being responded to is both more personal (a single human death) and profound (the end of a royal lineage): "Because Prince [Apsirto] is the only heir to the throne, his death means the end of their kingdom and the destruction of their future."[79]

Of course, Apsirto's obvious homosexual leanings complicate this moment even more and raise a question: Had he lived, what sort of queer-but-procreative reign might he have had, and just how queer, really, has this now-dying kingdom been all along? All of this is simply to suggest that Apsirto's death does not have to be thought of as the end of a heteronormative lineage. It can just as easily be thought of as the end of a primitive queer one. With that in mind, Medea's decisive and irrevocable acts, both to side with the heterosexually defined (or instrumentally heterosexual) Jason and to give up an archaic culture for one defined by women's conscription to men, make her tragedy the tragedy of an individual's betrayal of her own identity. In other words,

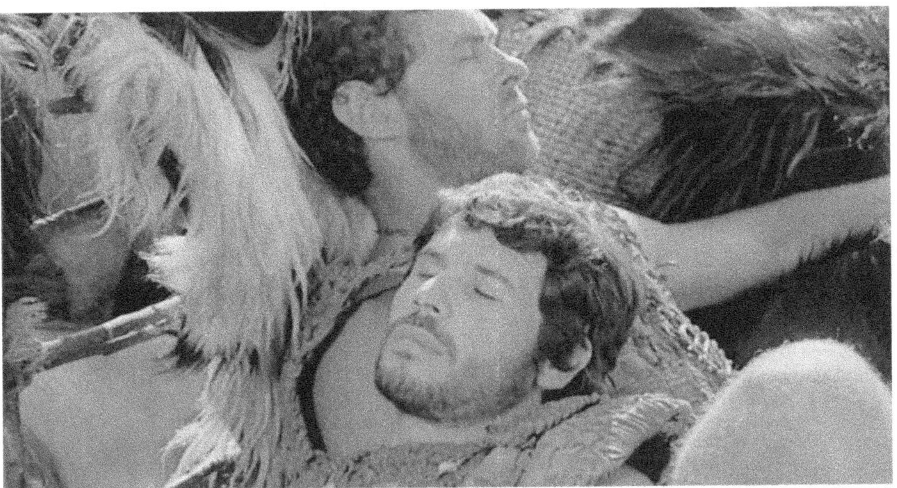

FIGURE 23. The men lie on the ship.

it is the tragedy of a queerly defined woman (she is, after all, played by a gay icon and opera diva) who, against any reasonable judgment, betrays her queer brother and culture only, finally, to be betrayed by the representative of a heterosexually defined civilization in which she had put her faith.

Alienated Distances

Doubts about Medea's wisdom become apparent almost immediately during the voyage back to Greece, which, as several scholars of the film have pointed out, takes place on the same decidedly unheroic raft the Argonauts took to Colchis, one that is about as far as can be imagined from the legendary *Argos* of the original myth. Beyond the simple demythologizing involved in the presented craft, the voyage home offers some of the most homoerotic images in the film; nevertheless, they are hardly queer in their resonances. Many may be described using D. A. Miller's apt term for images of groups of extras in Pasolini's work: "clump shots." As Miller describes it, "the men look awkward, barely competent, at their appointed . . . colonialist tasks," suggesting a world of male collusion and female alienation.[80] This is particularly true when we see Medea separated from the men (including the man she gave everything up for, Jason), who lie on the ship in erotic but sexless relation to each other (see figure 23). For instance, we experience, much more fully than most directors would allow, the quotidian boredom of a long voyage across the Black Sea from Colchis to Greece. Seemingly silent, the victors of a great prize aboard the vessel behave like sullen losers. At this moment, one does almost feel that *Medea* may be, in fact, turning into a proper "slow film."

In another strange swing in an opposite direction, formally, a film that has rushed through significant plot points and filmed others from alienating distances—the killing of Apsirto, the scattering of his body, and so on—now lingers in precise ethnographic detail on what would seem to be lesser material: lesser with regard to both narrative import and emotional-cultural resonance. And moving farther and farther from what Colchis represents, we, along with the ambivalent yet eroticized characters, return to Greece: Pasolini's analogy for the modern world. Here, archaic queerness is temporarily banished (it will return at the end of the film), and an oppressive, masculine homosociality, born of a heterosexually determined conquest, functions to oppress radical difference.

Once finally on dry land, Medea surveys the landscape and seems to suspect that she has made a grave error in betraying and abandoning her people. Her lamentation, at first almost nonsensical—"This place will sink because it has no foundation. You are not praying to God that he bless your tents. You are not repeating the first act of God. You are not seeking the center. You are not marking the center. No! Look for a tree, a post, a stone!"—is performed as Callas runs back and forth across a flat, desolate landscape that is very different from the majestic rocky geography of her home in Colchis. For Colleen Ryan-Scheutz, Medea's significance as a maternal figure is connected to her profound relationship to both her spiritual and environmental reality. Regarding the latter, Pasolini's use of establishing long shots featuring Callas in Colchis "effectively join[ed] Medea with her environment" and "ma[de] her one with each setting." But now, far away from her rocky and sublimely arresting mountainous homeland, on the parched, flat earth where she now stands, "the [long] shots do not connote communion with, and immersion in, that world. Rather, they suggest disorientation, discomfort, and difference with respect to the foreign and desecrated land."81

Again, risking the derision of critics and audiences who might accuse him of directorial ineptitude, Pasolini chooses to underscore this change of scenery and Medea's traumatized change of identity with a poetic sense of the felt presence of the camera, even as the camera's operator, who centers the key shot in this sequence awkwardly, far above Medea's head, might be accused of the basic professional failure of not being able to keep his subject appropriately within the frame. (Pasolini gives himself another martyr's wound, filming according to the logic of the scene as he radically sees it but, as a result, looking utterly incompetent to a filmgoer who might not remember that, by contrast, the shots of Callas in Colchis were extremely well composed.) Medea screams out, "Speak to me, sun! You're disappearing, perhaps never to return again. . . . Stone, speak to me! Perhaps you're disappearing! I no longer hear what you say! You, grass, talk to me! You, rock, talk to me!" And yet, in a supreme moment of harsh cinematic conformation, the earth below Medea, as well as Medea on it, "disappears" even as she protests. The camera lets the earth disappear due to its strange interest instead in prioritizing the vast, *sunless*, bright-gray sky above her. Furthermore, it cannot escape notice that the flat-crusted mud across which Medea runs conspicuously lacks the grass and stones she references. "Earth, where are you? Where can I find you again? Where is the bond that joined you to the sun?" As she cries in despair, Jason and his Argonauts sit around their campfire, variously smirking at or ignoring her. Time and again throughout Callas's dramatic tour de force, the camera is either looking too high, looking too low, or stationed too far away from her, this in a scene in which her character is crying about the importance of the landscape and the relationship between it and the human beings who exist in relationship to it (see figures 24, 25, and 26).

In John Osias's review for the UC Berkeley student newspaper in 1971, he offers a memorable description of this scene, one that insightfully distinguishes between camera and character:

> Suddenly the flesh and "camera-beings" *disengage*: the former moving lineally across the caked mosaic-work of a flat coastal plane; the latter swinging backwards and upwards until a lofty height is attained.
>
> The resultant image is an overpowering skyscape which literally *consumes* the upper three-fourths of the screen. . . . The lower extremities of the now-minuscule human figure have been sliced out of the picture; only its upper half remains to "frame" the picture's lower periphery.[82]

Osias's term "camera-beings" is a useful and evocative one, and we might well regret that it has not entered the lexicon. In the context of this film, it perhaps implies anthropologists from the future or another world, extraterrestrial Margaret Meads and Gregory Batesons, filming a primitive culture with their advanced technology.

But perhaps the term "camera-beings" is a bit misleading, in that it does not take into account how the image in question functions according to the logic of Pasolini's free indirect point of view, in which a film character's subjectivity is imperfectly implied by the strained attempt of the filmmaker both to honor it (from afar) and to exemplify it (through a sympathetic imagination). The vertiginous shots of Medea in a new and foreboding land reflect both her panicked disequilibrium and her newfound sense of rootlessness (not to mention a barbaric lack of the kind of "professional Hollywood style" that would befit a prestige picture such as this). The shots also signify the class consciousness of the author (Pasolini, the camera-being). Here, the director awkwardly comments on a subaltern's subjectivity by showing, for instance, the immense

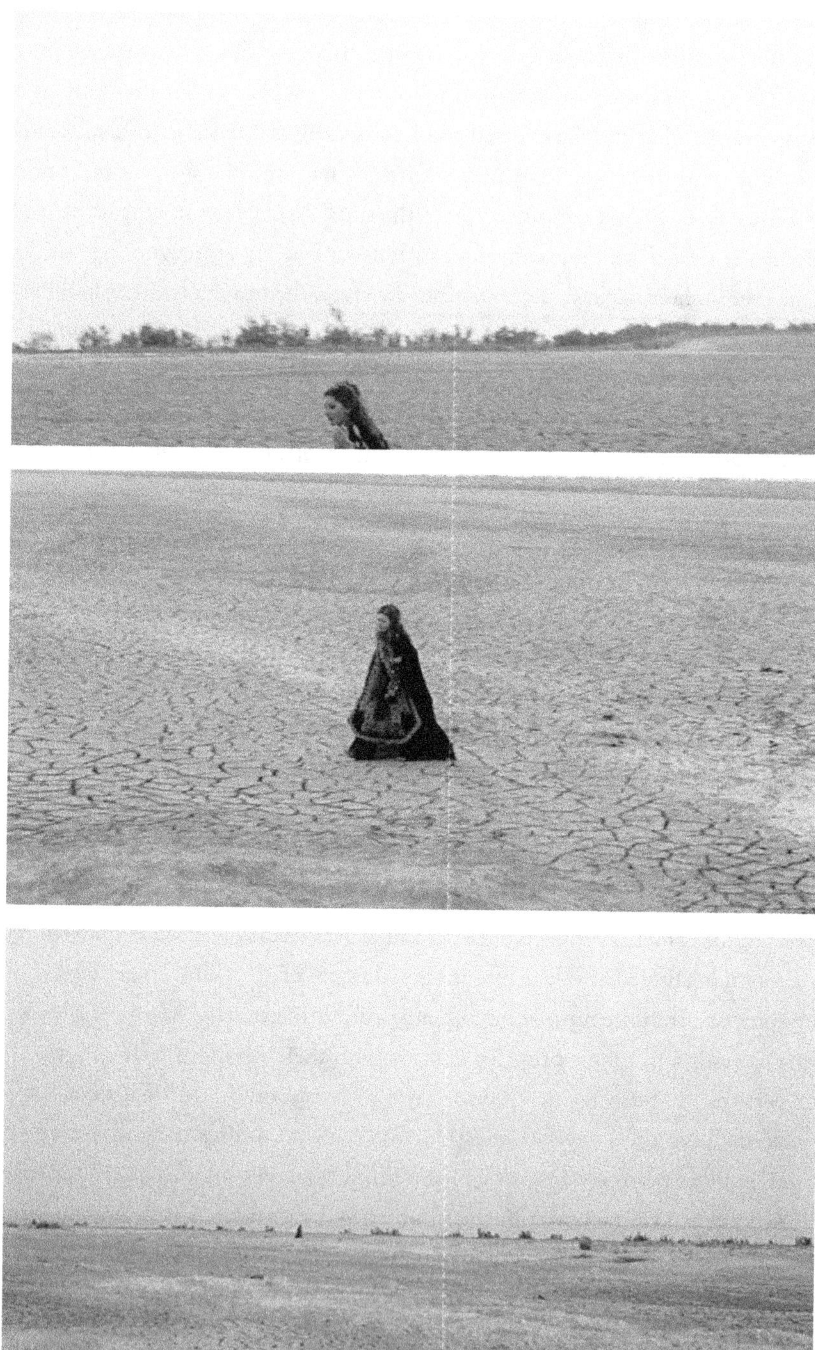

FIGURES 24-26. The camera is pointing too high to fully capture Medea in the frame; the camera is looking too low to capture the sky that Medea references; the camera is stationed too far away from Medea for her to be clearly seen in the image.

sky just when his subject is talking about the lost *earth*. Through another constructed tension, the spectator is pulled both toward Medea's subjectivity and away from it toward the filmmaker, both of which signify contrasting queer energies.

Finally, in a disturbing coda to this scene, Jason eventually walks out to Medea, who is sitting resignedly on the desolate mud flats, and violently pulls her back to the camp that he and his men have set up. He takes her into his tent and for the first time on-screen lays claim to her body. The last step in Jason's plundering of a foreign world has been taken, and Medea has lost the majesty of her homeland to become the Western hero's conscripted woman.

Home

When Jason returns to Iolcus to trade the Golden Fleece for his throne, he finds himself, not unexpectedly, betrayed. "Today you will experience something unexpected," Pelias intones. "You'll find out that kings are not always obliged to keep promises." While Jason seems curiously unfazed by this turn of events, the shock that registers on Medea's face suggests that she realizes anew the seriousness of her situation; she gave up her role as a leader in one country not, it turns out, to be queen in another but to be the wife of a mere citizen. In the following scene, when the "lowly" women of Iolcus remove Medea's holy, royal vestments and replace them with a plain dress like those they are wearing, her descent is complete. She has lost everything except Jason, and when back in their tent, her eyes travel the length of his body, as if to console herself through erotic desire. In a shot that is often noted for its homoerotic celebration of the male form, it does seem that Jason might be enough to compensate her for her loss of her culture and her savage selfhood. (Surely many queer men and women know what it is like to lose everything else in order to lay claim to sexual satisfaction.) But as with the images of male beauty on the raft during the return from Colchis, the spectacle of Jason's body here cuts two ways. First, it stands as an example of an objectified male put in relation to a woman-as-subject, in sharp contradistinction to standard practice in narrative cinema at the time; but, second, it does so by investing him with a real degree of, passive as it may be, confident, seemingly effortless, patriarchal authority.

As Ryan-Scheutz writes,

> When Jason takes [Medea] to his tent to make love, she is inspired by the physical closeness and fulfillment to consecrate him. . . . During the night, she sits up to watch Jason sleep. From her point of view, the camera slowly pans down the length of his body, from head to foot, which gives the effect of an adoring caress. Beyond the homoerotic content of this sequence . . . ,

Medea's silent observation of Jason reflects the expression of her spiritual subjectivity in earlier scenes. Throughout this private ritual, she designates Jason's body as her new spiritual center, and the emotion is so powerful that she rouses him from sleep to make love (i.e., make contact with the sacred) once more.[83]

Ryan-Scheutz's interpretation of this scene is not, ultimately, antithetical to mine.[84] (Certainly for many gay men, homoerotic passion can take the place of what others call spiritual passion.) For Ryan-Scheutz, the tragedy of the title character is that "Jason is not interested in Medea's spiritual life or her religious beliefs" and that "his connection with her is purely utilitarian."[85] This is true as far as it goes. But I would argue that it is not Jason's personal betrayal that is at issue. Rather, as a representative of Western patriarchy, Jason functions according to the logic of that system, and his behavior is a manifestation of it.

As Jason awakes and he and Medea begin to make love again, Jason stops just long enough to look away from Medea and directly at the spectator with a complicitous gaze (see figure 27). It is, in some ways, analogous to the celebrated image from Ingmar Bergman's *Sommaren med Monika* (*Summer with Monika*, 1953), in which that film's eponymous character breaks the "fourth wall" and look directly at the camera, daring (according to most interpretations of the scene) the spectator to pass judgment on her imminent betrayal of her newlywed husband.[86] In *Medea*, too, such a shot makes us realize, with a shiver, that a betrayal is on the horizon—indeed the subsequent shot is of the vast sea and an endless horizon beyond it and functions as the point-of-view shot for the previous close-up of Jason—and we, the Western audience, are in league with it.

Pasolini's Euripides

At this point, sixty-two minutes into the 110-minute film, the narrative suddenly, and without notice, jumps ten years into the future and to Corinth.[87] Now, Medea lives on the outskirts of the city, raising her and Jason's two young boys. It is here, after 56 percent of the film is over, that Pasolini finally shifts to the part of Medea's story that was famously dramatized by Euripides and Seneca. As he did with the "Jason and the Argonauts" section, however, Pasolini "queers" this material, and the spectator watching it, in subtle, complex, and unexpected ways. In this portion of the film, however, a more negative form of queer desire—modern queer desire, to be precise—is revealed. First, we see a scene in which Jason, all these years later, is reunited with the centaur Chiron. He greets his long-lost friend with a noticeably emphatic, forceful kiss. One

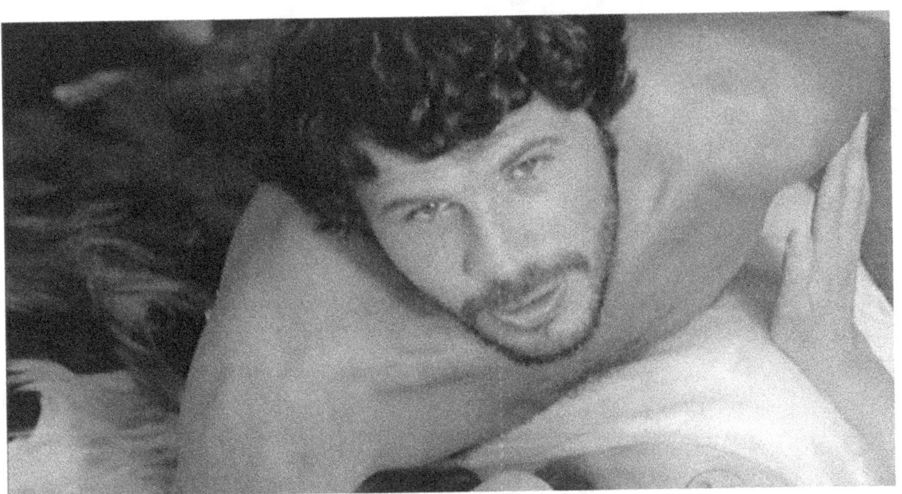

FIGURE 27. Jason looks directly at the spectator.

would probably make nothing of this "innocent" same-sex intimacy except, coming as it does in the film almost immediately after Jason's kiss of Medea in his tent, one cannot avoid comparing and contrasting the two identical acts. While it would be an overstatement to suggest the juxtaposition sexualizes the male-male kiss, Jason's kissing Chiron is demonstrated to be more passionate than his kissing Medea.

As the denouement of the tragedy begins to unfold, it becomes clear that a story about Medea's desire for Jason is being replaced with one revolving around Jason's orthodox homoerotic/homosociable enthusiasms, connected to a desire for power, in an androcentric universe: Jason's desire to marry Glauce (Margareth Clémenti) is evoked as a way to connect him to the young woman's father, Creon (Massimo Girotti), in order than he might rise in the political class of his adopted land. As we have seen, the queer creature Chiron has transformed from a half-human/half-horse centaur into a fully human and not-so-queer stepfather. Because Chiron's transformation occurred slowly as Jason was growing up, it stands as a thought-provoking allegory that compares individual maturation with the heteronormative historical development associated with certain cultures.[88] Here, in Corinth, through Jason's subjective vision, the spectator sees on the screen simultaneously the two versions of Chiron, suggesting that both versions continue to live side by side in his consciousness. Only the modern version, however, the purely human (rational) not-so-queer Chiron, can speak to the adult Jason (see figure 28).

Although it is just a simple process shot, the image in which both versions of Chiron appear on-screen at the same time is impressively seamless. (Conversely, we will

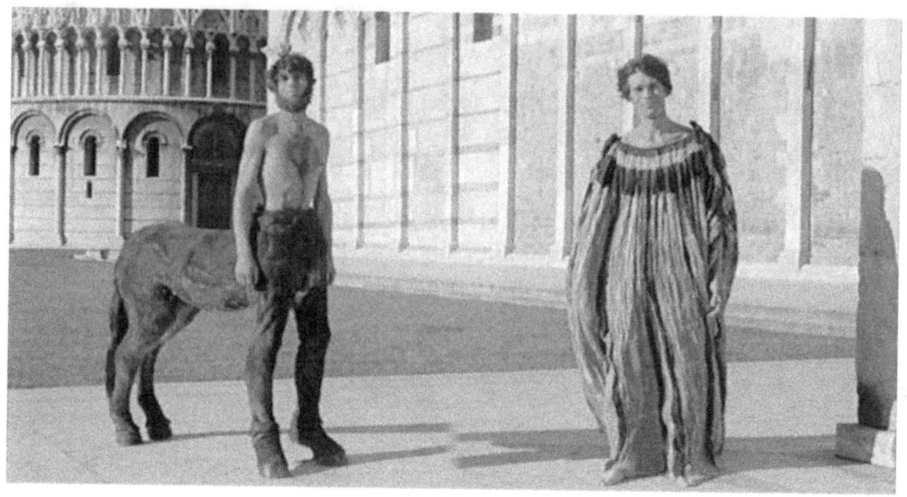

FIGURE 28. We see through Jason's subjective vision both versions of the centaur.

see nearly laughable process shots a few years later in *Il fiore delle mille e una notte*.) In contrast to the successful special effect, the horse body crafted for the centaur, most clearly seen in the beginning of this film, remains unconvincing, to say the least (John David Rhodes astutely remarks that it looks like "something . . . seen on the stage of an amateur theatre").[89] But Pasolini gives us utter realism for the impossible image of the side-by-side Chirons. It suggests that while the fantastic is best understood as queer *écriture*, the deep division within the mind of our heterosexualized hero, though visualized through a fantasy image, is beholden to a different register within the real.

According to the human Chiron, the queer centaur can no longer "speak, because we can't understand his logic." Pasolini suggests here that rational man can only indirectly understand prerational forms of thinking. In other words, a nonqueer subjectivity (hard won by Jason) can understand a queer perspective only through cognitive, rather than empathetic, forms of thought; "It is under his [the centaur's] sign," says Chiron-the-man, "that you, despite your plans, love Medea." Here we come to see that Jason's love for the once-savage Medea was an irrational, queer love after all. In this sense, too, then, *Medea* (imperfectly) reflects *Edipo re*, in that the adapted myth's central and paradigmatic heterosexual relationship is unveiled as queer, as a heterosexuality that incorporates and expresses queer desires; Jason's attempt to leave Medea for the social power he would have as the husband of Glauce can now be seen as a betrayal of the not-yet-extinguished (good) queer part of himself for the (bad) form of homosocial desire that is also often labeled, misleadingly, as queer.

Jason, for his part, seems strangely upset by the fact that, although he is rationally endeavoring to discard Medea for Glauce and claim the throne of Corinth as a result, he might actually love the woman who has honored him with her world-destroying passions. Chiron's claim challenges the utilitarian practices that Jason has favored throughout the narrative, utilitarian practices that include the film's only overt sexual acts, between Jason and Medea, and that, as D. A. Miller points out, Jason "accedes to . . . only having first rationalized [them] . . . in the service of exclusively social ambitions."[90] Bluntly put, Jason was happy to fuck Medea to get what he wanted in terms of political power, just as he is now willing to marry/fuck Glauce for the same reason. But what Jason cannot easily master is the idea of love and irrational—perhaps suicidal—queer passion, the kind that Medea represents throughout the film. The fact that the film implies multiple potential motivations for Jason's fear—is Jason afraid of true heterosexual love, or is he afraid of the queerness that Medea represents?—results in the kind of indeterminacy that Pasolini's cinema consistently offers. Like Pasolini's Oedipus, we thus have a man whose tragic and supremely destructive heterosexual affair may be little more than displaced queer desire after all.

Queer (Mis)Understandings

The scene with the centaur(s) is immediately followed by one of the most deliriously misleading sequences in the film, especially for a queer spectator. It is a sequence that comes very close to outing the entire Medea story as a homosexual/homoerotic allegory while, at the same time, contorting the exact nature of that allegory. For the time being, things remain complicated and more than a little unclear.

In Medea's residence outside the walls of the city, Medea (who, like Jason, does not seem to have aged despite the fact that ten years have elapsed) tells her wet nurse and confidante (a character carried over faithfully from Euripides) that they are journeying into the acropolis. The reason is not made clear, nor is the reason for the wet nurse's sudden and vociferous resistance. Nonetheless, the two make the journey. And again, after so many important plot details having been hastily skipped over, spectators find themselves exasperated to discover that a full fifty seconds of footage will present the two women walking from point A (Medea's home) to point B (inside the city's walls). Yet it is precisely the moment of exasperation that gives life to the Barthesian spectator who sits in the back of the auditorium. The extended presentation, in real time, of the characters' walk along the trail into the city does not have the kind of hypnotic resonance associated with much of the latter-day slow cinema, but it does create an opportunity for any cruising spectator to check out the hot guy who meanders in during the last half hour.

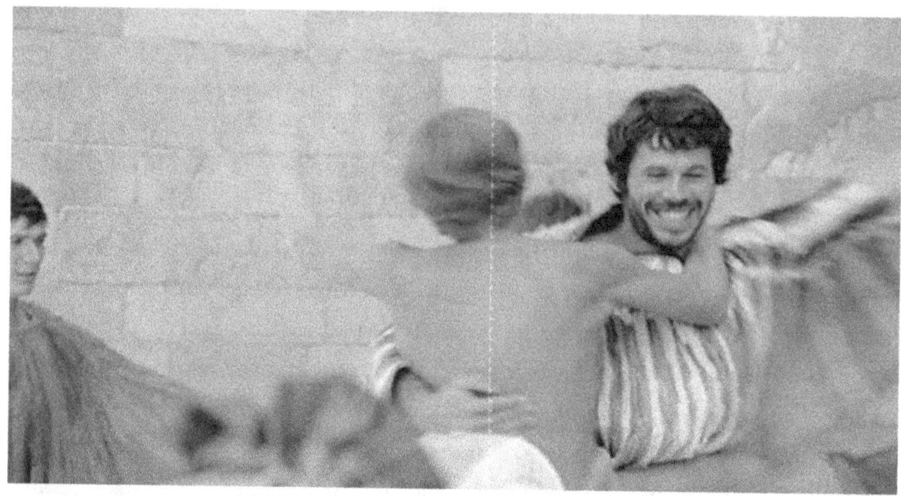

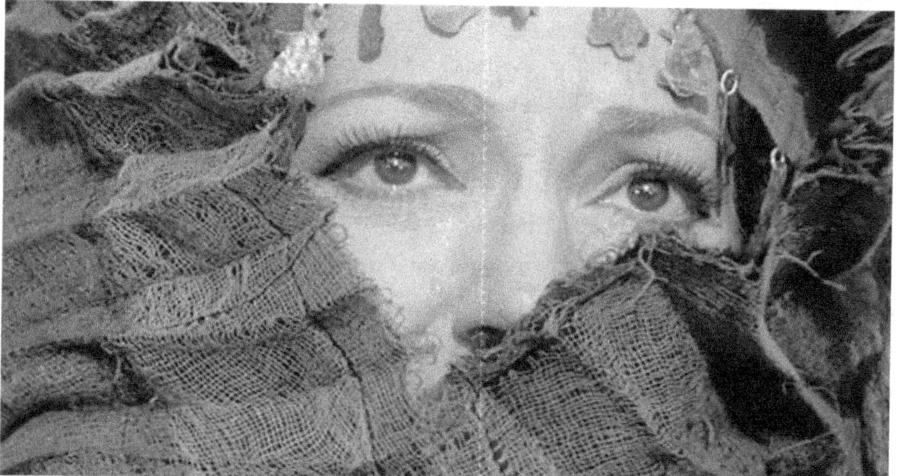

When the narrative once again commences inside Corinth, the two women witness Jason dancing with a group of attractive young men, two of whom are shirtless (see figure 29). Seeing this, Medea is horrified (see figure 30). We may eventually come to understand this as some sort of ancient-world (heterosexual) engagement celebration, but to the contemporary queer viewer, it appears as a scenario in which a wife discovers a closeted husband in the act of enjoying homosexual predilections that were previously hidden from her view. There is certainly nothing presented to us in the film to lead us to any other conclusion.[91] Pasolini's point is, however, finally darker and more ambivalent.

Indeed unsettling, this sequence, properly contextualized yet also with the aura of homoeroticism maintained, reveals male-to-male sexual desire in the most repressed and therefore utilitarian way, in the sense that Eve Sedgwick lays out in *Between Men*. As such, Medea, correctly understanding the celebration, is nevertheless right to recoil in horror: she is losing her man to a woman but not because Jason essentially desires the new woman sexually but because he wants the power that will be transferred to him from other men (more precisely, Glauce's father). Through the kind of hermeneutics of suspicion that Pasolini's style occasions, what seems to be a straightforwardly queer form of sexual desire is ultimately revealed as patriarchal homosociality. More radically, the filmmaker fully blurs the lines between the homosocial and homosexuality in such a way that the one finally destabilizes the other. In effect, and to follow Edelman, Pasolini's homo*cinécriture* presents itself as "a mode of strategic or analytic resistance." Furthermore, "by exposing the non-coincidence of what appears to be the same, the homograph . . . confounds the security of the distinction between sameness and difference."[92]

Again, in D. A. Miller's apt phrasing, "Pasolini's decision to retell the Medea legend goes hand in hand with a refusal to tell it *well*."[93] Although it is tempting to suggest that refusing to tell the story well is, in so many words, simply a refusal to tell it (hetero)normatively, this is not exactly right either. At least it is not exactly what Miller is saying. Indeed, Miller rightly suggests that many of the queerly resonant threads in the narrative (those involving Apsirto and the sacrificial boy or Apsirto's own desire for Jason, to name just two) seem to be evoked precisely to be quickly and frustratingly brushed aside.[94] The slow pan across Giuseppe Gentile's body that Ryan-Scheutz identifies as homoerotic is, in Miller's estimation, very nearly the opposite. In Miller's estimation, the film seems resolutely heterosexual. Since Pasolini cuts away from Medea's point-of-view shot of Jason's body, just as her eyes were passing across his crotch, to a shot showing her face in private satisfaction, Miller argues that, "once again, Medea puts a damper on homoerotic fantasy, not in the male characters this time, but in the male audience. She intrudes as the one who 'naturally' gets to see what the pan promises, and her interpolated image denies us." In other words, "There is something about *Medea*—something about Medea, too—that inhibits all sexual relations except hers with Jason."[95]

Miller's argument is persuasive regarding the themes the film presents, but as a spectatorial experience, in which the frustrations of the cinematic cock-tease can often be said to add to, rather than take away from, an erotic experience, *Medea* maintains a queer affect. But by the time we get to the Euripides section of the film, this queerness registers more on the thematic than the visual level, the shot of the men dancing notwithstanding. It does so, through Medea's horrifying filicide, largely in the form of a fantasy abolition of the heterosexual logic of institutional straight marriage and what Gayle S. Rubin famously called "the traffic in women," in which forms of wealth and power are circulated through a society, from a powerful older man to a younger one through the marriage of the former's daughter to the latter.[96] Medea, in a revolutionary act, thwarts Jason's attempt at a patriarchal family expansion arrangement with King Creon while destroying the original family business he had set up with her by fathering her two sons. It is far too simple to say that from *Medea's* first to its second half it progresses from surface-level homoeroticism to a deeper queer critique of heterosexual structures. And yet it is important to understand that the queer phenomenological pleasures of the first half give way to a relentless, apocalyptic sense of fatefulness. The film speaks of the end of a savage but fully alive, fully free archaic universe and then one where (Medea's) destructive political resistance is the only conceivable form of freedom. Keeping the two halves of the film in mind at once offers us a crucial instance of Pasolini's archaic modernism.

(Don't) Look into the Camera

Considering that Pasolini is, in the second half of this film, adapting a dramatic text, it is hardly surprising that the narrative becomes more dialogue driven as it approaches its bloody conclusion, just as it did in the nearly identically structured *Edipo re*. This gives him the opportunity to develop an unnerving technique that he touches on in "The 'Cinema of Poetry.'" For Pasolini, "In cinema, direct discourse corresponds to the point-of-view shot," and a shot that replicates the vision of a character directly looking at another character, resulting in the two characters' eyes locking together, can result in one of the most disconcertingly intimate uses of the point-of-view shot.[97] Something very different happens near the end of the film in *Medea's* *seemingly* (as we shall see) point-of-view/eye-contact-with-a-character shots. First, the spectator is essentially transported out of the auditorium and placed in the film world on the screen as one of the diegetic characters. But Pasolini, except for the shot of Gentile looking directly at the camera discussed earlier, is not interested in *direct* cinematic discourse of the kind that would interpolate a spectator into the film. Instead, he argues for a cinema of poetry based on free *indirect* point-of-view shots, which aligns the filmmaker with the perspective of the character(s) but does so too noticeably, imperfectly. As a result, what seem to be shots from the points of view of specific characters turn out not quite to be so. In other words, those people whom Medea seems to be making eye contact with are not, once we get the reverse angle, actually making eye contact with her.

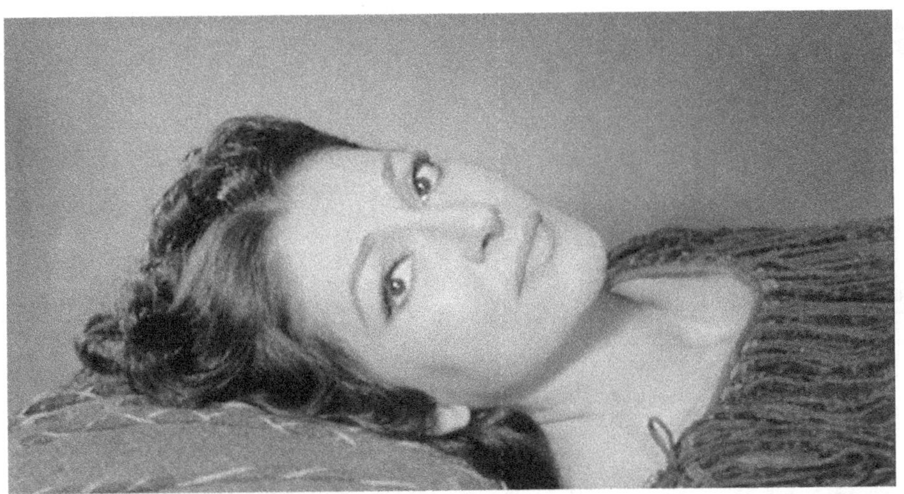

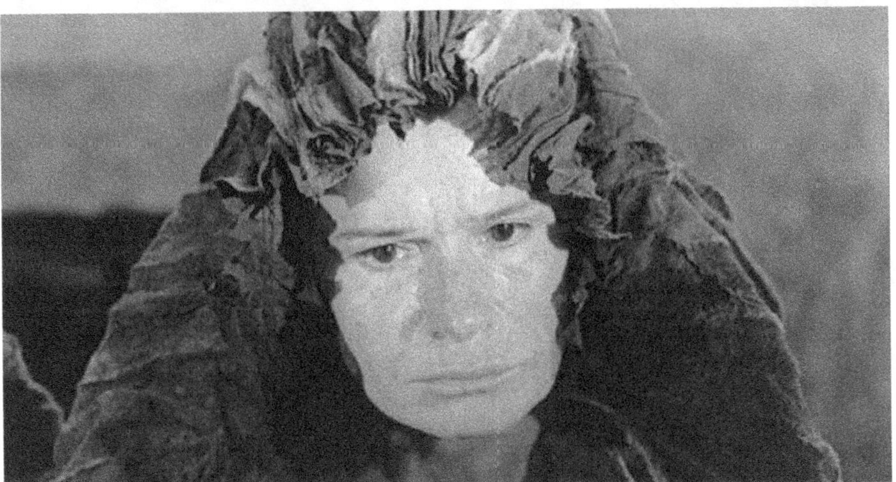

Consider an exchange between Medea and her wet nurse and then another, between Medea and Creon. Ultimately, the effect engendered, in this most remarkable example of the strategy, is of a *failure* of what promised to be a union between not just two but four perspectives: Character A (Medea), Character B (the wet nurse, then Creon), the filmmaker (Pasolini), and the spectator (us). That it falls apart so noticeably for the spectator reveals the (mis)workings of the cinematic apparatus (see figures 31, 32, 33, and 34). In a slight variation on this effect, Pasolini gives us instances of characters looking almost directly, but not quite, at the camera when the camera represents

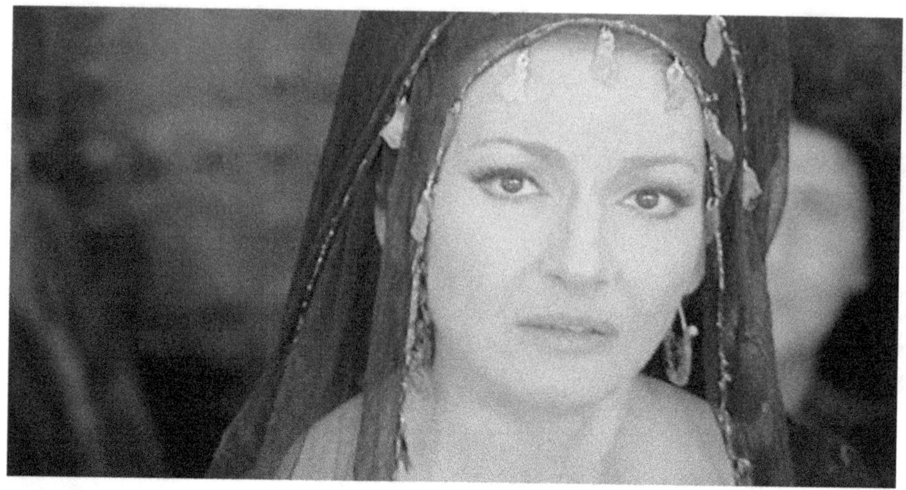

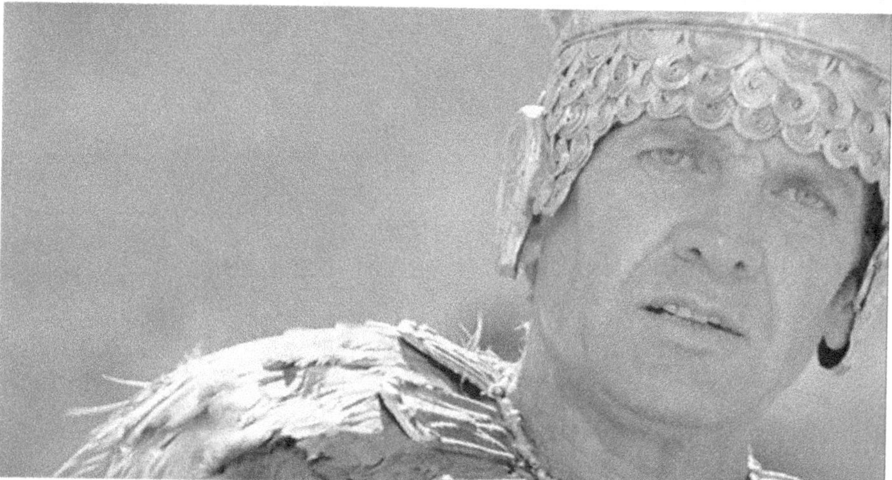

FIGURES 33 AND 34. Medea seems to be making eye contact with Creon; Creon is not quite making eye contact with Medea.

another character, without following up with the expected countershot of the other character (see figure 35). The proximity of the camera position to the eye line of the character is such that we may wonder whether or not the character is or is not looking at the camera/the other character/us. The effect is uncanny, particularly in scenes that alternate with those in which the characters *do* look directly at a camera. The effect is one of being imperfectly sutured into the film, beckoned by it but not fully embraced by it. One is engaged but not completely interpellated.

Pasolini uses another technique to similar ends in the film's second half when we get a series of shots of Medea kneeling on the floor awkwardly superimposed onto dissimilar shots, for instance, a rapid panning shot of her maids rushing in to attend to her (see figure 36). The narrative motivation for these examples of pure (but very rough) style seems to be to convey both the return of Medea's irrationality and that this section of the film is a fantasy or vision on Medea's part rather than reality. But the effect, as with the ill-fitting point-of-view shots, evokes the archaic materiality of cinema and reminds spectators of their position vis-à-vis it. We have seen shots filmed by cameras not quite lining up with shots to which they are joined and shots that are filmed by cameras that just do not seem to have been placed correctly in relation to the eye lines of the actors. Now we have superimpositions that seem to speak more

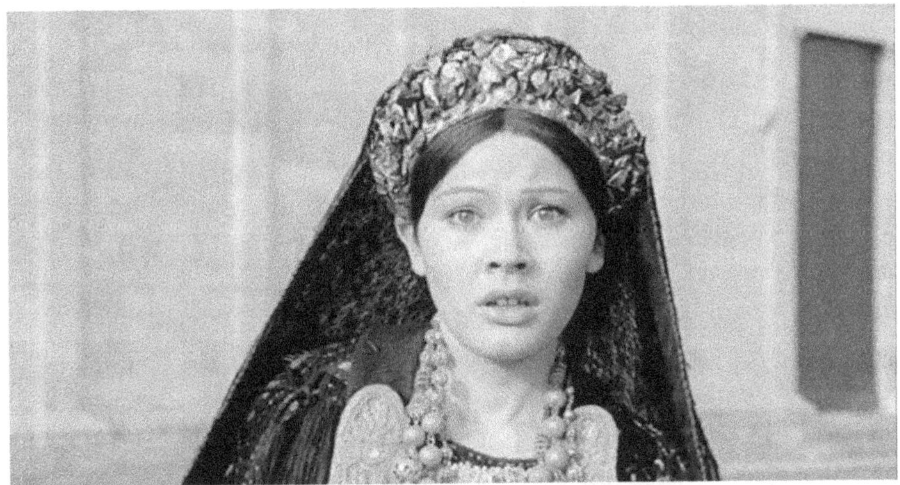

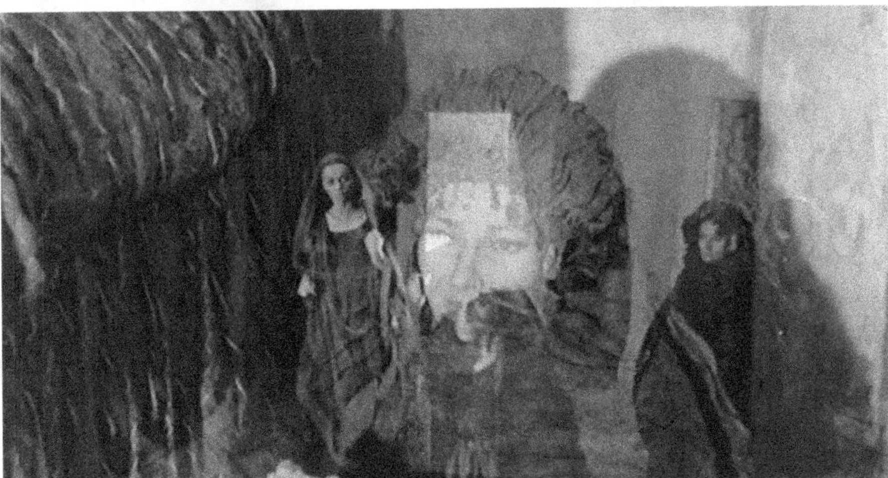

FIGURES 35 AND 36. A character looking almost, but not quite, directly at the camera; Medea kneeling on the floor, superimposed onto a shot of her maids rushing in to attend to her.

to some sort of glitch in a processing lab than to Medea's supernatural powers or visionary insights.

To return to Barthes, who called for an awareness of the split between the spectator as narcissist (identifying with the attractive cast in beautiful costumes in stunning locations, larger than life on the big screen) and the spectator as pervert (contending with grittier misbehaviors by enjoying a film that fails to follow the basic narrative, stylistic, and technical rules of the cinema and thus compels one to think about the film as a film), *Medea*'s split spectators achieve delirious goals. They are both "in the story" and "*elsewhere*," Barthes says: "a slightly disengaged image-repertoire, that is what I must have—like a scrupulous, conscientious, organized, in a word *difficult* fetishist."[98] For Barthes, this elsewhere is halfway between the image on the screen and the reality of the theater in which one watches it. Pasolini's genius is that he was able to create the sense of being halfway between the movie and the tawdry theater, the kind of theater seen clearly in Hernández's and Tsai's films and now, more indirectly, as a result of watching Pasolini's million-dollar *Medea*.

Barthes's comparison of a sexual fetishist to a film spectator, aware of elements that surround the film itself and that give meaning to it, is an ever-insightful one. Just as the shoe that Freud's classic fetishist requires his sex partner to wear is not physically necessary for coitus itself, a theater (maybe one with damaged speakers, bad projection, and sticky floors) is hardly necessary for a film to be viewed and understood. This is especially true today, at the height of gay bourgeoisification, when the intersection between sex and the cinema (the latter loosely defined) is epitomized by the phrase "Netflix and chill" and diminished by video-on-demand for the sedate viewer in the privacy of the home, a home where one's partners have been preselected via a smartphone app before they have even entered the physical locale. One *can*, however, posit that the fetish object incorporated during sex facilitates coitus while functioning as something else. The fetish object, be it a shoe or a theater or even a film that inspires a certain kind of theatrical experience, becomes a symbol of, and compelling, psychically liberatory *evidence for*, a phallocentric logic that makes fetishism possible under the patriarchy. By extension, the all-but-extinct theatrical-experience-as-fetish allows for a *more liberated* relationship based on similar invested-but-distanciated understandings of the ideology that surrounds it. In such a dynamic, the film is fetishistically related to whatever sex might be taking place in the auditorium; conversely, the sex becomes a fetishistic talisman for a successfully archaic and savage cinema experience. This cinema becomes the reflection of the desire that the extrafilmic sexual activity performatively evokes. But the result, for Barthes, is not just two perversions in some sort of symbiotic relationship. It is a matter of love: "I complicate," he writes, "a 'relation' by a 'situation.' . . .

It is, one might say, an amorous distance."[99] Unlike Medea's possessive love for Jason or Jason's selfishly deployed love for Medea, the love that is born (and borne) by the spectators watching Pasolini's film is a love of disengagement, deconstruction, collaboration, refusal, and all manner of erotic and intellectual desire.

Of course, in the case of Pasolini's film, the subject matter, or *object matter*, on the screen is critical. *Medea* is, at heart, about the love of, or rather the *desire for*, the other: a queer desire for the other sex and for someone informed by a pronounced cultural otherness. This makes it a perfect accompaniment for the enterprise epitomized by movie-theater cruising. In "Sociability and Cruising," Leo Bersani argues for "an ecological ethics, one in which the subject, having willed its own lessness" through anonymous sex in public, "can live less invasively in the world." Such sexual hygienics occasion "intimacy with an unknown body" as a practice that reveals a profound "distance at the very moment we appear to be crossing an uncrossable interval." This finally, in Bersani's model, "threaten[s] the security of . . . the hyperbolic ego's destructive illusion of power over the objects of knowledge."[100] Jason had already lost the Golden Fleece, privileged avatar of power and authority, when it was unceremoniously taken without requital by Pelais. His only compensation in the emerging patriarchal order was the set of children Medea bore him and, eventually, the possibility of marriage with Glauce, daughter of the king, a possibility dashed after Medea has her killed in the reign of terror leading up to the murder of her children. All this is lost in the narrative unfolding on the screen in fits and starts. In the implied audience of the film, then, the productive loss of ego-based relationality functions as its contemporary referent.

Medea's last scenes, laboriously, slowly focusing on Medea bathing her children to prepare them for the penetrating knife and the immolating fire, are followed almost perfunctorily by a brief last scene in which she offers her final defiant justifications to Jason, which concludes the film decisively while offering no sense of closure whatsoever. The film leaves us adrift in the modern world but awakened to an archaic past that is still with us as a part of our sociable sexuality and our nonhyperbolic sense of self. More simply, *Medea* leaves its audience bewildered, queerly hot and bothered, in a way that makes its members feel productively, freely, and erotically (dis)engaged from/with the film. All the while, there is, in the fragments, a tale of tragic desire turned into murderous liberation, one that has been there all along. But this film has offered an experience that exceeds the screen and thus one that has required and indeed mobilized the spectators' actively desiring, erotic intelligence.

The ancient myths of Medea as preserved in archival manuscripts and recorded in our textbooks recount many more events taking place after this horrifying moment in the character's life story, but Pasolini leaves us, almost as if in midconversation, with a quick cut away from the final scene of Medea and Jason arguing over their now-dead children. Our first sight of Medea showed her preparing to kill a child; our last sight has her having just done so again. She has moved from committing a sacrifice for a better future to a sacrifice to destroy the future. As a result, even as spectators leave the theater, they have a sense that the film is both playing again and again in their brain in a loop and, at the same time, going onward to some unknown destination. According to myth, Medea escapes Corinth in a dragon-drawn chariot and is granted asylum in Athens, where she has many more adventures. It is sometimes said that she returns to Colchis, where "the rest of her legend is lost in the ingenious fancies of individual authors."[101] Like Pasolini's interpretation of Oedipus, it is another eternal ideological and psychoanalytical looping.

Whatever Medea's ultimate end, the sense that her life story both moves onward to an unknown future and returns full circle to where it began is particularly apt when discussing Pasolini's cinematic experience as a whole. His spectator is similarly positioned through cinematic form—*a cinema of poetics*—beyond the theatrical experience of this one film while cradled within the ever-present stasis of a productive, illuminating, and vengeful desire: the spectator radically changed, triumphantly retains, or regains, a sense of primitive sexuality, one that is of both the distant past and a terminal future.

BEFORE THE BEGINNING / AFTER THE END

Appunti per un'Orestiade africana (1970/1973/1975)

(Re)*Écriture* Aeschylus

Appunti per un'Orestiade africana is arguably the queerest of Pasolini's texts. Like "homosexual difference," which Lee Edelman posits to be an "unstable differential relation," the seventy-three-minute film constantly challenges one's attempt to even define its status in relationship to the cinema.[1] As such, it brings into focus the text as a fraught and unsettling site for meaning and representation. Ostensibly, it is a documentary or essay film about a proposed feature adaptation of Aeschylus's *Orestia* set in twentieth-century sub-Saharan Africa. The film, or whatever one considers it, was commissioned by the director's friend Angelo Romanò for Italian television but was ultimately never broadcast.[2] Pasolini shot footage in December 1968 and February 1969 on 16 mm black-and-white film stock while engaged in preproduction on the much-bigger-budgeted *Medea*; that film, in turn, would be shot in 35 mm Eastmancolor over the summer of 1969. Although begun first, *Appunti* was not completed until after *Medea*'s December 1969 debut. Indeed, its first (semipublic) screening was as a work in progress, presented on April 16, 1970, at the MIDEM trade show in Cannes. Its official premiere finally took place in Venice in 1973. Finally, after Pasolini's death, in November 1975, it had a brief commercial run in Italy. With the exception of another trade showing, it was not released in the United States until 1980.

In *Appunti per un'Orestiade africana*, Pasolini combines his own material with newsreel imagery shot by others of the 1967–70 civil war in Nigeria. Pasolini's own footage includes a number of disparate sequences, rather intricately edited together: purported location scouting in Tanzania and Uganda for the anticipated feature, a heated classroom discussion about the proposed film with black African students back in Italy at the University of Rome, rough enactments of scenes planned for the finished film, and a jazz-recording session captured by Pasolini's camera in "a Western city" meant to contribute to the film's ultimate soundtrack.[3] All told, Pasolini's footage presents material from both the western and eastern regions of Africa, as well as Europe, in order to construct a mythic, all-too-broad conception of "Africa," one that, in Pasolini's formulation, is like the Greece of the *Oresteia*. And like the ancient Mediterranean country's history, Africa is positioned on the verge of an evolutionary leap forward from a constellation of tribal societies oppressed under colonialism to postcolonial, free democracies.

The mythological character of Orestes is first found in Homer's *Odyssey* (approximately 900–800 BCE). He and his vexed family appear repeatedly in later Greek drama, including tragedies by both Euripides and Sophocles. Pasolini, however, focuses on Aeschylus's "trilogy" (*Agamemnon*, *The Libation Bearers*, and *The Eumenides*), first performed in 458 BCE, as his referent.[4] Across the three plays, Aeschylus chronicles the saga of the house of Atreus: first, the murder of Agamemnon by his wife, Clytemnestra, and her lover, Aegisthus, and then the eventual revenge against the murderers by the victim's son, Orestes. But in avenging his father's death, Orestes is pursued by the Erinyes (or Furies, infernal goddesses of revenge) for his act of matricide. In the play cycle's final extant drama, Orestes travels from Delphi to Athens, where he undergoes a trial at the court of the Areopagus; there his is judged not by the gods but, for the first time in history, by a jury of human beings, a jury of Orestes's peers.

Apollo defends Orestes, who is finally acquitted by the goddess Athena, who, called on to break a tie vote by the mortal jury, releases the tormented hero from the charge of matricide. At the same time, he and his family are also freed from a multigenerational curse characterized by repeated cycles of pride and violence imposed by the gods. The Erinyes/Furies are thus appeased and transformed into the Eumenides (or Kindly Ones). As the trilogy draws to its end, the ancient traditions of bloodguilt and revenge are rejected; they are replaced by justice according to established law and the self-government of humankind.[5] According to Pasolini, "The Oresteia synthesizes the history of Africa over these last one hundred years: the sudden passage from an almost sacred society to a civil and democratic one."[6] It thus allows for an exploration of the tensions between an archaic worldview, what Sam Rohdie in his study of Pasolini calls the "real, primitive, terrible," and what he describes as "the rationality and controllability of signs and language."[7]

While we watch the filmmaker's purported location scouting for his proposed film, we hear Pasolini's voice on the soundtrack. This voice, however, performs not exactly as a narrator; instead, it is the vocal performance of a filmmaker in the preparatory stages of a film. With this voice-over, we hear audio notations linked to footage already shot that the speaker intends to reference later. In other words, the voice-over gives the sense of an observer who takes notes pondering the possibilities the images offer in the service of connecting the past and present. This is not to say that Pasolini is unaware of his audience. As we will see, *Appunti per un'Orestiade africana* is presciently aware of the spectator. At the same time, the footage accompanied by the voice-over has the quality of a private archive or scrapbook. The material is presented to the audience as if they were in a private home, invited to gather with friends and watch a slide show or silent home movies or perhaps in a lecture hall listening to an anthropology professor offering extemporaneous narration of the footage recently shot on an excursion.[8] However, unlike a neighbor's travel photographs, the intimacy of the cinematic experience offered by *Appunti per un'Orestiade africana* ultimately proves less than inviting and nostalgic.

As the filmmaker's "notes" unfold, the proposed film's fidelity to the spirit of the original myth becomes increasingly doubtful. Something more troubling is at stake for the spectator who is so intimately engaged with this filmmaker's voice. As Gian Maria Annovi reminds us, the filmmaker's voice is never synchronized to Pasolini's image, although we do see the filmmaker on-screen on a few occasions. Therefore, "we are . . . called upon to experience a separation of gaze and voice, which corresponds to the author's double position as observer and commentator in the film."[9] The filmmaker's separation between sound and image, seen yet unseen, is replicated in the spectator's experience. Although a certain critical distance is constructed between filmmaker and text in Pasolini's other mythic films explored in this book, the specific cinematic strategy here troubles meaning in an even more radical and, at the same time, more fundamental way. This becomes starkly clear as the film proceeds.

It is tempting to consider that the African *Oresteia* (the red-herring film-to-be-made that is not made) would have served as the third feature in an easily recognizable cinematic trilogy, one based on Greek myths, alongside *Edipo re* and *Medea*. But if we are to take *Appunti per un'Orestiade africana* itself as a significant work by Pasolini, we can rightly claim it, in fact, to be the key work in, indeed the climax of, what is undoubtedly a proper, fully realized trilogy.[10] As I posit in my introduction, it stands as Pasolini's "Trilogy of Myth." Like *Edipo re* and *Medea* but more directly, *Appunti per un'Orestiade africana* explores the "Third World" of the mid-twentieth century. In the overall exploration, the three films envision the implications for European colonies when they are suddenly liberated, or at least suddenly insistent on their own cultural autonomy, yet constrained by the terms of Western mythology. But with one eye focused on painful, personal issues associated with familial and extrafamilial sexual desire, Pasolini metaphorically shifts the contested ethical relationships between the colonizer and its "family" of colonized subjects beyond typical postcolonial concerns.

As Massimo Fusillo points out, Pasolini's first and second Greek mythology films engage with the two paramount, revolutionary human sciences of the twentieth century: *Edipo re* with psychoanalysis and *Medea* with anthropology.[11] They, along with *Appunti per un'Orestiade africana*, itself filtered, perhaps unconsciously, through the logic of deconstruction (the film certainly ends up asserting almost the opposite of what it claims it intends), constitute the entirety of their director's cinematic pre-occupation with Hellenic tragedy. However, it must be noted that Pasolini's interest in the topic predated his work as a filmmaker, with a translation of the *Oresteia* commissioned by actor-director Vittorio Gassman in 1959; it was also reflected in a series of original tragedies written quickly in 1966 when Pasolini was bedridden.[12] They are all, in Fusillo's view, "clearly inspired in their formal structure by ancient theatre."[13] The stage versions of *Orgia* and *Porcile* (together the source for the film *Porcile*) and *Affabulazione* (recently translated into English) are internationally best known among the six.[14] However, *Pilade*, a free adaptation of the last two plays in Aeschylus's trilogy, is considered by David Ward to be "the most topical of all Pasolini's verse tragedies," functioning as a "thinly veiled allegory of post–World War II Italy."[15] Moving from an allegory of the recent past in Pasolini's own Italy to one imposed on sub-Saharan Africa, however, raises problematic ethical concerns that Pasolini, as we shall see, deconstructs.

Over the years, our understandings of the colonialist imaginary and of "Oriental-ism" have been rigorously debated. And an initial viewing of *Appunti per un'Orestiade africana*, from our twenty-first-century perspective, predictably raises questions regarding Pasolini's ostensible naiveté about the Third World in general and Africa more specifically. As Annovi argues,

> The alleged protagonists of the film, the African people, are never asked anything about democracy or the Western world: they are just bodies, faces and profiles, possible embodiments of Greek characters, completely deprived of any individual or collective voice. This presentation of them is of course in open contradiction with Pasolini's claim that "the great protagonist" of his film is the people. The men and women of Uganda and Tanzania are muted, subalterns who cannot speak. Despite the film's anticolonial intentions, its voice is that of the author—male, white, Western, representative of a country with a shameful colonial past—speaking *for* and *about* Africa.[16]

Even more sharply, Keith Richards points to the film's "composite Africa bereft of any cultural specificities." Pasolini, "in his effort to allegorise and celebrate African independence, . . . falls into almost every trap provided by the colonial legacy; strip-ping Africa of its own heritage he attributes both the concept of social order, and the means by which it is achieved, to Europe."[17]

These criticisms should not be roundly dismissed. Although to answer Annovi's remarks, I would contend that in some sense Pasolini is answering no to the question posed by Gayatri Chakravorty Spivak's that Annovi alludes to, "Can the subaltern speak?" With regard to the traps Richards believes Pasolini falls into, I argue that Pasolini falls into them willingly. Ultimately, I wish to understand *Appunti per un'Orestiade africana* through a lens that *reinscribes*, queerly and disruptively, Western ancient mythology and Greek tragedy. In this regard, Pasolini is part of a notable tradition of artists that includes Jean Cocteau, Gregory Markopoulos, George Platt-Lynes, and Jack Smith who draw on myth and mythic figures to express homoerotic desire, queer subjectivities, and a radical contestation of the heteronormalization of high culture. Unlike the more romantic work of those four artists, I argue that Pasolini's final "Greek film" presents something more trenchant, if similarly perverse, in its faltering, in its even noble conscious embrace of a kind of failure.

Simply put, Pasolini—the homo-white director—rewrites (*reécriture*) his ideological position of this period in his career from within the text.[18] *Appunti per un'Orestiade africana* is, therefore, an exercise in *homographesis*: (re)writing to activate destabilizing queerness, in bodies and as desire. It opens yet another perverse angle on Edelman's provocative concept. In other words, it is a text that queers the terms for Western understandings of Africa and the bodies who inhabit that continent. In reconfiguring the text, really two texts (Aeschylus's and, broadly speaking, the colonialist text(s) about the character of Africa), Pasolini discomforts the invited guests to his intimate screening. Rather than reassure a "normative" (Western) audience of its cultural superiority, Pasolini painfully, embarrassingly deconstructs the whole colonial enterprise. The project's very failure, its "note-taking" voice-over that seemingly naïvely meanders across a series of disjointed imagery, invariably uncovers Western notions of metaphysical-being-through-representation as duplicitous shards of ideological production.

Furthermore, by calling a film "notes," Pasolini collapses the distinction between written language and cinematic language. And just as the voice-over narration in a classical Hollywood film can function either to validate the "reality" it visualizes (as in Martin Scorsese's *Goodfellas* [1990]) or to undercut it (as in Stanley Kubrick's *Barry Lyndon* [1975]), Pasolini's ambivalent narration points to a queer erasure (*sous rature*). This is to say, *Appunti per un'Orestiade africana* bears the strong trace of false hierarchies at play in discourse—spoken/written, literary/cinematic, documentary/fiction, and, finally, reality/myth—while showing both the all-but-irresistible pull of their logic and their fragmented impossibility. As such, *Appunti per un'Orestiade africana* is essential to, in retrospect, grasping Pasolini's (only slightly) more traditional adaptations of Greek myth. Ultimately, this film is crucial to understanding the entirety of Pasolini's cinematically queer adaptations, both before and after its production.[19] In

Teresa de Lauretis's words, Pasolini's filmmaking—nowhere more obviously than in this work—institutes "a cultural consciousness of thought as representation."[20]

Inscribed Myths and Autocritical Ethnography as Queer Orientalism

Franco Cordelli defended Pasolini's last completed work, the scandalous *Salò*, in the following way: *Salò* is "above all the description of its own language . . . and therefore a critique of language, an auto-critique."[21] I contend that *Appunti per un'Orestiade africana*, even more than *Salò*, is an autocritique; but in this instance, it is an auto-critique of the director's own Eurocentrism and Orientalism—certainly his culture's own Eurocentrism and Orientalism, broadly defined.[22]

The term "autocritique" took hold in the mid-twentieth century within leftist political discourse in France, where it received its most detailed definition in Edgar Morin's 1959 book *Autocritique.* In this work, Morin engages French Communist intellectuals who were coming to terms with the newly revealed horrors that Stalin unleashed in the Soviet Union as well as Eastern Bloc suppression. Coupled with these oppressive histories, the as-troubling political and ethical questions raised by the French-Algerian War triggered significant debate within the Communist movement. As Alfonso Montuori summarizes, "*Autocritique* is a remarkable document from an 'engaged' intellectual grappling with the complexities of politics and self-deception" that rattled the PCF (Parti communiste français/French Communist Party) in this period. From this point forward in Morin's career, as Montuori explains, the French thinker's "effort would be to develop a form of thinking—and of being in the world—that is always self-reflective and self-critical, always open and creative, always eager to challenge the fundamental assumptions underlying a system of thought, and always alert for the ways in which, covertly or overtly, we create inviolate centers that cannot be questioned or challenged."[23]

For Pasolini, such a willingness to challenge the supposedly "inviolate centers" of Communist orthodoxy was second nature and deeply embedded in his critical thinking. Much of his work is, to be sure, in deep sympathy with the strategies and goals we encounter in Morin's writing, ideas directly alluded to in two major sequences in *Appunti per un'Orestiade africana.* The first reference to Morin's work in the film occurs at the University of Rome, where the students, having just viewed some of Pasolini's footage from Africa, criticize it while Pasolini appears almost clueless in regard to their criticisms. The scene echoes the conclusion of *Chronique d'un été (Paris 1960)* (*Chronicle of a Summer*, 1960), Morin's single work as a filmmaker—in collaboration with Jean Rouch—in which the filmmakers show their documentary to the subjects they have documented. Indeed, *Chronique* cannot be overlooked if one is to understand Pasolini's own understanding of what he intended with *Appunti per un'Orestiade africana*.

Chronique d'un été follows an ethnographic approach in its examination of postwar Parisians as it queries to what extent they are "happy." It concludes with its subjects watching a rough cut of the cinematic result of this ethnographic project and then offering a critique of it. Their opposing viewpoints about the film then stands as that project's final words. But the fact that the question-and-answer session in the Morin/Roach film is presented at the end of what is essentially a finished project, one an audience has already had a chance to make an assessment of, gives it, structurally, the function of a mere postscript or addendum. The analogous scene in Pasolini's film, for its part, operates as a challenge of the film itself *as it unfolds*. Pasolini's question-and-answer session is split into two, with the first half occurring about seventeen minutes in and the second occurring very near to the film's end. As a result, it has a far greater impact on a spectator's developing understanding of the project. With many of the students offering particularly sharp criticism in the first of the two halves, a pall of suspicion becomes cast on the middle third of the film as it unfolds.

One interviewee, a shy but astute man, reluctantly expresses his concerns in response to Pasolini, who offers a broad comparison between Africa and ancient Greece. At one point, the student politely offers Pasolini the reminder that "Africa isn't a nation; it's a continent." Pasolini, on the defensive, attempts to salvage the moment by asking the young man which specific African nation he might recommend as most analogous to ancient Greece. The student responds that he has not "traveled around Africa." (We learn later that this young man was born in Ethiopia.) His response implicitly condemns the Western tendency that assumes all Africans are experts in all things "African." After Pasolini references African tribal culture as a key component for his proposed film, another student advises that the director "shouldn't make too much of the issue of tribalism in Africa, because Europeans generally made too much of tribalism [seen as a primitive and violent form of social organization by the outside world] to justify their crimes." At this point, one can actually become more than a little embarrassed for, and perhaps even by, Pasolini. The looks of annoyance, impatience, and sullen discomfort by a significant number of the students regarding the proposed Afro-Greek project only increase one's suspicion that Pasolini may indeed be engaged in a monumental act of intellectual and ethical misjudgment, in late-twentieth-century Orientalism. It seems likely that had Pasolini seriously entertained a big-budget African *Oresteia* as his follow-up to, or precursor to, *Medea*, this tense and profoundly awkward encounter would have surely had the effect of dissuading him from doing so.

However, after one of the university students argues that Africa must be understood not in terms of tribal geographies but in terms of the continent's contemporary nation-states, Pasolini hastens to remind the students that African "nation-states" were "constructed by European leaders" by simply drawing "lines on a map." In pointing this out, Pasolini consciously challenges the students (and the spectators) to recall their (differing) ideologically inscribed place in postcolonialism. In challenging the viewer this way, Pasolini asserts that modern Africa—that which the students ostensibly defend—is a false reality, false in ways that link but also separate spectator and postcolonial subject. The ramifications, as Pasolini illuminates them throughout the rest of the film, are profound. Pasolini's archaic modernism will be revealed in this film as the conceptual and aesthetic tool through which colonizer and colonized must engage to recognize the tragic existence that has befallen them.[24]

Unlike the other films in this "Trilogy of Myth," *Appunti per un'Orestiade africana* most clearly demonstrates the complex relations in the colonizer-colonized dynamic. For example, footage that immediately precedes the first of the two segments showing Pasolini's encounter with the adult students at the University of Rome puts the segment into tension with what may be perceived as the filmmaker's Orientalist visions. Here we see purportedly straightforward documentary images of Africa. But this footage demonstrates Pasolini's eroticizing lens as it is trained on the notably younger men of the continent, and it is through these images that Pasolini's offers the cinematic terms for his queer desire, an eroticization of the Other born of the ideological imperatives obliged by European colonialism. In his "location-scouting" footage, where dirt roads articulate to the Western viewer an impoverished African village and an African schoolroom shows children attaining a European-style education, Pasolini introduces his most complex and ideologically difficult autocritique.

Pasolini's narration here claims that the young schoolchildren, "presented with knowledge that still seems to them like a gift, are obedient, passive, and humble." The point made is indeed clear *as* a progression, if only in the structural sense. That is, it is presented as a progression from poverty on the streets to a Westernized classroom where students read (what we see is a student reading a book not so subtly seen to be titled *Europe*) to, finally, that European university in Rome where "older . . . and . . . by no means obedient or passive" students, in Karen T. Raizen's words, are able to confront their colonizer in the form of an anthropologist/filmmaker.[25] Hence, male Africans are seen as moving in a preordained logic, from the status of beautiful children to adolescent students—still, for Pasolini, objects of desire—being instilled with European values and, finally, to young-adult men fulfilling an ideological dream in which they attend college and become citizens of the world. Moreover, once they become students at the University of Rome, they turn the so-called Enlightenment against their colonizer. There, they critically rehearse what Homi Bhabha calls "catachrestic reversal," and Pasolini's illustration that "the desire of the colonized to identify with the humanistic, enlightenment ideal of Man" is powerfully but negatively returned. The students, in other words, critically rehearse "the cultural supremacy and racial typology upon which the universalism of Man is founded."[26] Ultimately, then, the University of Rome sequences put on display Pasolini's authorial self-destruction, not under the weight of the dominant hegemony but as its sacrificial victim—*autocritique.*

For the moment, a defeated Pasolini retreats from these adult Africans. This entire series of scenes—from the African roads to the African school to the European university—represents in miniature an essential component of the film itself but also of Pasolini's work as a whole: Orientalist sexual desire is methodically brought to the point of failure; it finds itself at a loss precisely, it has to be said, as these men reach adult maturity. With the terms of colonizer and colonized collapsed, male sexuality (pederastic or heterosexual) in particular collapses along with the terms for its authoritative existence. Following this scene, then, Pasolini, returns us from Italy to Africa, where a more complex negotiation of myth, text, and the weight of history on the postcolonial era undoes not only the subjects in the film but also the Eurocentric spectator.

Queer Postcolonialism?

With so much common sense (and solid evidence) to the contrary, can it nevertheless be argued that Pasolini's "Trilogy of Myth" (especially *Appunti per un'Orestiade africana*) resists or transcends an all-too-common urge to mythologize the Other through Western ideologies of representation? Is it possible that Pasolini's queer turn on European colonialism is, in fact, disturbingly queer precisely because the director refuses to deny his complicity in the Western project of domination? If this is true, and if there is no recourse for the Western homosexual artist to intervene against the practice—aesthetically, politically—I would like to further investigate the terms for autocritique that are so central to this film, whatever one's ultimate judgment about it may be. I contend that Pasolini's *Appunti per un'Orestiade africana* is precisely a deconstructive force, not meant to claim the authority of Western tradition for Africa; instead, the film is an address to that intimate audience that Pasolini seeks to make ill, in other words, those whose bourgeois homosexual sentiments he seeks to queer. If the gentle and informative voice we hear throughout the film suggests a command of the spaces Pasolini occupies, his camera lens lends itself to an eroticization of the young (read: "wild") African body. And yet, in doing so, the liberal Western audience (for whom this film is presumably made) is dislodged. Their humanist expectations for the colonized are distorted, made critically uneasy, through Pasolini's equivocally expressed project.

Pasolini's eroticization of the black male body, saddled with his confident, authoritatively seductive, and Western voice, brings to bear the colonizer's benevolent paternalism. Seen this way, the erotically charged footage of the African landscape and its young men creates an odd effect for the spectator. To render the youth *as erotic objects*, Pasolini insists on containing his young subjects within a film frame, even as some literally try to escape it. Put simply, these male figures all too clearly appear exploited. They are, after all, poor children and adolescents from an underdeveloped region of the world, seen through an erotically invested lens of a postcolonial European auteur. However, as Pasolini cinematically records his homoerotic investment in the enframed bodies, the camera's presence is profoundly *felt*. Through the formalistic devices of Pasolini's craft, the camera articulates a complex and ambivalently homoerotic relationship to the young men. To recall "The Written Language of Reality," what we experience during this sequence is Pasolini practicing what he preaches. *Appunti per un'Orestiade africana*, more than any other Pasolini film and as a perfect conclusion to his mythic trilogy, effectively "demystif[ies] the 'innocence of technique' to the last drop of blood."[27]

In one passage, for example, Pasolini's camera spends a significant amount of time lingering on the young men, following them determinedly with a quick pan or a tilt, only to, in turn, cut away from them a bit too quickly, as if reflexively indicating some trepidation. It is similar to the ambivalent objectification of the young Colchian Others in *Medea*, discussed in chapter 2, but felt even more obviously, in this cinema verité context, as the cameraman's desire. Pasolini is inviting us to see them *as he sees them*. More precisely, he shows *how* he is *coming to see them in the moment*. Pasolini's desire, rendered all the more perverse as a desire generated *through hegemonic ideology*, presents the African male as a (homo)erotic object of desire (see figure 37). To what extent is it possible, then, to rethink Pasolini's position in this colonized land as a "queer Orientalist"? And, in describing him as such, what critique does Pasolini bring to the colonizer-spectator who watches the film?

Through the queer Orientalist filmmaker's lens, the African male subject troublingly and seductively transforms before our eyes. He is no longer a simple, pitiable poor boy from Africa who is presented in the form of concretized queer desire, as disturbing—to be sure, *consciously* disturbing on the part of Pasolini—as the momentary consideration of the possibility of that may be. He is every bit as much a constructed sight of subjectivity for the Western queer man as the Western queer man is or, to better invoke Foucault, the Western homosexual is within European modernism. In short,

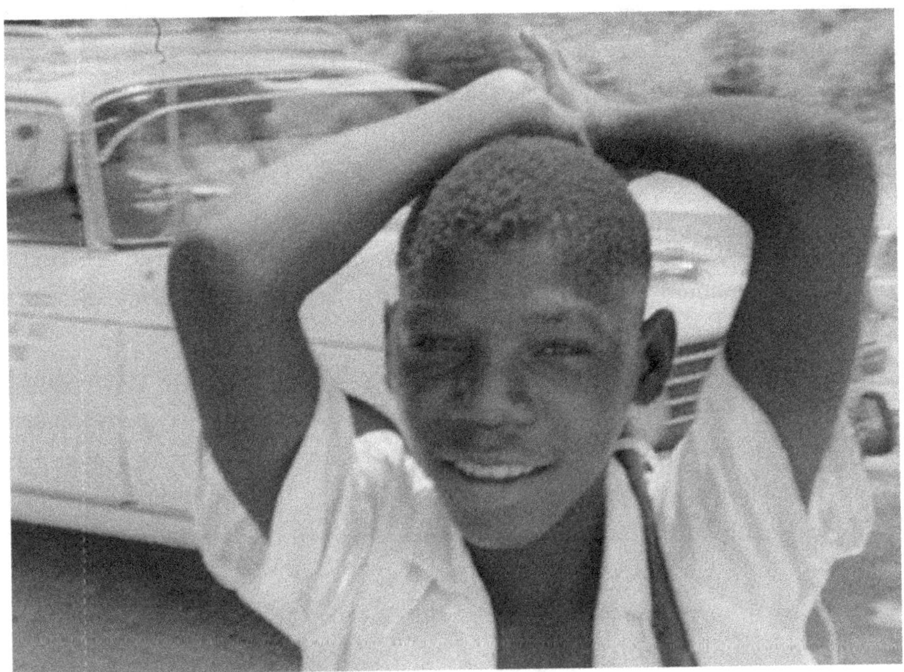

FIGURE 37. The African male as a homoerotic object of desire.

Pasolini rewrites the prohibited sites of erotic desire, unleashing the hypocrisies and reductive negations that give shape to so-called left and right politics. Pasolini inserts himself into the film as an ideologically inscribed bourgeois who refuses to ignore the terms for desire established precisely through Eurocentric hegemony. In the colonialist imagination, therefore, the status of the African boys as the *subjects of queer erotic fantasy* confers on them the status as *rerealized, homographetic subjects*. In other words, a palpable form of homosexual desire has been *rewritten on* their faces and bodies through Pasolini's *cinehomographesis*.

That desire is provocatively analyzed, troublingly so, through what Jean-Paul Sartre calls the "wounds" and "shackles" of the colonized subject in his preface to Frantz Fanon's *The Wretched of the Earth* (1961).[28] Two "purposes are at work in Sartre's preface" to Fanon's text, according to Judith Butler. She argues that "the scars and chains of the colonized here are brought to light reflect[ing] back the colonizer to himself." She further makes the case that these marks of violence "become instrumental to the European task of self-knowledge. On the other hand, . . . as the animating traces of a subjugation just short of death, these scars and chains mobilize an inexorable historical logic that . . . culminates in the demise of colonial power. . . . The scars and chains reflect not only the actions of European power, but also the default implications of European liberalism." Butler thus suggests "that the scars and chains are *in this regard* considered instrumental, producing a reflection of the violence of European liberalism, but only as part of the larger reflexive project of self-knowledge, self-critique, and even self-deconstitution on the part of a European elite."[29]

Whereas Butler points to Sartre's seemingly paradoxically blind self-recognition in the colonial project, I posit that precisely through Pasolini's queer autocritique, a metacinematic homographesis challenges an "inviolate center" (to invoke Morin's practice) of postcolonial criticism. Pasolini's *cinehomographesis* is not, therefore, merely a critical homoeroticization of the colonized Other; it is a cinematic lens turned on the way homosexuality and heteronormativity function within colonialism discourse. Pasolini's formulation makes meaning more complex because the viewer's own terms for homosexual *and*, ultimately, heterosexual desire are thrown into uncertain and vexed ideological terrain. As Joseph Allen Boone summarizes a key argument in his epic recent study, one focused on Arabia and Persia rather than sub-Saharan Africa, he almost seems to be referencing Pasolini's project when he describes a process that Pasolini's endeavor epitomizes, in this film, this way: "The unsettling reverberations set into motion by Western encounters with homoeroticism in the Middle East begin to 'provincialize' not only Europe but also its received histories of sexuality, calling into question the self-defeating logic that has traditionally posited East and West, hetero- and homosexuality, pre-modern and modern, as mutually exclusive terms."[30]

To better understand this idea, it is worth recalling Edward Said's turn on Gustave Flaubert and Gérard de Nerval in his study *Orientalism* (1978). If, as Said contends, Flaubert and Nerval "produced work that is connected to and depends upon . . . Orientalism," they did not do so to "dominate or set down the Orient." Instead, they "continually elaborated their Oriental material and absorbed it variously into the special structures of their personal aesthetic projects." Similarly, to use Said's words to describe Pasolini, the filmmaker has not simply "grasped, appropriated, reduced, or codified" the racial and cultural Other; instead, he *lives in* "and exploit[s] aesthetically and imaginatively" these foreign lands "as a roomy place full of possibility."[31] Pasolini's desire thus materializes on the faces and bodies he records. Like Flaubert's landscape of the Orient, which, Said tells us, "becomes a living tableau of queerness," Pasolini's "Third World" is similarly one of radical passive engagement. Like Flaubert, the traveler "tours. . . . [He] is a watcher, never involved, . . . always ready for new examples of what [Flaubert's] *Description de l'Égypte* called 'bizarre jouissance.'"[32]

What Butler, Said, Boone, and Pasolini foreground are the ways in which simple binary, oppositional assertions (good/bad, Orientalist/*not*-Orientalist) underestimate a critical discourse through which "queer" reminds the reader/viewer how "unconsumable" a text remains in a "post"-colonial era.

Back to Africa

Immediately following the scene at the university, Pasolini discusses an abstract and poetic way of writing the myth of Orestes onto the continent of Africa. Here we see huge, majestic trees. Pasolini suggests they might take on the role of the Furies in his adaptation of Aeschylus, the figures who haunt Orestes for the crime of matricide. He further muses over the image of a wounded lion, positing that it, also, might make a suitable Fury. But the variously elegiac or schoolchild-heroic sensibility that Western cultural ascribes to mythology is here violently discarded. Now, Pasolini proposes something more disturbing, immediate, and concrete. Following a relatively unremarkable series of shots where we see soldiers training, Pasolini presents raw, if nearly traumatizing, archival footage of the Nigerian Civil (or Nigerian-Bafrian) War. During the period Pasolini visited Africa, this conflict was a sustained human tragedy.[33]

Watching the footage (presumably acquired from a news archive; he admits in his narration that he did not shoot it), we hear Pasolini muse that one shot "could be an image of Troy burning" and, of others, that "these could be images of the sack of Troy, of massacres and destruction it suffered after it was conquered." As if both recognizing and misunderstanding the ethical dilemma of appropriating this war footage to describe what is proposed to be a cinematic-mythological narrative, Pasolini claims, "this war should not be understood as a specific war, as the Bafrian war, but as an abstract war. Its images are metaphorical images of what should be the actualization of the war between the Greeks and the Trojans." Spectacularly inverting the commonsensical expectation one might have for a project such as this—that the Trojan War might be employed as an analogy for contemporary social and political violence—Pasolini anticipates precisely what he would be accused of/credited with when making *Salò*: taking a very real, recent historical wound and, by superimposing it onto a classic text, exposing the representation of the "real" as a system of discursivity that both draws on a material past and rewrites it to interrogate the present.

Following the presentation of the footage of the war, the film continues with scenes that resemble those found in Pasolini's scripted, more traditionally crafted films. The first is set at the grave of a recently buried individual, where Pasolini films a father and daughter making offerings and praying for a deceased family member. Although Pasolini's footage was shot in East-Central Africa, nowhere near Nigeria/Bafria, which is on the continent's west coast, the footage of familial grief is situated to immediately follow the archival/newsreel footage of the war and thus connects the two. Here, however, Pasolini links his own footage not to the Trojan War but to Agamemnon's death at the hands of his wife, suggesting that it represents notes for a scene in which Electra visits her father's grave. It is all just a bit too much for the spectator to sort out, let alone contest, but the slippage from direct historical referent (Nigerian Civil War) to analogy (one war is like another) to synecdoche (a single death represents all the historical violence that surrounds and has led to it) to, finally, allegory (the story of postcolonial Africa can be understood through a specific Greek tragedy) serves to destabilize referentiality itself. It does so across both the bodies of the dead and the bodies of the living.

With regard to the latter, the graveside scene of the elderly father and his daughter is immediately followed by one featuring an imposing young-adult African male. It was directed by Pasolini "as if," as he states in his narration, "it were the real scene in my film." The African, of unknown occupation, temporarily employed by Pasolini as an actor in the role of Orestes, is shown also to be visiting his father's grave. The seemingly tall (he is shot from low, admiring angles), handsome individual, who is first seen shirtless walking through tall grass, is roughly the black equivalent of the kind of white (really bronze) beefcake actor one would find in a Hollywood film about Greek mythology. He is also, in his fit state of seminakedness, a likely source of gay male desire, and as such, he is this film's prime example of the practice of writing sexually resonant meaning onto the human body for broadly ideological goals.

Soon, however, this man will find himself clothed in Western attire, therefore losing his sheen of Western-situated homoerotic attractiveness only to embody another facet of Western desire regarding the subaltern postcolonial subject: the noble savage tamed. As with the street boys who become schoolchildren who in turn become European university students questioning their European colonizers during the first section of the film, the director effectively expresses the containment (perhaps strategic containment), if not abolition, of primitive erotic desire through Western culture. For Pasolini, this historically contingent denial of eroticism, facilitated by the West's sexually moralistic self-oppression, momentarily suggests Alexandre Kojève's formulation of the master-slave dialectic, in which the subordination of the sensually felt, and erotically framed, freedom of others fulfills the needs of the dominating group.[34]

Pasolini follows this man out of the grasslands and into an urban setting, narrating the story of this African Orestes as he seems to finally have envisioned him in his updated, transplanted story. This urban setting is Kampala, the capital of Uganda, which, in Pasolini's conception, "could represent the ancient and modern city of Athens." One quick cut later, however, the African is seen staring upward and off screen. We assume he is looking toward the Kampala/Athens we have just been shown but are told, "Now Orestes is before the Temple of Apollo," which is seventy-one miles from Athens in Delphi and which is represented by the university of Dar es Salam in Tanzania, 1,480 miles to the southeast of the Ugandan capital. The editing strategies that Pasolini imposes collapse space just as his narration collapses time: Athens collapsed into Delphi, Uganda into Tanzania, and ancient Greece into modern Africa. More specifically, Pasolini collapses the meaning of the Temple of Apollo into the meaning of twentieth-century academia, proclaiming an institute of higher learning to be an appropriate substitute for the center of ancient Greek civilization.

According to Pasolini's narration, "The university of Dar es Salam, which, seen from afar, immediately displays disquieting signs of resembling typical Anglo-Saxon, neocapitalist universities. Its external aspect . . . [and] its internal organization make of it a typical university, such as you see all over black Africa. These . . . conform to the neocapitalist, progressive model. They are the seat of the future local intelligentsia, of the culture of knowledge of the young African nations. And these, in fact, represent all the internal contradictions of these young African nations." Laudably, Pasolini points out the disquiet that emerges as African universities are seen to resemble those in the West, a result of internal contradictions that the film hints at. More importantly, in complicated cinematic play that toggles between the historical past and the contemporary scene while constantly, problematically invoking the tradition of Western mythology as the premise for a new film, Pasolini suggests that the most horrific historical *and* contemporary realities are readable *and return* as only texts. These include the texts of a myth, a film, or even the buildings, layout, and organizational logic of a university campus.

To be sure, Pasolini's oeuvre rests on this theoretical concept. When making *Il vangelo secondo Matteo*, Pasolini explained his rejection of a "positivist or marxist [*sic*] reconstruction" of the life of Jesus, despite the fact that he did not believe in the divinity of Christ: "I am not interested in deconsecrating. . . . I want to re-mythicize. . . . I wanted to do the story of Christ plus two thousand years of Christian tradition, because it is two thousand years of Christian history which have mythicized this biography. . . . My film is the life of Christ plus two thousand years of story-telling about the life of Christ."[35] On the one hand, keeping this in mind, it is clear that Pasolini considers his cinematic texts as palimpsests. More radically, on the other hand, it is clear that he understands that human subjectivity, at both the conscious level and the unconscious, is a textual accretion, an ideological and materialized anatomy on which history, the body, and the "reality" that is the material world are written. In this way, therefore, history and subjectivity are an etching into the unconscious, not dissimilar to words etched with a stylus onto a wax tablet through a sheet of plastic.

Pasolini's texts are thus more akin to Freud's "Mystic Writing-Pad," an apparatus not lost on Derrida and, later, Edelman.[36] They reveal the traces of once-registered events that have been forgotten or neglected by the conscious mind and in official histories. His cinema is thus the practice of making the deeply embedded but unseen etchings visible again.

Back to School

We finally return to the university classroom in Rome, tellingly, as Raizen points out, directly after Pasolini describes Orestes's fateful appearance before the tribunal in Athens: "The scene cuts from the imagined tribunal setting to an implicit tribunal—that of the students themselves, with Pasolini himself positioned as a man on trial."[37] Finally, after wending our way through Pasolini's recounting of his proposed film, the director asks the students if they "feel like Orestes." "Yes," one responds, "because we came here to study, to discover the Western world. Now we have—how do you say it?—we have discovered many things in terms of civilization, in terms of progress, of study. I mean—how to put it?—Orestes was a man who discovered something. So, in a way, we could represent Orestes." During this sequence, we do not see the student who responds to Pasolini. On the basis of the direction in which the other students' heads are turned, he seems to be just out of the frame, on the right side of the screen and close to where Pasolini stands. The handheld camera pans and tilts during this fraught sequence as it shows us the faces of the unseen student's classmates. They listen intently, never, however, affectively conveying their agreement, and to be sure, the smile that crosses one of the faces of those assembled is clearly sardonic. But what seems crucial is the odd way the comment, more or less affirming Pasolini's project, is presented in the film. The voice represents, to use Derrida's terms, an "unmediated presence," and yet it also functions here as an absent presence that invariably speaks that which is always already ideologically inscribed. However, in this instance, heard but conspicuously not seen, its status as conveyor of documentary truth or, again in Derridean terms, its logocentric value is not so subtly questioned. Image and sound are awkwardly, ill-fittingly joined together in ways that simultaneously contradict and complement each other.[38] It is with this vocalization, "written" into the soundtrack by Pasolini, that the ideological constraints with which the film has wrestled become crystallized. The sequence dramatically marks the impasse at which the colonized and colonizer find themselves.

As the scene continues, another student largely agrees with the unseen man but reminds Pasolini that they are not all the sons of tribal chiefs (in the way that Orestes was the son of a king) and that therefore the analogy is limited at best. In another

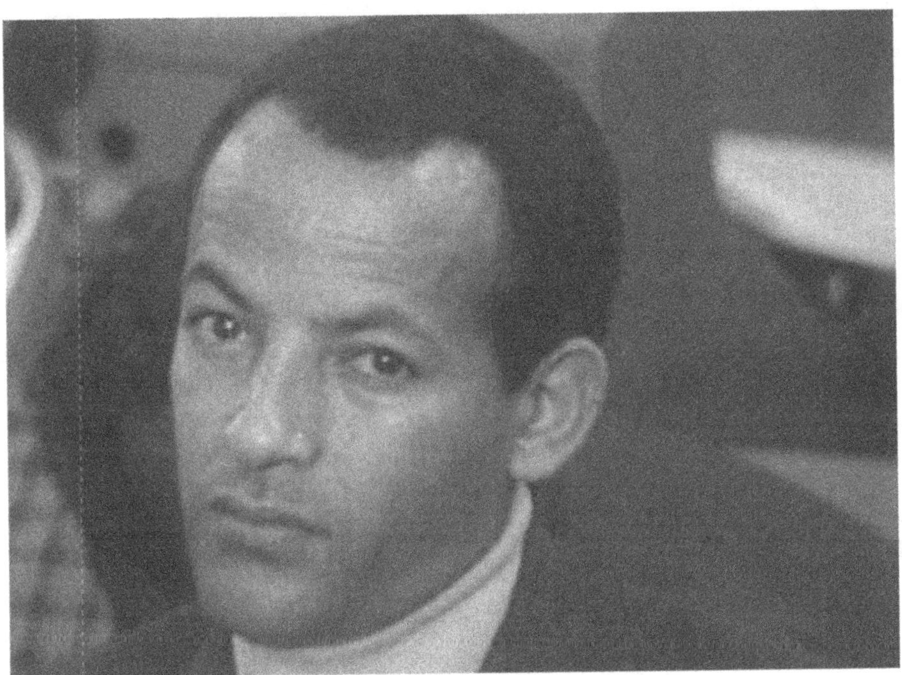

FIGURE 38. An African student in Rome looks directly into the camera lens.

instance, the camera returns to the shy, unnamed student who earlier contested Paso-lini's seemingly naïve comments (by reminding him that "Africa isn't a nation; it's a continent"). In the context of this final accounting, and through his silence and pained facial expression, this young man remains unreconciled to Pasolini's conceptualization of postcolonial ideology. Indeed, at one point, he looks directly into the camera and, in doing so, forcefully challenges the postcolonial Italian filmmaker and his international audience (see figure 38). When it becomes clear that the camera refuses to turn away or, in fact, lacks the sense of shame to break its "eye contact" with this gently defiant youth, the young man finds himself at the crosshairs of the Western lens. As a response, he simply closes his eyes. He breaks eye contact not in the panicked or shameful way that many people do when someone is staring at them, by looking off to the side or down into his own lap, but with this ultimate refusal: he simply and elegantly shuts out the Western gaze of Pasolini's camera.

As the film draws to a close, in its penultimate sequence, Pasolini showcases mem-bers of the Tanzanian Wagogo tribe dancing. In voice-over, the filmmaker expresses his position on the Westernization/modernization of indigenous people. Here, he comes across as remarkably optimistic, considering many of the dire predictions he would elsewhere make regarding indigenous cultures under the crushing weight of rapidly expanding Western capitalism. Pasolini concludes his film by telling us,

> This new Africa, the Africa of the future, must be a synthesis of modern, independent, free Africa and of ancient Africa. . . . This ancient dance—ancient, so to say, let's say, up to just a few years ago—was, of course, a rite, with a precise, religious meaning, perhaps even cosmogonic meaning. Now, though, as you see, the Wagogo people, in the same places where they once performed this dance in earnest, imitate it, in jest, to divert themselves, divesting these gestures, these movements, of their ancient sacred meaning and making them almost *out of pure joy*. Here is a metaphor of what might be the transformation of the Furies into Eumenides.

On a first viewing, the images of tribal dancers appear to connote an empty emulation of traditional customs that have lost their original mythopoetic logic in the era of alienating and regressive modernism. Or, perhaps, Pasolini is predicting a postmodern understanding of style-as-substance or play-instead-of-meaning that emerges out of late modernity. One might, therefore, imagine that this dancing would invite the displeasure of Pasolini, who wrote with apocalyptic fury about the erasure of indigenous cultures' beliefs and customs. Or, perhaps, we have been misunderstanding Pasolini all along. If so, how do we, in the years to come as Pasolini scholarship approaches its sixth decade, return to, in order to queerly revise, this cinema?

The final images in *Appunti per un'Orestiade africana* present another celebration, one immediately following the Wagogo dancers. It is a wedding filmed in the Tanzanian capital of Dodoma.[39] As M. D. Usher, quoting Pasolini, points out, these festivities take the "form of tradition, an ancient, indigenous spirit that will not allow itself to be lost." And yet "the scene then cuts to the inner courtyard of the house where an even more secularized party is going on, 'a party very similar to any European party of ours' [Pasolini says] where couples dance to contemporary Afro-pop played on Fender Stratocasters and electric bass guitars. 'But even here, in this modern attitude and this modern music,' Pasolini remarks, 'you can feel the residue of the ancient sprit I've been talking about, transformed, as you can see, into moments of happiness, of festivity and grace, and lightheartedness—these traits very typical of the African spirit.'"[40] It is as if Africa's sense of (heterosexual) origins has been replaced by a sense of queer *jouissance*, an *archaic modernism*, in which pleasure and death continually dance with each other.

Considering that *Appunti per un'Orestiade africana* and *Medea* were made almost simultaneously, with the former going into production first but the latter receiving earlier public screenings, it is reasonable not to situate the African "documentary," in the final analysis, as the last film in Pasolini's "Trilogy of Myth"; instead, it may be accurate to position the film as an unstable, protean link between the director's Euripides adaptation and his *Trilogy of Life*. As such, one is compelled to reconsider those mythic films, perhaps Pasolini's queerest, in the vein that the filmmaker proffers at the end of his sketch film dedicated to an African *Oresteia*.

Pasolini's cine-*écriture*, reconfiguring the archaic past for twentieth-century film readers, rewrites space and time. It gives the filmgoer a modernist mytho-history pointing forward to a postmodern twenty-first century. Africa as the seminal origin of humanity and Greece as the seminal origin of the West are reaffirmed, reconfigured, and reappropriated. In other words, Pasolini offers a queer remapping of polymorphous pleasures for bodies precisely through the ideological constraints that myth allows. The Furies, those essential demons of heterosexist inviolability, thus become the Eumenides in Pasolini's cinema. The playful, relational, and untamed Eumenides, while nonbarbarous, are certainly mischievous and troublesome. In short, then, we are in the presence of the sinthomosexual. After another, more widely recognized trilogy, the sinthomosexual will return one last time. But if *Salò* is more obviously a text of pure negation, indeed a full-throttled and terrifying denial of the future, *Appunti per un'Orestiade africana*, despite its final scenes of laugher and dancing, is perhaps no more optimistic in its implications. (*Salò*, of course, ends with dancing, too.) The laughter and dancing at the end of Pasolini's African notes, however, are more bearable. They collapse the archaic and the modern. For a moment, the bitterness abates. For a few seconds, there is just queer poetry.

CONCLUSION
The Aesthetics of Death

Viewed in chronological order and within a time frame corresponding to the production dates of the films—something not possible for most viewers during Pasolini's lifetime—the "Trilogy of Myth" reveals a clear progression or, perhaps more aptly, a *regression*. In that way, these films resemble, surprisingly enough, Ingmar Bergman's "Silence of God" trilogy, *Såsom i en spegel* (*Through a Glass Darkly*, 1961), *Nattvardsgästerna* (*Winter Light*, 1963), and *Tystnaden* (*The Silence*, 1963), and perhaps Michelangelo Antonioni's trilogy—*L'avventura*, *La notte*, and *L'eclisse*—more than the *Trilogy of Life*. Only here, the reduction is at the level of form itself. Pasolini in the "Trilogy of Myth" takes us from what one can consider a finished, if somewhat rough-hewn, art film to what seems like a rough assemblage to what might seem sketchy notes for an utterly dubious project. By reevaluating the three films through an abridged timeline as I have done, Pasolini's film practice presents itself as one that moves both backward and forward: back to an archaic period before the rules of classical cinema, including the distinctions between fiction and documentary, were codified and forward to meet the late-capitalist world and the Western civilization it overtook in rapid disintegration.

A Reduction

Edipo re is the most traditionally crafted film when measured against *Medea* and *Appunti per un'Orestiade africana*. Although it offers passages that disorient or disturb one's filmgoing experience (particularly those focused on the death of Laïus and Oedipus's encounter with Tiresias), it nevertheless operates for extended periods as a traditional adaptation of a classic text. It subtly and modestly embodies the "cinema of poetry" to the extent that it echoes the Antonioni and Bertolucci stylistics that Pasolini describes in his 1966 essay.

Indeed, the fact that *Edipo re*'s release in the United States was delayed until 1984 probably has little to do with fears that any potential distributor might have had about its challenging nature; instead, the film was almost surely pushed into the shadows by the wide release of Universal Pictures' *Oedipus the King* (1968), directed by Philip Saville and featuring the star power of Christopher Plummer, Lilli Palmer, and Orson Welles. Where it was given a timely release in the English-language markets, such as the United Kingdom, Pasolini's adaptation received generally favorable reviews from mainstream critics.[1] It certainly received better notices than *Medea* a few years later, suggesting that the oppressive powers-that-be in Hollywood, rather than distributors' fears of an unconsumable product, might have kept this art-film alternative version of Sophocles's play off American screens.

International critics and audiences had more opportunities to see *Medea* in the late 1960s, perhaps due to the star power of Maria Callas and the lack of a competing Hollywood version. But, as we have seen, it was met with a mixed response. It bore some resemblance to *Edipo re* aesthetically and dramatically (a backstory foregrounded to become the film's first half), yet for many viewers, it seemed to be both a rough cut that had been mistakenly released to the public and some sort of fragmentary text seemingly sent to us from a distant past.[2]

For years, *Appunti per un'Orestiade africana* remained almost completely unseen by general art-cinema audiences—a bit of Pasolini ephemera that, to this day, is only available in a high-resolution, English-subtitled version as an "extra" on the British Blu-ray/DVD edition of *Il Decameron* (BFI). The fact that it can claim three different original release years—1970, 1973, and 1975—depending on how one defines "release year," indicates its status as a slippery subject within the filmmaker's oeuvre. As noted, a recent American edition exists with Pasolini's voice removed from the soundtrack, replaced by another utterly betraying the director's sensibility. The English speaker's voice is arrogant and complacent, whereas Pasolini's narration is humble and tentative. The original is the voice of a man offering himself up as a sacrifice. The replacement epitomizes the haughty voice of untroubled authority. The implications about Pasolini's voice-over in this film cannot be underestimated.[3]

Although I have suggested we think of these three films as a "Trilogy of Myth," I realize such an assertion suggests a fully realized accomplishment on the part of the filmmaker. This, however, is not quite what we as spectators are left with. We move from a poetically "flawed" feature overshadowed by a Hollywood production to a film all but in fragmented form to a series of "notes" about a film that is never made. I always feel a bit saddened by the thought of *Appunti per un'Orestiade africana* not first appearing at the 1970 Cannes Film Festival, as some people mistakenly contend. Instead, it was presented at a trade show that happened to be in the city of Cannes. Here, on display as a desperate product, rejected by the television company that commissioned it, *Appunti per un'Orestiade africana* was unveiled in the futile hopes of acquiring another distributor, only to find itself essentially shelved for five years.

The history of the film's European release was essentially repeated in the United States, where it appeared at the Los Angeles Film Exposition in March 1977, on a

Tuesday, two p.m. matinee, as part of a free double feature. Its companion film was a "making of" documentary about a film that does actually exist, Bernardo Bertolucci's *Novecento*.[4] Bertolucci's Italian epic, shot in 1975, would further eclipse Pasolini's work, in that case, his final film, the posthumously released *Salò*. Another three years following its Los Angeles Film Exposition screening transpired before *Appunti* again appeared in America, finally in regular commercial release, this time at a series of small cinematheques around the country before a brief run in New York in January 1981.

Unfinished Business

In "Orson Welles as Ideological Challenge," Jonathan Rosenbaum points to that director's many unfinished films to consider the value of "incompletion as an aesthetic factor," which results in a "confounding of the notion of art as commodity." Hastening to assure the reader that he was "not claiming that this challenge was always or necessarily intentional," Rosenbaum offers an illuminating way to think of Welles that yields even stronger results when applied to Pasolini, whose radical forms engaged with radical content.[5] Massimo Fusillo, for his part, addresses "a true poetics of the unfinished" in Pasolini's late work, "notes, projects, fragments, conceived not as preparation for real works, but as new forms that negate and subvert artistic conventions, that is to say the Aristotelian idea of an enclosed organism."[6] As Luca Caminati reminds us, *Appunti per un'Orestiade africana* is also thought to have been intended as part of a larger work that Pasolini proposed in the late 1960s, one to be titled *Appunti per un poema sul Terzo Mondo* (Notes for a poem on the Third World).[7] Pasolini's outline of it, however, describes a very different conception of the African chapter than he ultimately prepared.[8]

All of this suggests that, in addition to the fragmentary and transmedial status of Pasolini's works, there is a protean quality to many of the filmmaker's projects.[9] This quality causes the work to function not just as a challenge to the idea of completion but also as a challenge to notions of singularity or unity. But for all the discussion of ideological challenges being implied by aesthetics of fragmentation, incompleteness, and work without works, it should be remembered that, in the commonplace understanding of such things, many people would simply say that Pasolini failed. Perhaps his failure is not in the punitive sense that one generally assumes and certainly not in the rather simple sense that Jack Halberstam means when positing a "queer art of failure."[10] More accurately, we can say that he succeeded, perhaps quite consciously, in failing. Discussing the theme of failure in Pasolini's first three films, *Accattone, Mamma Roma,* and the short "La ricotta" (1963), as well as some of his later writings, Krzysztof Rowiński reminds us that "the other important term, in addition to *progress,* that failure positions itself against is *future*."[11] Beyond, but connected to, Edelman's queer critique of futurity, the complex heretical Marxism that Pasolini proffered also looked at the concept of "the future" with suspicion. Summarizing ideas of Franco Berardi, Rowiński reminds us that "the origins of the myth of the future" can be traced to "the development of modernity and modern capitalism. The only possible response to the expectation of future, then," from the perspective of post–World War II Marxism, "is an attempt to 'stop the machine,' which may be understood both individually (as a personal, libidinal reorientation from the future to the present [itself, of course, very queer]) or socially (as, for instance, through the general strike)."[12]

Put another way, as if defiantly ignoring the futurity inherent in a coherent, marketable body of work resulting from a well-ordered career, one that is meant to *stand the test of time*, Pasolini simply *refused to succeed*. And when he did "succeed," he renounced that unwelcome development as quickly as possible.[13] It comes as no surprise, then, that many critics and scholars have traced a martyr's complex in Pasolini's life and work, including Armando Maggi. Maggi "considers both [Pasolini's] unquestionable death drive and his sexuality" as a fused and single impulse. For him, Pasolini, exemplifying the "sodomitical subject," in effect, "embodies death and speaks death."[14] Seen this way, Pasolini's pessimism is not simply Bersanian/Edelmanian negativity; for Maggi, it is literally apocalyptic. Pasolini's self-aware role in life is as the buggered prophet who announced the end of days.

Even more controversially, Giuseppe Zigaina, a close friend of the filmmaker, has long argued that Pasolini's death was an intricately staged suicidal performance, or rite, planned at least as early as 1962. Zigaina holds that Pasolini repeatedly alluded in coded, poetic language to his planned aestheticized suicide throughout much of his work.[15] This theory, while hardly suppressed, has not been granted much credence within Pasolini studies or by his biographers, and probably for good reason.[16] And yet Zigaina can point to an impressive amount of compelling material in Pasolini's corpus as evidence that the filmmaker, poet, and theorist tacitly acknowledged his work/life as a "death project." This testifies to something undeniable: Pasolini created work and lived in the world as an artist who elucidated the *value in* the terminal.

Hence, Zigaina maintains that Pasolini initially wanted to take his life in 1969, with *Medea* "planned to be his last work."[17] It would certainly have been a stunning finale to his film corpus: Maria Callas seen screaming, "Niente è più possibile, ormai!" (Nothing more is possible, now!). Infamously enough, Callas's legendary voice was silenced and replaced with another performer's, but her annihilating facial expression was all her own. It would have punctuated the queer filmmaker's death in grand fashion. But after Pasolini decided, in Zigaina's account, to postpone his self-deliverance until 1975, *Salò* became his consciously planned, utterly fitting final feature. Still, one must quickly recognize that almost all of Pasolini's feature films would have served as a fitting epigraph to his own life and to the postwar era's disingenuous futurity.

The Death of Tragedy

Evoking end times in a series of adaptations of Western myths might seem a particularly odd gesture, or a queer one. Like the literary sources for the *Trilogy of Life*, those Greek myths and their tragic stage adaptations are long considered accounts of cultures' births, hence profoundly archaic. Considering Pasolini's penchant for incompleteness, it should not go unnoticed that the trio of mythological films ends up dramatizing the three paramount poets of Greek tragedy: Sophocles, Euripides, and Aeschylus. Fragmented though Pasolini's work may be, he covers the bases. In doing so, he connects his pessimistic vision, his queer *écriture*, and his refusal to produce "successful" takes on formative texts to the very failures that define tragedy.

In a short 1996 lecture belatedly published as "Is There a Gay Art?," Leo Bersani summarizes, "The art I'm thinking of involves a massive and double negativity: the negation of relationality as we now know it, and an attack on the cult of difference that supports the dominant mode of relations."[18] It seems to me that much of Pasolini's work that is so easily criticized for naïvely embracing gay relationality and celebrating cultural and personal difference, in fact, does just the opposite. Bersani argues that absolute "negativity can be more prominent in canonical authors than in culturally marginal art. The latter frequently celebrates minority cultures, thus unwittingly supporting the differential barriers that the dominant culture is only too happy to see reinforced."[19]

For all the criticism about Pasolini's Eurocentric gaze, seen as objectifying the young, the lower classes, and the people of the Third World, the self/other distinctions that are presupposed in those criticisms *and that serve to reinforce murderous forms of relationality* collapse through the filmmaker's processes of queer *écriture*. As such, the criticism is untenable. Pasolini's attempt to project Western concerns onto the people of the Third World fails. More importantly, any "positive value" that might have come out of the encounter between the Italian filmmaker and his subaltern subjects is forestalled. Even the finished film about the unmade film fully accounting for that impasse just falls between the cracks. It has no official English-language title (it has variously been marketed in English as *Notes for an African Orestes*, *Notes towards an African Orestes*, *Notes for an African Oresteia*, etc.) and no clear year of release.

Before that, in the Euripides adaptation, Jason and Medea, allegorical representatives of Western civilization and Eastern exoticism, in turn, also fail to relate. There is no future for their children either. In D. A. Miller's assessment, *Medea* "ends, quite explicitly, by going nowhere." The "absence of any catharsis that would allow Medea, Jason, or any other survivor of the plot's cataclysmic events to 'move on'" results in a denouement of stunning negativity.[20] Before that, Oedipus's journey out of and back into his womb is shown as the ultimate failure of relationality. His incestuous desire for his mother reveals a preexisting desire for his father. In the end, however, Oedipus only fucks himself. In Bersani's words, "Negativity in art attacks the myths of the dominant culture," and in Pasolini's films, that negativity serves to attack the myths of the dominant culture directly. Attacking our myths gets at our myths, "the pastoral myth, for example, of sexuality as inherently loving and nurturing, of sexuality as continuous with harmonious community."[21] Pasolini's own appalling ending is, of course, an unbearable, apposite testament to that—these films only somewhat less so. They remain, however, dramatizing the past, the beginning of a civilization with no future. Now, regarding this work from a moment in history that seems even more apocalyptic than Pasolini's own, we must reckon with what this artist's cinema has left behind.

APPENDIX
Filmography of Motion Pictures Directed by Pier Paolo Pasolini

Accattone (1961)

Italy, 35 mm, black and white, 117 mins.

Screenplay by Pier Paolo Pasolini with dialogue collaboration by Sergio Citti

Produced by Alfredo Bini

Director of photography: Tonino Delli Colli

Editor: Nino Baragli

Sound: Luigi Puri

Art director: Flavio Mogherini

Music: Johann Sebastian Bach

Cast: Franco Citti (Vittorio Cataldi/"Accattone," dubbed by Paolo Ferrari), Franca Pasut (Stella), Silvana Corsini (Maddalena), Paola Guidi (Ascenza, dubbed by Monica Vitti), Adriana Asti (Amore), Romolo Orazi (Accattone's father-in-law), Massimo Cacciafeste (Accattone's brother-in-law), Luciano Conti (the Mohican), Luciano Gonini (Gold Foot), Renato Capogna (Renato), Galeazzo Riccardi (Cipolla), Leonardo Muraglia (Mammoletto), Giuseppe Ristagno (Crazy Peppe), Roberto Giovannoni (the German), Mario Cipriani (Balilla), Roberto Scaringella (Carthage), Silvio Citti (Sabino), Giovanni Orgitano (Scucchia), Piero Morgia (Pio), Umberto Bevilacqua (Salvatore), Franco Bevilacqua (Franco), Amerigo Bevilacqua (Amerigo), Sergio Fioravanti (Gennarino), Adele Cambria (Nannina), Edgardo Siroli (1st Farlocchi), Renato Terra (2nd Farlocchi), Emanuele Di Bari (Sor Pietro), Adriana Moneta (Margheritona), Danilo Alleva (Iaio), Francesco Orazi (the peasant), Mario Guerani (the commissioner), Stefano D'Arrigo (investigating judge), Sergio Citti (a waiter), Adriano Mazzelli (Amore's client), Elsa Morante (Lina, a prisoner)

Mamma Roma (1962)

Italy, 35 mm, black and white, 106 mins.

Screenplay by Pier Paolo Pasolini with dialogue collaboration by Sergio Citti

Produced by Alfredo Bini

Director of photography: Tonino Delli Colli

Editor: Nino Baragli

Sound: Leopoldo Rosi

Art director: Flavio Mogherini

Cast: Anna Magnani (Mamma Roma), Ettore Garofolo (Ettore), Franco Citti (Carmine), Silvana Corsini (Bruna), Luisa Orioli (Biancofiore), Paolo Volponi (the priest), Luciano Gonini (Zaccarino), Vittorio La Paglia (Signor Pellissier), Piero Morgia (Piero), Leandro Santarelli (Begalo the Roscio), Emanuele di Bari (Gennarino the troubadour), Antonio Spoletini (the fireman), Nino Bionci (the painter), Nino Venzi (a client), Roberto Venzi (the airman), Maria Bernardini (the bride), Santino Citti (the father of the bride), Lamberto Maggiorani (a patient), Franco Ceccarelli (Carletto), Marcello Sorrentino (Tonino), Sandro Meschino (Pasquale), Franco Tovo (Augusto), Pasquale Ferrarese (Lino), Renato Montalbarno and Enzo Fioravanti (nurses), Elena Cameron and Maria Benati (female prostitutes), Loreto Ranalli and Mario Ferraguti (male prostitutes)

"La ricotta," an episode within the anthology film *RoGoPaG* (1963)
Italy-France, 35 mm, color, 35 mins.
Screenplay by Pier Paolo Pasolini
Produced by Alfredo Bini
Director of photography: Tonino Delli Colli
Editor: Nino Baragli
Art director: Flavio Mogherini
Costume designer: Danilo Donati
Cast: Orson Welles (the director, dubbed by Giorgio Bassani), Mario Cipriani (Stracci), Laura Betti (the "star"), Edmonda Aldini (another "star"), Vittorio La Paglia (the journalist), Maria Berardini (the stripper), Rossana Di Rocco (Stracci's daughter)

"La rabbia" (1963)
Italy, 35 mm, black and white, 92 mins.
Screenplay by Pier Paolo Pasolini; two-part film, with the second part by Giovannino Guareschi
Produced by Gastone Ferranti
Editors: Pier Paolo Pasolini, Nino Baragli, Mario Serandrei
Narrators: Giorgio Bassani (poetry voice), Renato Guttuso (prose voice)

Comizi d'amore (*Love Meetings*, 1964)
Italy, 35 mm, black and white, 92 mins.
Screenplay by Pier Paolo Pasolini
Produced by Alfredo Bini
Directors of photography: Mario Bernardo, Tonino Delli Colli
Editor: Nino Baragli
Sound: Oscar De Arcangelis, Carlo Ramundo

Participants: Alberto Moravia, Cesare Musatti, Camilla Cederna, Oriana Fallaci, Adele Cambria, Peppino di Capri, Giuseppe Ungaretti, Antonella Lualda, Graziella Granata, Ignazio Buttitta, Graziella Chiarcossi

Sopralluoghi in Palestina per "Il Vangelo secondo Matteo" (1964/1965)
Italy, 35 mm, black and white, 55 mins.
Produced by Alfredo Bini
Commentary written and narrated by Pier Paolo Pasolini
Directors of photography: Aldo Pennelli, Otello Martelli, Domenico Cantatore
Sound: Domenico Cantatore

Il vangelo secondo Matteo (*The Gospel According to St. Matthew/The Gospel According to Matthew*, 1964)
Italy, 35 mm, black and white, 137 mins.
Screenplay by Pier Paolo Pasolini
Produced by Alfredo Bini
Director of photography: Tonino Delli Colli
Editor: Nino Baragli
Sound: Mario Del Pozzo
Art director: Luigi Scaccianoce
Costume designer: Danilo Donati
Cast: Enrique Irazoqui (Jesus Christ, dubbed by Enrico Maria Salerno), Margherita Caruso (young Mary), Susanna Pasolini (old Mary), Marcello Morante (Joseph), Mario Socrate (John the Baptist), Settimio Di Porto (Peter), Otello Sestili (Judas Iscariot), Enzo Siciliano (Simon), Giorgio Agamben (Philip), Ferruccio Nuzzo (Matthew), Giacomo Morante (the Apostle John), Alfonso Gatto (Andrew), Guido Cerretani (Bartholomew), Rosario Migale (Thomas), Luigi Barbini (James of Zebedea), Marcello Galdini (James of Alfeo), Elio Spaziani (Thaddeus), Rodolfo Wilcock (Caiaphas), Alessandro Clerici (Pontius Pilate), Paola Tedesco (Salomè), Rossana Di Rocco (angel), Amerigo Bevilacqua (Herod the Great), Francesco Leonetti (Herod Antipas), Franca Cupane (Herodias), Eliseo Boschi (Joseph of Arimathea), Natalia Ginzburg (Mary of Bethany), Renato Terra (a pharisee), Ninetto Davoli (young shepherd)

Uccellacci e uccellini (*The Hawks and the Sparrows/Hawks and Sparrows*, 1966)
Italy, 35 mm, black and white, 86 mins.
Screenplay by Pier Paolo Pasolini
Produced by Alfredo Bini
Directors of photography: Tonino Delli Colli, Mario Bernardo
Editor: Nino Baragli

Sound: Pietro Ortolani

Art director: Luigi Scaccianoce

Costume designer: Danilo Donati

Original music: Ennio Morricone

Cast: Totò (the father, Friar Cicillo), Ninetto Davoli (the son, Friar Ninetto), Femi Benussi (Luna the prostitute), Rossana di Rocco (a friend of Ninetto), Francesco Leonetti (voice of the crow), Riccardo Redi (the engineer), Lena Lin Solaro (Urganda), Gabriele Baldini (Dante's dentist), Rosina Moroni (peasant woman), Umberto Bevilacqua (Incensurato), Ricardo Redi (mansion owner), Vittorio Vittori (Ciro Lococo), Giovanni Tarallo (starving peasant)

"La terra vista dalla luna" ("The Earth as Seen from the Moon," an episode within *Le streghe* [*The Witches*], 1967)

Italy, 35 mm, color, 30 mins.

Screenplay by Pier Paolo Pasolini

Produced by Dino De Laurentiis

Director of photography: Giuseppe Rotunno

Editor: Nino Baragli

Sound: Vittorio Trentino

Art directors: Mario Garbuglia, Piero Poletto

Costume designer: Piero Tosi

Original music: Ennio Morricone

Cast: Silvana Mangano (Assurdina Caì), Totò (Ciancicato Miao), Ninetto Davoli (Basciù Miao), Luigi Leoni (a tourist), Laura Betti (the tourist's wife), Mario Cipriani (priest)

Edipo re (*Oedipus Rex*, 1967)

Italy, 35 mm, color, 110 mins.

Screenplay by Pier Paolo Pasolini

Produced by Alfredo Bini

Director of photography: Giuseppe Ruzzolini

Editor: Nino Baragli

Sound: Carlo Tarchi

Art director: Luigi Scaccianoce

Costume designer: Danilo Donati

Cast: Franco Citti (Edipo), Silvana Mangano (Jocasta), Alida Valli (Merope), Carmelo Bene (Creon), Julian Beck (Tiresias), Ninetto Davoli (Anghelos/Angelo), Pier Paolo Pasolini (high priest), Luciano Bartoli (Laïus), Ahmed Belhachmi (Polybus), Giandomenico Davoli (Polybus's shepherd), Francesco Leonetti (Laïus's slave), Ivan Scratuglia (priest)

"Che cosa sono le nuvole" (an episode of *Capriccio all'italiana*, 1968)
Italy, 35 mm, color, 22 mins.
Screenplay by Pier Paolo Pasolini
Produced by Dino De Laurentiis
Director of photography: Tonino Delli Colli
Editor: Nino Baragli
Sets and costumes: Jürgen Henze
Original music: Domenico Mondugno, Pier Paolo Pasolini
Cast: Totò (Iago), Ninetto Davoli (Othello), Laura Betti (Desdemona), Adriana Asti (Bianca), Franco Franchi (Cassius), Ciccio Ingrassia (Roderigo), Francesco Leonetti (puppeteer), Domenico Modugno (garbage man), Carlo Pisacane (Brabanzio)

Appunti per un film sull'India (*Notes for a Film on India*, 1968)
Italy, 16 mm, black and white, 34 mins.
Story and commentary written and narrated by Pier Paolo Pasolini
Produced by Gianni Barcelloni
Camera operators: Federico Zanni, Roberto Nappa
Editor: Jenner Menghi
Original music: Ennio Morricone

Teorema (*Theorem*, 1968)
Italy, 35 mm, color, 98 mins.
Screenplay by Pier Paolo Pasolini
Produced by Manolo Bolognini and Franco Rossellini
Director of photography: Giuseppe Ruzzolini
Editor: Nino Baragli
Sound: Dario Fronzetti
Art director: Luciano Puccini
Costume designers: Roberto Capucci, Marcella De Marchis
Original music: Ennio Morricone
Cast: Terence Stamp (the visitor), Silvana Mangano (Lucia, the mother), Massimo Girotti (Paolo, the father), Anne Wiazemsky (Odetta, the daughter), Andrés José Cruz Soublette (Pietro, the son), Laura Betti (Emilia, the first servant), Ninetto Davoli (Angelino, the postman), Adele Cambria (the second servant), Susanna Pasolini (old countrywoman), Carlo De Mejo (Lucia's first trick), Ivan Scratuglia (young man), Luigi Barbini (the boy at the station), Alfonso Gatto (doctor), Cesare Garboli (interviewer)

"La sequenza del fiore di carta" (an episode of *Amore e rabbia* [*Love and Anger*], 1969)
Italy/France, 35 mm, color, 12 mins.
Screenplay by Pier Paolo Pasolini
Produced by Carlo Lizzani
Director of photography: Giuseppe Ruzzolini
Editor: Nino Baragli
Original music: Giovanni Fusco
Cast: Ninetto Davoli (Riccetto), Rochelle Barbieri (girl), Voices of God: Graziella Chiarcossi, Aldo Puglisi, Bernardo Bertolucci, Pier Paolo Pasolini

Porcile (*Pigsty*/*Pigpen*, 1969)
Italy/France, 35 mm, color, 98 mins.
Screenplay by Pier Paolo Pasolini
Produced by Gian Vittorio Baldi
Directors of photography: Armando Nannuzzi (archaic story), Tonino Delli Colli, Giuseppe Ruzzolini (modern story)
Editor: Nino Baragli
Sound: Alberto Salvatori
Art direction and costumes: Danilo Donati
Original music: Benedetto Ghiglia
Cast: Pierre Clémenti (cannibal), Franco Citti (second cannibal), Jean-Pierre Léaud (Julian), Alberto Lionello (Klotz, the father), Ugo Tognazzi (Herdhitze), Anne Wiazemsky (Ida), Marco Ferreri (Hans Günther, dubbed by Mario Missiroli), Ninetto Davoli (young man/Maracchione), Margherita Lozano (Frau Bertha Klotz, dubbed by Laura Betti), Luigi Barbini (soldier), Sergio Elia (servant)

Medea (1969)
Italy/France/West Germany, 35 mm, color, 110 mins.
Screenplay by Pier Paolo Pasolini
Produced by Franco Rossellini and Marina Cicogna
Director of photography: Ennio Guarnieri
Editor: Nino Baragli
Sound: Carlo Tarchi
Art director: Dante Ferretti
Costume designer: Piero Tosi
Cast: Medea (Maria Callas, voice dubbed by uncredited performer), Giuseppe Gentile (Jason), Laurent Terzieff (Chiron, the centaur), Massimo Girotti (Creon), Margareth Clémenti (Glauce), Sergio Tramonti (Apsirto), Anna Maria Chio (wet nurse),

Paul Jabara (King Pelias), Luigi Masironi (Jason at age five), Michelangelo Masironi (Jason at age thirteen)

Appunti per un'Orestiade africana (*Notes for an African Orestes*, 1970/1973/1975)
Italy, 16 mm, black and white, 73 mins.
Screenplay by Pier Paolo Pasolini
Produced by Gian Vittorio Baldi
Photography: Giorgio Pelloni, Mario Bagnato, Emore Galeassi, Pier Paolo Pasolini
Editor: Cleofe Conversi
Sound: Federico Savina
Original music: Gato Barbieri
Musical performers: Gato Barbiere (sax), Donald F. Moye (drums), Marcello Melis (bass, as Marcello Melio), and sung by Yvonne Murray and Archie Savage

Il Decameron (*The Decameron*, 1971)
Italy, 35 mm, color, 111 mins.
Screenplay by Pier Paolo Pasolini
Produced by Franco Rossellini
Director of photography: Tonino Delli Colli
Editors: Nino Baragli, Tatiana Casini Morigi
Sound: Pietro Spadoni
Art director: Dante Ferretti
Costume designer: Danilo Donati
Cast: Franco Citti (Ciappelletto), Ninetto Davoli (Andreuccio of Perugia), Angela Luce (Peronella), Pier Paolo Pasolini (Giotto's pupil), Giuseppe Zigaina (a friar), Vincenzo Amato (Masetto of Lamporecchio), Guido Alberti (a rich merchant), Gianni Rizzo (father superior), Elisabetta Genovese (Caterina), Silvana Mangano (the Madonna), Vincenzo Ferrigno (Giannello), Vittorio Vittori (Don Giovanni), Mirella Catanesi (Donna Gemmatta), Monique Van Vooren (Queen of Skulls), Giovanni Davoli (Pietro)

I Racconti di Canterbury (*The Canterbury Tales*, 1972)
Italy/France, 35 mm, color, 110 mins.
Screenplay by Pier Paolo Pasolini
Produced by Alberto Grimaldi
Director of photography: Tonino Delli Colli
Editor: Nino Baragli
Sound: Primiano Muratori

Art director: Dante Ferretti

Costume designer: Danilo Donati

Original music: Ennio Morricone

Cast: Hugh Griffith (Sir January), Laura Betti (the Wife of Bath), Ninetto Davoli (Perkin the fool), Josephine Chaplin (May), Pier Paolo Pasolini (Chaucer), Franco Citti (the devil), Alan Webb (the old man), Steve Whitton (young man), Tom Baker (Jenkin), Jenny Runacre (Alison), Peter Cain (Absalom), Dan Thomas (Nicholas), Michael Balfour (John the carpenter), J. P. Van Dyne (the cook), Vernon Dobtcheff (the franklin), Adrian Street (the miller), Derek Deadman (the pardoner), Nicholas Smith (the friar), Peter McGregor (the merchant), George Bethell Datch (host of the tabard), Robert Brook Howard (the nun's priest), Selwyn Roberts (the knight), Charlotte Kell (the prioress), Pinky Martin (the nun), Ray Parks (sergeant at law), Terry Hooper (jester), Judo Al Hayes (wrestler), Michael Derrek (Robin), Alan McConnell (Master Gerveys), Martin Philips (Martin), Patrick Duffet (Alan), Eamonn Howell (John), Albert King (Simkin the miller), Eileen King (Simkin's wife), Heather Johnson (Molly), Richard Hughes (the manciple), Gordon King (the monk), Andrew Dymock (Bill), Laurie Itch (Mary), Norman Mcglen (Perkin's father), Dorothy Everall (Perkin's mother), Charles de la Tour (innkeeper), Stephen Calcutt (groom), Diana Fisher (bride), Charles de Wolf (father of the bride), Leonard S. Brooks (shopkeeper), Patrick Newell (priest), Chris Greener (Sir Elephant), Reg Stuart (fourth husband), Judy Stewart-Murry (Alice), Oscar Fochetti (Damian), Wiloughby Goddard (Placebo), Peter Stephens (Justinus), Giuseppe Arrigo (Pluto), Elizabetta Genovese (Prosperina), Tony Moore (the spy), Hugh Mckenzie-Bailey (Thomas), Anita Sanders (Thomas's wife), Robin Asquith (Ruffo), Martin Whelar (Jack the Justice), John McLaren (Johnny the Grace), Edward Monteith (Dick the Sparrow), David Hatton (poor sodomite), Athol Coats (rich sodomite), Settimio Castagna (the angel), Karl Howman (first effeminate man), Philip Davis (second effeminate man), John Francis Lane (friar)

Il fiore delle mille e una notte (*Arabian Nights*, 1974)

Italy/France, 35 mm, color, 129 mins.

Screenplay by Pier Paolo Pasolini with the collaboration by Dacia Maraini

Produced by Alberto Grimaldi

Director of photography: Giuseppe Ruzzolini

Editors: Nino Baragli, Tatiana Casini Morigi

Sound: Luciano Welisch

Art director: Dante Ferretti

Costume designer: Danilo Donati

Original music: Ennio Morricone

Cast: Franco Merli (Nur-ed-Din), Ninetto Davoli (Aziz), Franco Citti (the genie), Ines Pellegrini (Zumurrud), Teresa Bouché (Aziza), Salvatore Sapienza (Prince Yunan), Alberto Argentino (Prince Shahzaman), Margareth Clementi (Aziz's mother), Francesco Paolo Governale (Prince Tagi), Abadit Ghidei (Princess Dunya), Salvatore Verdetti (Barsum), Fessazion Gherentiel (Berhané), Gian Idris (Giana)

Le mura di Sana'a (*The Walls of Sana'a*, 1974)
Italy, 35 mm, color, 13 mins.
Commentary and narration by Pier Paolo Pasolini
Produced by Franco Rossellini
Director of photography: Tonino Delli Colli
Editor: Tatiana Casini Morigi

Salò o Le 120 giornate di Sodoma (*Salò or the 120 Days of Sodom*, 1975)
Italy/France, 35 mm, color, 115 mins.
Screenplay by Pier Paolo Pasolini with the collaboration of Sergio Citti
Produced by Alberto Grimaldi
Director of photography: Tonino Delli Colli
Editors: Nino Baragli, Tatiana Casini Morigi
Sound: Domenico Pasquadibisceglie, Giorgio Loviscek
Art director: Danto Feretti
Costume designer: Danilo Donato
Original music: Ennio Morricone
Cast: Paolo Bonacelli (the duke), Giorgio Cataldi (the bishop), Umberto Paolo Quintavalle (the magistrate Curval, dubbed by Giancarlo Vigorelli), Aldo Valletti (Durcet, the president, dubbed by Marco Bellocchio), Caterina Boratto (Signora Castelli), Elsa De Giorgi (Signora Maggi), Hélène Surgère (Signora Vaccari, dubbed by Laura Betti), Sonia Saviange (pianist), Ines Pellegrini (servant), Sergio Fascetti, Bruno Musso, Antonio Orlando, Claudio Cicchetti, Franco Merli, Umberto Chessari, Lamberto Book, Gaspare Di Jenno (male victims), Giuliana Melis, Faridah Malik, Graziella Aniceto, Renata Moar, Dorit Henke, Antiniska Nemour, Benedetta Gaetani, Olga Andreis (female victims), Tatiana Mogilansky, Susanna Radaelli, Giuliana Orlandi, Liana Acquaviva (daughters), Rinaldo Missaglia, Giuseppe Patruno, Guido Galletti, Efisio Etzi (soldiers), Claudio Troccoli, Fabrizio Menichini, Maurizio Valaguzza, Ezio Manni (collaborators), Paola Bieracci, Carla Terlizzi, Anna Maria Dossena, Anna Recchimuzzi (procuresses/servants)

NOTES

Introduction

1. Pasolini, "Confessioni tecniche," 44. Translation for the author by Francesco de Dilectis. Hereafter cited parenthetically in the text.

2. Sitney, *Cinema of Poetry*, 15.

3. Joseph Luzzi, *A Cinema of Poetry: Aesthetics of the Italian Art Film*, P. Adams Sitney, *The Cinema of Poetry*. (While Sitney's book has a 2015 copyright date, it was released well before the end of 2014.)

4. Pasolini, "Written Language of Reality," 197. Two of the most significant and valuable examples, in English, of studies that do apply Pasolini's theory to Pasolini's cinema remain Patrick Rumble's *Allegories of Contamination: Pier Paolo Pasolini's "Trilogy of Life,"* and Maurizio Viano's *A Certain Realism: Making Use of Pasolini's Film Theory and Practice*. One extended study in Italian of Pasolini's theories of the "Cinema of Poetry" is Luciano de Carolis's *Pasolini e il cinema: Il progetto di una teoria semiotica in "Empirismo eretico."* There is also a significant body of work in Italian that focuses on some of the same areas of concern within Pasolini's oeuvre that I do, including, most directly, Massimo Fusillo's *La Grecia secondo Pasolini: Mito e cinema* (on Pasolini's interest in the Greek myths involving Orestes, Medea, and Oedipus), Luca Caminati's *Orientalismo eretico: Pasolini e il cinema de Terzo Mondo* (on issues of Orientalism and Pasolini's eroticization of the third-world body), and Giovanna Trento's *Pasolini e l'Africa, l'Africa di Pasolini: Panmeridionalismo e rappresentazioni dell'Africa postcoloniale* (on the problematics of Pasolini's use of Africa in his work). This study's primary focus, however, remains dedicated to looking queerly at the texts I have chosen to review. One of the things I hope to suggest in these pages is that for Pasolini this is fundamentally connected to looking at things poetically, through the cinema.

5. Pasolini, *Pier Paolo Pasolini*, 73. Following his criminal conviction in 1949 (later absolved due to lack of evidence) for "lewd acts in public" with teenage boys, Pasolini was expelled from the Italian Communist Party. See Siciliano, *Pasolini*, 134–36. From that point forward, his relationship with the official party, from a position outside it, was both fiercely engaged and fraught with animosity. Furthermore, as he was "nearly blocked by Togliatti personally from appearing in the party's publication *Vie nuove* (New Pathways) because 'such a man is unfit for family readers'" (Schwartz, *Pasolini Requiem*, 77), one can understand Pasolini's negativity toward the party leader and the Italian Communist establishment. As a mature political thinker, Pasolini maintained a

deep skepticism toward orthodox Communism, while developing and elucidating his own form of heretical Marxist thought.

6. I. Aitken, *European Film Theory and Cinema*, 238.

7. In a fecund study that approaches this dynamic more through the concept of the sacred than the archaic, Stefania Benini posits that "to Pasolini, the sacred embodies the nemesis of modernity, the return of the uncanny archaic that shatters the apparent coherence of bourgeois existence" (*Pasolini*, 23). Her reading of the sacred/archaic in antagonistic relationship to modernity in Pasolini's work is persuasive and often brilliant. I, however, want to stress the ambivalent, if surely vexed, relationship between the archaic and the modern in Pasolini's late 1960s/early 1970s work.

8. Lavelle, *Archaic Greece*, 15.

9. All three films in the *Trilogy of Life* can be said to take near-archaic texts that participate in the establishment of mature cultures and translate them into works of modernism. Naomi Greene points out that "each of the three films [of the trilogy] was based on a book that had founded not only a literary tradition but an entire culture" (*Pier Paolo Pasolini*, 184).

10. Lavelle, *Archaic Greece*, 21, 24–25.

11. Lemke, "Primitivist Modernism," 409.

12. Patrick Ramble's excellent study of the *Trilogy of Life* posits that such a germinal/terminal dialectic informed Pasolini's interest in the source material for those three films. He reminds us that "there may be something within these proto-novels that is shared with the 'post-novel' of the culture of late capitalism" (*Allegories of Contamination*, 9).

13. Greenberg, "Modernist Painting," 200.

14. Bordwell, *Narration in the Fiction Film*, 209, 210.

15. In developing his concept of a reverse discourse, Foucault argues that "we must not imagine a world of discourse divided between accepted discourse and excluded discourse, or between the dominant discourse and the dominated one; but as a multiplicity of discursive elements that can come into play in various strategies." (*History of Sexuality, Volume 1*, 100). The term has more generally come to refer to the practice of arguing against a proposition while conceding some of the basic terms that ground it.

16. The first noted appearance of the term "queer theory" was in February 1990, as part of the title of a conference held at the University of California, Santa Cruz, organized by Teresa de Lauretis. See de Lauretis, "Queer Theory," iii. (De Lauretis later resisted incentives to define her own work as queer theory.) Queer Nation was founded in New York the following month. The concept of the New Queer Cinema dates to an essay, released in several iterations by B. Ruby Rich, that seems to have first been published in the program of the Sundance Film Festival in January 1992, in which Rich enthusiastically announced, "the new season of queer cinema is upon us" ("Gay Nineties," 60).

17. See de Lauretis, "Queer Theory," iii–xviii.

18. One is reminded of a concern voiced by J. L. Austin, in his work on performative speech acts, which is subsequently examined by Eve Kosofsky Sedgwick and Andrew Parker. Austin considered performative acts that are, in fact *performed*, for instance, wedding vows made onstage in the course of a play, to be "not indeed false but in general *unhappy*" and to be "an ill to which *all* acts are heir which have the general character of a ritual or ceremonial, all *conventional* acts. . . . Language in such circumstances is in special ways—intelligibly—used not seriously, but in ways *parasitic* upon its normal use—ways which fall under the doctrine of the *etiolations* of language" (*How to Do Things with Words*, 14, 18–19, 22, emphases in original). For Parker and Sedgwick, the ways in which Austin pathologizes theatrical, ritualistic, and ceremonial performative gestures represents a moralism that, in their words, links the "theatrical" with the "abnormal, the decadent, the effete, the diseased." As such, the theatrical, ritualistic, and ceremonial aspects of Pasolini's films can be seen to fall within the sphere of what Parker and Sedgwick call the "quarantine" of what we might finally label the queer performative (introduction to *Performativity and Performance*, 3–4).

19. While queer theory has been applied to Pasolini's cinema less often than one might expect in the past, its citation in a handful of fine papers delivered at the conference "Pier Paolo Pasolini: Image, Object, Sound" at New York University in the fall of 2015 suggests that this has started to change.

20. Pasolini, "'Cinema of Poetry,'" 172. Hereafter cited parenthetically in the text.

21. The reasons why Bertolucci's tendencies toward a cinema of poetry lead him toward palpably queer states of being while Antonioni's do not is a subject beyond the scope of this book. One might provisionally argue that Antonioni's emotional reserve would guard against such an evolution, while Bertolucci's comparatively open (and essentially confessional) expressions of desire would invite it. Pasolini, a close family friend of Bertolucci's, seems to be implying as much in the passage quoted earlier. For a discussion of the queerness in Bertolucci's early work, see W. Aitken, "Leaving the Dance."

22. Rumble, *Allegories of Contamination*, 130. The form of contamination Pasolini discusses in Bertolucci's work is a narrower form than that Rumble addresses in his own study of Pasolini, which is focused on broader forms of transcultural and transhistorical contamination. Rumble effectively argues that these broader contaminations are at the core of Pasolini's ideological project.

23. Bruno, "Body of Pasolini's Semiotics," 91.

24. Heath, "Film/Cinetext/Text," 109.

25. Eco, quoted in Viano, *Certain Realism*, 23.

26. Metz, *Film Language*, 212–13.

27. One of the best, sustained studies of Pasolinian reality remains Maurizio Viano's *A Certain Realism*.

28. Pasolini, "Written Language of Reality," 198 (emphasis in original).

29. De Lauretis, *Alice Doesn't*, 50, 49 (emphasis in original). The embedded quotations are de Lauretis's own translation of a passage from Pasolini's "Written Language of Reality."

30. As if in anticipatory support of Pasolini's controversial thesis, Lacan said many times that the unconscious "is structured like a language" (*Psychoses*, 166–67).

31. Pasolini, "Written Language of Reality," 221–22.

32. Derrida, "Deconstruction and Its Other," 115–16.

33. Derrida, *Of Grammatology*, 52, 9. Since Derrida mentions cinematography and music, one can only conclude that the soundtrack of a film, not just the music, is part of his conception of *écriture*.

34. I want to thank David Gerstner particularly for our discussions on *cinematic écriture* throughout the past couple of years, a concept I first encountered in his book *Queer Pollen* (11, 18) and then again in the monograph he coauthored with Julien Nahmias, *Christophe Honoré: A Critical Introduction* (14–15, 28–29), both of which greatly inform this project. As I have long been interested in the ways in which Derrida's understandings of writing and speech relate, queerly, to the cinema, the formulation that Gerstner and Nahmias develop have proven invaluable in my own thinking on Pasolini.

35. Edelman, *Homographesis*, xiv. A survey of Edelman's work suggests his sympathy with Derrida's fundamental critique of Foucault, particularly Foucault's *History of Madness* (1961) and thus more generally his entire New Historicist project. As Derrida argues, Foucault claims to interrogate historical discourse, particularly its origin, but does so through a narrativization of discourse that is itself historical. Therefore, for Derrida, Foucault's project ultimately reproduces the metaphysics of history it claims to interrogate. See Derrida, "Cogito and the History of Madness" (1964).

36. Edelman, *Homographesis*, xv–xvi (emphasis added).

37. Edelman, 9 (emphasis added).

38. Of course, a study of the male bodies in Pasolini's cinema cannot neglect the bodies of women, as we will see in my discussion of Maria Callas in *Medea*. A recent and excellent study of, specifically, the male body in Pasolini's late cinema is Sergio Rigoletto's "Pier Paolo Pasolini's Erotic Imagery and the Significance of the Male Body."

39. For a critical assessment of this tendency within the *Trilogy of Life*, see Viano, *Certain Realism*, 263–93. For a valuable short defense of Pasolini in this regard focused solely on *Il fiore delle mille e una notte*, see Boone, *Homoerotics of Orientalism*, 416–21.

40. See Muñoz, *Cruising Utopia*.

41. Ruti, *Ethics of Opting Out*, 170 (emphasis added).

42. Ruti, 169–70 (emphasis added).

43. Bersani, *Homos*, 7.

44. Bersani and Dutoit, "Merde Alors," 22, 24.

45. Bersani and Dutoit, 25.

46. Bersani, *Homos*, 7.

47. Edelman, *No Future*, 27.

48. Edelman, 35, 37 (emphasis added). In offering his own translation, Edelman provides more accuracy and greater nuance than the recently published English edition of Lacan's *Book XXIII*. There, "C'est une façon ancienne d'écrire ce qui a été, ultérieurement, écrit 'symptôme'" (*No Future*, 159n5) becomes "*Sinthome* is an old way of spelling what was subsequently spelt *symptôme*" (Lacan, *Sinthome*, 3, emphasis in original). The English reader of *The Sinthome* unhelpfully considers "spelling," while *No Future*'s reader, seeing *écrire* as "writing," more clearly sees the link to Derrida's theory of *écriture*.

49. Edelman, *No Future*, 35.

50. In what seems to be the first sustained analysis of a Pasolini film in English specifically in the wake of queer theory's negative turn, Filippo Trentin explores "*Porcile* as a text that allows us to glimpse potential forms of life and being that escape the endorsement of queerness in any affirmative or reparative way" ("Pasolini's Anti-relationality," 217). Trentin's short essay is exemplary in its application of queer antirelationality to illuminate Pasolini, Bersani, and Edelman's embracing of "suspension, interruption, silence and void" as a way to "think outside the limits of a political order in which the space for otherness and incoherence seems to have been drastically reduced" (223).

51. These three films have been referred to casually as a trilogy by a handful of scholars, including Kvistad, "Spectres of Euripidean Refusal," 134; Todini, "Pasolini and the Afro-Greeks," 219; and Fusillo, "Pasolini's *Agamemnon*," 229.

52. See Humphrey, *Queer Bergman*.

Chapter 1. Queer Oedipus

1. Rhodes, "Watchable Bodies," 456.

2. For the sake of clarity, I will always refer to Pasolini's film as *Edipo re* and Sophocles's play as *Oedipus Rex*, just as Pasolini's 1975 film will be called *Il fiore delle mille e una note* while its source material will be referred to as *Tales of 1001 Nights*.

3. See Gibbs, *Poetics of Mind*, 363.

4. Muecke, *Irony and the Ironic*, 15.

5. Holland, *Divine Irony*, 34.

6. Garmendia, *Irony*, 11.

7. Admittedly, in virtually every English-translated version of the written tale that I have consulted, the older prince enthusiastically declares the younger prince to be, as a recent version puts it specifically, "cast in the mould of splendour and perfection to the extent that his beauty deserved to be proverbial" (*Arabian Nights*, 94). However, considering the frequency with which male characters comment on other males' beauty in the *1001 Nights*, such a description should not necessarily be seen as always sexually

charged. On the other hand, Joseph Boone flatly declares that the "tale details the gay love-affair of a fifteen-year old boy" ("Framing the Phallus," 26). Boone's most persuasive evidence for this is a mid-twentieth-century translation (from an earlier French translation) by Matthew Powys. See Boone's "Rubbing Aladdin's Lamp," 172–73n16. The translation I default to in this study is the first English version of the twenty-first century to be derived from the Arabic "Macnaghten edition" (or Calcutta II), Malcolm C. Lyons's 2008 Penguin Classics edition (*Arabian Nights*).

8. *Arabian Nights*, 96.

9. Schwartz, *Pasolini Requiem*, 556.

10. The older prince is named Ajib in the original tale, not Yunan.

11. The argument that intercourse, both vaginal and anal, functions as a metaphor for corporeal violence is now a well-established axiom in both feminist and queer theory, while at the same time it is almost universally conceded that the inverse is also the case: a knife piercing any portion of the skin can function as a dark reflection of sexual penetration. See Dworkin, *Intercourse*; and Bersani, "Is the Rectum a Grave?"

12. Bukhārī, *Sahih Bukhari*, vol. 3, book 48, number 832. Aḥmad ibn Yūsuf Tīfāshī's *Nuzhat al-albāb fīmā lā uūjadu fī kitāb*, a well-known collection of Arab erotic texts, contains an oft-quoted lyric that also points to the importance of one's fifteenth year in the erotic imaginary:

    > When barely past his fifteenth year
    > Tendrils of hair begin
    > To form on his cheeks
    >
    > . . . .
    >
    > A boy at that age no longer fears
    > The things we dream of doing
    > With him, and he's lost his childish soul
    > That never thought of screwing!

    Quoted in al-Tīfāshī, *Delight of the Hearts*, 60. In "Tale of the Third Dervish," the time frame is slightly vague, with the prophecy stating that the boy will "live for fifteen years, after which he will be faced by a danger." The 2008 English translation implies that the boy is killed fifty days after his birthday, but it is not entirely clear (*Arabian Nights*, 95). Pasolini's film is more precise. The fateful encounter between Yunan and the boy occurs on his fifteenth birthday.

13. Bersani, "Is the Rectum a Grave?," 18–19.

14. Foucault, *History of Sexuality, Volume 2*, 215–17.

15. This logic—in which penetrating a male with a penis "kills" male subjectivity as citizen and patriarchal figure as surly as a knife's penetration would literally kill him—is the subject of Bersani's "Is the Rectum a Grave?"

16. While some versions of the myth stress that the slave was aware of a nearby shepherd who would probably rescue the baby, as Pasolini films the episode, the infant's rescue comes across as an unforeseen happenstance.

17. Pasolini, *"Oedipus Rex,"* 44.

18. The costumes and other indicators from the mise-en-scène suggest the late 1930s or early 1940s.

19. In a remarkable passage, Louis Althusser bemoans the casualties required to turn a "small biological being" into "a human child (having escaped all childhood deaths, many of which are human deaths, deaths punishing the failure of humanization)." According to Althusser, in the "war" deemed necessary for developing the unconscious mind, each of humanity's "sons, who, projected, deformed and rejected, are required, each by himself in solitude and against death, to take the long forced march which makes mammiferous larvae into human children, *masculine* or *feminine subjects*." Althusser, "Freud and Lacan," 57 (emphasis in original). Pasolini's project, like that of queer theory writ large, is to account for and transcend, if not undo this damage.

20. Lewes, *Psychoanalytic Theory of Male Homosexuality*, 36.

21. Freud, "Some Neurotic Mechanisms," 221–32.

22. Lewes, *Psychoanalytic Theory of Male Homosexuality*, 42.

23. Pasolini, *My Cinema*, 110.

24. Pasolini, "Why That of Oedipus Is a Story," 9; Pasolini, *Pasolini on Pasolini*, 120.

25. Devereux, "Why Oedipus Killed Laius." The author's first name is correctly spelled as Georges; however, it was Anglicized to George in the instance of this publication.

26. Devereux, 133.

27. Rank, *Incest Theme in Literature and Legend*, 221.

28. Pasolini, *"Oedipus Rex,"* 20 (emphasis in original).

29. As with many other sequences in Pasolini's oeuvre, he creates meaning here expertly utilizing the Kuleshov effect, which results when a series of shots generate meaning completely absent from the same shots in isolation (or sequenced in some other order). One of the ways Pasolini queers reality is by the queer meanings and resonances he creates through such editing. Faces, objects, and settings may seem to reflect little more than heteronormative reality, but as Pasolini shows, when looked at through a different structure of desire, the reality of them betrays different meanings.

30. For an interesting discussion of the etymological significance of Oedipus's name in relation to seeing, knowing, and castration, see Schur, "Jocasta's Eye and Freud's Uncanny," 112.

31. I am not sure whether the homosexual connotation associated with a male lifting another male's legs up in the air bears mentioning in this context.

32. Devereux, "Why Oedipus Killed Laius," 134. As Devereux explains, in at least one account (the now-lost *Oidipodeia*), after killing him, Oedipus deprives his father of

his sword—a form of castration—and takes his belt, symbolic of a man performing intercourse with a woman: "The undoing of a woman's belt was a preliminary to intercourse." Of course, the engorgement of a part of a male's body also strongly suggests an erection and therefore male desire.

33. Regardless of one's personal judgment, it is certainly true that this adolescent male, with his black, tightly curled hair and dark skin, represents Pasolini's idealized sexual type. He is essentially a slightly darker-skinned Ninetto Davoli, with somewhat more chiseled facial features.

34. Chow, *Sentimental Fabulations*, 183.

35. Bersani, *Thoughts and Things*, 50–51.

36. Bersani, 51.

37. Sinfield, *Out on Stage*, 284.

38. Bersani, "Is the Rectum a Grave?," 212.

39. Bersani, 217.

40. Pasolini, *"Oedipus Rex,"* 57.

41. Pasolini, 58.

42. Viano, *Certain Realism*, 176.

43. Lacan, *Four Fundamental Concepts*, 95–96. For a discussion on the queer ramifications of this process, see Humphrey, "In and Out."

44. Pasolini, *"Oedipus Rex,"* 92. In the play, one finds the wording to be,

> Nor need this mother-marrying frighten you;
> Many a man has dreamt as much. Such things
> Must be forgotten, if life is to be endured.

Sophocles, *Theban Plays*, 52.

45. Pasolini, *"Oedipus Rex,"* 94. In the play the wording is,

> What does it matter
> What . . . he means? It makes no difference now . . .
> Forget what he told you . . . It makes no difference.

Sophocles, *Theban Plays*, 55.

46. Belau, "Sublimation, Myth, and the Work of Dreams," 102–3.

47. Pasolini, "Why That of Oedipus Is a Story," 9–10.

48. Viano, *Certain Realism*, 178.

49. Viano, 179.

50. Raglan, *Jocasta's Crime*, 81.

51. Edelman, *Homographesis*, 107–8.

52. Pasolini, *"Oedipus Rex,"* 99 (ellipses in the original).

53. Pasolini, 104 (emphasis added).

Chapter 2. A Cinema of (Queer) Poetry

1. Pasolini, "'Cinema of Poetry,'" 167–86.

2. Tsai specifically refers to Pasolini as a member of a small group of "outstanding film-makers of the world," in an interview with Nick Pinkerton, saying he is "always astonished by how many new discoveries" he finds in their work "each time" he revisits them. Pinkerton, "Reverse Shot." Hernández, for his part, according to B. Ruby Rich, considers Pasolini "the third point on [his] holy trinity of influences," along with Derek Jarman and Michelangelo Antonioni. Indeed, references to *Accattone* and *Mamma Roma* are as thick in Hernández's *Mil nubes de paz cercan el cielo, amor, jamás acabarás de ser amor* (*A Thousand Clouds of Peace Encircle the Sky*, 2003) as are those from *Edipo re*, *Medea*, and *Il fiore delle mille e una notte* in *Raging Sun, Raging Sky*. Rich, "Walk in the Clouds," 99.

3. For a discussion of this episode, see my book *Queer Bergman*, 15–17.

4. Baldwin, *Another Country*, 3. One likes to imagine it was a Pasolini film, although this novel's late-1950s setting means that at best, it could only have been a film *written* by Pasolini, perhaps Fellini's *Le notti di Cabiria* (*The Nights of Cabiria*, 1957).

5. The work of David Bordwell exemplifies this position. See his *Narration in Fiction Film*.

6. Barthes, "Leaving the Movie Theater," 349 (emphasis on "twice over" in original; other emphases added).

7. Quoted in Smith, "Caress of the Camera," 85.

8. Chan, "*Goodbye, Dragon Inn*," 91.

9. Schoonover and Galt, *Queer Cinema in the World*, 276. Scholars have posited varying definitions and histories of slow cinema. One of the most thorough and helpful has been articulated by Ira Jaffe in *Slow Movies: Countering the Cinema of Action*, which asserts, "These movies are slow by virtue of their visual style, narrative structure and thematic content and the demeanour of their characters. With respect to visual style, the camera often remains unusually still in these films, and when it moves, as it does persistently in Béla Tarr's work, it generally moves quite slowly. Curtailed as well is physical motion *in front of* the camera. Furthermore, editing or cutting in slow movies tends to be infrequent, which inhibits spatiotemporal leaps and disruptions. Not only do long takes predominate, but long shots frequently prevail over close-ups. Consistent with these stylistic elements, which may distance and irritate the viewer, is the austere mise-en-scène: slow movies shun elaborate and dynamic decor, lighting and colour. Moreover, the main characters in these movies usually lack emotional, or at least expressive, range and mobility" (3; emphasis in original).

10. Schoonover and Galt, *Queer Cinema in the World*, 276–77.

11. One wonders if *Medea*, in fact, played at cruising-ground theaters when it first appeared. A thorough historical investigation into this intriguing question is beyond the scope

of this study, but briefly researching the film's release in the United States' two largest cities in 1971, the answer seems to be probably, though I have only indirect evidence. *Medea*'s first commercial theatrical run in Los Angeles, after a three-day engagement at a UCLA campus theater, was at the Los Feliz repertory theater. The venue "catered to Europeans and academics as well as buffs" (Thomas, "Repertory Approach Used," 20), and it actually had something of a Pasolini retrospective that year, showing five of the director's films. Located three blocks west of Silverlake in East Hollywood, right at the edge of Los Angeles City College, the Los Feliz would probably have been a cruising ground for gay men at the time. In New York, *Medea* opened at the Fifth Avenue Cinema in Greenwich Village, a somewhat middle-brow art theater that occasionally brought queer films such as *Lot in Sodom* (1933) and *Le sang d'un Poète* (*The Blood of a Poet*, 1932) to Manhattanites. It also hosted the first US commercial screenings of *Accattone* in 1968. Generally, the Fifth Avenue Playhouse was not known to have a particularly large queer clientele, although, as an art-film theater, almost by definition, it had to have attracted some queer cineastes, looking for cinema and more on a regular basis. The lower Manhattan theater best known for queer cruising at the time of *Medea*'s US release was Theatre 80 St. Marks. It, however, was almost exclusively showing revivals of classic Hollywood films in the early 1970s.

12. Bersani, "Sociability and Cruising," 45–62.

13. Russell, "Crowd Laughs during *Medea*," 29.

14. Kelly, "Film: Maria Callas a Hypnotic *Medea*," 23.

15. Daley, "At the Movies," 53. "Empty," "confusing," and "devoid of humanity" are all terms that make some sense as descriptors of the film, but "passionless" could hardly be a more inappropriate word to describe it. The critic's use of the adjective almost seems to be an attempt to redefine the word in strictly heteronormative terms.

16. Reed, "Another Stanley Steamer."

17. Miller, "*Medea*," 12.

18. For example, an article in the *Colorado Springs Gazette Telegraph* headlined "Colorado Premiere Set for Fine Arts Center" describes it thusly: "Filmed on location in Italy, Turkey and Syria at a budget of over one million dollars, the film is also magnificent in setting, costuming and décor" (27D).

19. Canby, "Film: Callas Stars in Pasolini's 'Medea,'" 29.

20. Zimmerman, "Life with Mother," 192.

21. Zimmerman, 192.

22. Zimmerman argues that this consideration was probably behind the distributor's decision to book the film on college campuses before opening it commercially in the large urban North American markets. The strategy also suggests that the canny distributor might have been eyeing a student counterculture audience, rather than the upscale, arthouse market. Of course, college campuses have also always been queer spaces where

cruising has been known to offer "marvelous moments" for a brotherhood of men, right under the noses of those in their seats, facing the front of the room for an "educational, respectable, boring" lecture (Zimmerman, 192).

23. Pasolini, *Pier Paolo Pasolini*, 109.

24. Pasolini, "Unpopular Cinema," 267–75.

25. Ravetto, "Heretical Marxism," 227.

26. Pasolini, *Pier Paolo Pasolini*, 109.

27. As Naomi Greene points out, Pasolini "suggested that the films of the [*Trilogy of Life*] had a national-popular cast," that, essentially, he had returned, in his penultimate project, to his more optimistic Gramscian roots (*Pier Paolo Pasolini*, 184).

28. Mari Ruti adumbrates queer negativity in terms of "self-destruction, failure, melancholia, loneliness, isolation, abjection, despair, regret, shame, and bitterness." "For many," it is a stance that "represents an antidote to the valorization of success, achievement, performance, and self-actualization that characterizes today's neoliberal society" (*Ethics of Opting Out*, 2).

29. Pasolini, *Pier Paolo Pasolini*, 109.

30. Pasolini, "'Cinema of Poetry,'" 177.

31. Rhodes, "Pasolini's Exquisite Flowers," 149 (emphasis in original).

32. Rhodes, 155.

33. Truisms abound about a species of "self-hating" upper-class homosexuals, on their knees, masochistically fellating lower-class gay men with whom they would otherwise never interact; discussions about Pasolini's own sexual practices place him in similar situations.

34. Near the end of *Beyond the Pleasure Principle*, Freud offers a chilling summation: "The pleasure principle seems actually to serve the death instincts" (77).

35. Pasolini, "Unpopular Cinema," 267–68.

36. Pasolini, 268.

37. Pasolini, 269 (emphasis in original).

38. Barthes, "Death of the Author," 148.

39. Pasolini, "Unpopular Cinema," 269.

40. Pasolini, 269. Pasolini sometimes creates emphases with italics and at other times by capitalizing words. I follow his choices whenever I quote him.

41. Miller, "*Medea*," 12 (emphasis in original).

42. Greene, *Pier Paolo Pasolini*, 161.

43. Rosenfeld, "*Medea*: Callas," B11.

44. Rhodes, "*Medea*," 4.

45. White, *Content of the Form*, 5.

46. White, 10, 11 (emphasis added).

47. De Lauretis, *Alice Doesn't*, 118–19.

48. Edelman, *No Future*, 41–50.

49. Viano, *Certain Realism*, 238.

50. Sisto, *Film Sound in Italy*, 158–59.

51. In *Rabioso sol, rabioso cielo*, in both the first sequence and again later, characters imagine they are hearing a nearly ceaseless stream of babbling by a chorus of unseen others. In both scenes, the discussions are presented as nearly meaningless and oppressive. The silent eloquence of the characters' contrasting movements and affective behavior stands in poetic contrast to it.

52. Barthes, "Leaving the Movie Theater," 349.

53. *Oxford English Dictionary Online*, s.v. "discretion," accessed October 4, 2017, www.oed.com.

54. See Barthes, *Pleasure of the Text*.

55. Pasolini ended his career with four films that exemplify marathon storytelling as the construction of other beautiful/monstrous universes. Like *Il Decameron*, *I racconti di Canterbury*, *Il fiore delle mille e una notte*, and *Salò o le 120 giornate di Sodoma*, *Medea*'s beginning suggests a near-endless universe of materialized discursivity—a world seemingly made real through storytelling, which is, of course, what, in the final analysis, the Greek myths have been for many people.

56. Pasolini's selection of the remarkably handsome Italian Olympic triple jumper Giuseppe Gentile to play the adult Jason heightens *Medea*'s strong male homoerotic sensibility.

57. I use the term "introduced" lightly. With the exception of Jason and Medea, the names of most of the characters are never spoken in the film—which, among other things, makes it difficult to identify the actors who portray them forty-five years later. I use the names given these characters in the original Greek versions of the myths, being mindful of the fact that many of these characters have multiple names with multiple spellings in the Latin alphabet. For instance, the name of Medea's brother has been spelled Absyrtus, Apsyrtus, and, in the Italian context, Apsirto.

58. Pasolini, "'Cinema of Poetry,'" 184.

59. A similar sequence occurs about eighteen minutes into *Il vangelo secondo Matteo*, when, in one shot, the camera shows the face of a man among a group of men confronting King Herod's soldiers as they are about to slaughter the infant boys of Bethlehem. Behind the man at this tense moment, one sees the slightly out-of-focus chest of another, whose garment is partially open to rather erotically display a nipple. Just as we seem to register the body part, the nipple is made even more noticeable as the cameraman (and the camera operator is surely a man) refocuses the image to bring it into sharper clarity. The cameraman, as if embarrassed by his own palpable lechery, immediately pans left while tilting up, which has the effect of capturing part of the bare-chested man's face while moving beyond it. But the cameraman quickly seems to

decide that his desire to fully register the face of the bare-chested man is stronger than his sense of shame, and he pans back to the right to indulge in a long, clear view of it. Pasolini's cinema contains many of these moments registering the awkward-erotic ambivalence of the queer male's gaze. Indeed, his oeuvre all but demands a video essay cataloguing and demonstrating these curious, essential moments.

60. See, for example, *Trance and Dance in Bali* (Gregory Bateson and Margaret Mead, 1952) and *Dead Birds* (Robert Gardner, 1963).

61. Such as Cy Endfield's *Zulu* (1964) and George Roy Hill's *Hawaii* (1966).

62. Bersani, "Is the Rectum a Grave?," 30.

63. Viano, *Certain Realism*, 245–46.

64. Ravetto, "Heretical Marxism," 237.

65. In *Teorema*, released a year before *Medea*, Pasolini offers a trenchant account of an entire family erotically transfixed by a magnetic outsider. Arguably, that outsider's spell on each member of the household represents a reaction formation against long-denied incestuous desires.

66. This thus harks back to *Edipo re* and the triangle between Laïus, Oedipus, and Chrysippus.

67. Viano, *Certain Realism*, 245.

68. Rhodes, "*Medea*," 2.

69. Shapiro, "Pasolini's *Medea*," 105.

70. Kvistad, "Cultural Imperialism and Infanticide," 227.

71. McDonald, *Euripides in Cinema*, 5.

72. Kvistad, "Cultural Imperialism and Infanticide," 228.

73. In McDonald's sympathetic reading of the film, one that does a good job of trying to paper over the cracks in the narrative, she posits, "Somehow some silent communication [seems to have taken] place [between the two] because Medea does everything to help [Jason]" from this moment on (*Euripides in Cinema*, 10). As if desperately trying to account for the odd shot of the full moon at night stuck in the middle of what otherwise seems a single early-morning scene, McDonald also argues, "it seems that [another] night has passed and it is dawn [again]" when Medea rushes back to the royal chambers to enlist Apsirto's help (10). Perhaps the simple fact of the matter is that Pasolini attempted to film these scenes "day for night" (filming in the daytime but then underexposing the footage to make it look like night, a process that never looks very realistic and has largely been abandoned), and in postproduction, the underexposing of the footage was, for some reason, not done.

74. Wilson, "Hero Trouble," 32.

75. Geoffrey Nowell-Smith writes that "one is tempted to assume . . . technical incompetence" on the part of Pasolini when watching his first film, *Accattone*, "but there are a number of considerations which militate against this simplistic thesis. The first is that,

although at the time Pasolini may indeed not quite have known what he was doing, the fact remains that he . . . went on [ignoring or defying long established cinematic syntax] in subsequent films, by which time [he] could and should have 'known better,' if [he] had wanted to. . . . [Finally] there are effects produced . . . , which, if viewed with an attitude not too conditioned by conventional expectations, prove to be *at least provisionally comprehensible according to the terms of a system in many ways radically opposed to the usual narrative norm* ("Pasolini's Originality," 10; emphasis added).

76. In his study of Parajanov, James Steffen discusses the Armenian director's "deliberately archaic, radical stylized cinematic language, which encompasses such disparate influence as the visual style of medieval Armenian and Persian miniatures, the editing and narrative style of early filmmakers such as Georges Méliès, Pier Paolo Pasolini's fascination with the material culture of the ancient past and his tendency to stage shots as portraits or tableaux, and the decidedly modernistic technique of jump cuts" (*Cinema of Sergei Parajanov*, 116). Elsewhere in that study, Parajanov is quoted as saying, "I may have received [my] love for authentic texture in films thanks to Pasolini or Fellini, but through that truth which has it that when you film an old subject, the film acquires an archaic character and demands another style" (4).

77. Oeler, "*Nran Guyne*," 140.

78. Two of the most celebrated and characteristic films of these two representative directors, Rocha's *O Dragão da Maldade contra o Santo Guerreiro* (*Antonio das Mortes*, Brazil) and Sembene's *Mandabi* (Senegal), were released the same year as *Medea*.

79. Shapiro, "Pasolini's *Medea*," 109.

80. Miller, "*Medea*," 14.

81. Ryan-Scheutz, *Sex, the Self, and the Sacred*, 69.

82. Osias, "Pasolini's *Medea*," 7.

83. Ryan-Scheutz, *Sex, the Self, and the Sacred*, 70.

84. Miller offers his own, interesting reading of the scene: "Medea's first enchanted survey of that naked body—a head-to-toe pan interrupted at the interesting part by a smiling reverse shot and resumed below the knees suggests [Jason] has a point [when he says, "If you did anything for me, you did it for love of my body"]: she has replaced the sacred tree with his adorable pole as the *axis mundi* of her new life. For us, of course, there is a further point to be made: once again, Medea puts a damper on homoerotic fantasy, not in the male characters, but in the male audience. She intrudes as the one who 'naturally' gets to see what the pan promises, and her interpolated image denies us" ("*Medea*," 16; author's emphasis). I would argue that far from heterosexualizing Pasolini's homoerotic gaze, the reverse shot of Medea's face looking at Jason's penis actually serves to interpolate the queer spectator into the subjectivity of the titular character.

85. Ryan-Scheutz, *Sex, the Self, and the Sacred*, 70.

86. See Godard, "Bergmanorama," 59–60; and Hubner, *Films of Ingmar Bergman*, 45.

87. The transition may well have been less abrupt during Italian screenings of the film. In Italy, even films of under two hours were, during this time period, bifurcated with an intermission at some point, usually just past the halfway mark. It is difficult to imagine that this would not have been where such an intermission would have been placed in *Medea*.

88. The transition of the centaur from mythical being to fully human is handled with such a degree of subtlety that I did not consciously notice it the first time I saw the film. In the scenes with Jason as a child, the centaur is seen as half man, half horse. In the scenes with him bidding Jason farewell as an adult, we see him as fully human. Between those two scenes, in the oddly filmed sequence at the edge of the lagoon when Jason is thirteen, Pasolini keeps the lower half of Chiron-the-centaur's body obscured. We only see the actor Laurent Terzieff's head, neck, and torso in that scene, which suggests the transitional period of Jason's puberty as the moment when the queer father-creature becomes a mere human being.

89. Rhodes, "*Medea*," 3.

90. Miller, "*Medea*," 16.

91. Todd Haynes's *Far from Heaven* (2002), in which Julianne Moore travels from her suburban home into the city only to find her husband in the arms of a man when she gets to his office, offers a perfectly analogous scene.

92. Edelman, *Homographesis*, 13.

93. Miller, "*Medea*," 12.

94. Miller, 14.

95. Miller, 16, 15.

96. See Rubin, "Traffic in Women."

97. Pasolini, "'Cinema of Poetry,'" 176.

98. Barthes, "Leaving the Movie Theater," 347 (emphasis in original).

99. Barthes, 349.

100. Bersani, "Sociability and Cruising," 61–62.

101. Morford and Lenardon, *Classical Mythology*, 488.

Chapter 3. Before the Beginning/After the End

1. Edelman, *Homographesis*, 3.

2. Siciliano, *Pasolini*, 331.

3. This sequence features Gato Barbieri, Donald F. Moye, and Marcello Melis, as well as Yvonne Murray and Archie Savage, performing what is purported to be a musical interlude for the never-to-be-produced feature. Karen T. Raizen's essay "Voicing the Popular in *Appunti per un'Orestiade africana*" offers an important analysis of the film that focuses in large part on this musical interlude.

4. A fourth play in the series, *Proteus*, existed but is now lost.

5. See Morford and Lenardon, *Classical Mythology*, 343–49.

6. Quoted in Rohdie, *Passion of Pier Paolo Pasolini*, 87.

7. Rohdie, 87.

8. I have found no evidence that Pasolini wrote a screenplay or even a full treatment for the supposedly proposed "African Orestes" or otherwise seriously developed this project beyond what exists in the form of *Appunti per un'Orestiade africana*. According to Barth David Schwartz's exhaustive biography of Pasolini, Romanò "commissioned a film about how Pasolini *would* go about setting the Oresteia trilogy of Aeschylus [in Africa]," which suggests the proposed feature was only a hypothetical one (*Pasolini Requiem*, 550; emphasis added). Indeed, in 1968, Pasolini wrote a treatment not for an African *Oresteia* but for exactly what now exists, *Appunti per un'Orestiade africana*, which can be found in Pasolini, *My Cinema*, 143–44. Despite the widespread assumption that Pasolini was seriously planning to mount a scripted and acted film adaptation of the story of Orestes in Africa, such a film is as much an illusion as the feature Marguerite Duras references in her 1977 film *Le camion* (*The Truck/The Lorry*, 1977).

9. Annovi, *Pier Paolo Pasolini*, 149.

10. It is also tempting (and surely useful) to position this film as the third in a different trilogy preceded by *Sopralluoghi in Palestina per il vangelo secondo Matteo* (1965) and *Appunti per un film sull'India* (1968), as John David Rhodes pointed out to me during a postpanel discussion at the Society for Cinema and Media Studies in Toronto, on March 17, 2018. Having studied those earlier "notes" films in the process of preparing this book, I find that discussing them, along with *Appunti per un'Orestiade africana*, would take me far beyond the modest scope of this project. It could productively form the basis for its own monograph. In a way, the question of unofficial trilogies reminds me of the debate around Ingmar Bergman's late-1960s films: *Persona* (1966), *Vargtimmen* (*Hour of the Wolf*, 1968), *Skammen* (*Shame*, 1968), and *En passion* (*The Passion of Anna*, 1969). Most people consider the final three a discrete "Island Trilogy." For my part, I have always found it more useful to consider the first three to be something of a "Trilogy of Sexual Orientation" (lesbian, gay male/queer, and heterosexual), with *The Passion of Anna* representing both a postscript to the three and the beginning of a new phase for the director characterized by his belated embrace of color cinematography. Both ways of looking at these films, however, are certainly valid.

11. Fusillo, "Pasolini's *Agamemnon*," 226.

12. Siciliano, *Pasolini*, 301; Schwartz, *Pasolini Requiem*, 451–56.

13. Fusillo, "Pasolini's *Agamemnon*," 227.

14. There are, in fact, two relatively recent translations of the troubling play *Affabulazione* with its own queerly incestuous debts to *Oedipus Rex*: "Infabulation," trans. Thomas Simpson (2008), and *Fabrication (Affabulazione)*, trans. Jamie McKendrik (2010).

15. Ward, *Poetics of Resistance*, 158.

16. Annovi, *Pier Paolo Pasolini*, 151 (emphasis in original).

17. Richards, "Export Mythology," 59.

18. It is important to remember that there is no evidence that Pasolini was actually intending to embark on an African-set theatrical film version of the myth of Orestes and that these notes should best be considered open to a reading that concludes such a project to be politically and ideologically unviable. Indeed, a better title for what Pasolini offers might be "notes on a daydream about an African *Orestes*"; it is certainly a film that ends wistfully, without concluding that the feature proposed by the creator of this film would be a desirable endeavor. It is probably not a coincidence that one of the most disapproving assessments of Pasolini's *Appunti*, Keith Richards's, is one that assumes the filmmaker was serious about mounting a major African *Orestes* for the big screen and that this "documentary" was, in fact, "a 'work in progress' for a proposed later project . . . to transpose the play in the newly independent states of Uganda and Tanzania . . . never brought to fruition" (56, 57). Richards is also critiquing a severely compromised version of Pasolini's film, produced for the English-language market, in which an Anglophone narrator replaces Pasolini's voice on the soundtrack. While Pasolini's voice in the Italian-language original often expresses a quizzical humility and modesty about a project the director seems to realize is more than a little questionable, the English speaker's voice sounds wholly confident, condescending, often even impatient with those whom he is interviewing. As Richards points out, the English-language version does not even dub or subtitle Pasolini's "African interlocutors whose Italian and French is left [untranslated] in the original" (59). While Richards acknowledges that these choices "can be attributed to the distributor" (59), his critique of the film, which ascribes critical adverbs such as "glibly" and "unapologetically" (58) to Pasolini's authorial performance, raises the suggestion that the English-language narrator's vocal tone has negatively impacted his reading of the film.

19. In the years since the production of Pasolini's "Trilogy of Myth," the tradition has continued with Charles Henri Ford's *Johnny Minotaur* (1971), a little-known film with parallels with *Appunti per un'Orestiade africana*, Julián Hernández's *Rabioso sol, rabioso cielo*, and Christophe Honoré's *Métamorphoses* (2014).

20. De Lauretis, *Alice Doesn't*, 49.

21. Quoted in Greene, *Pier Paolo Pasolini*, 214.

22. Karen T. Raizen briefly raises the possibility of Pasolini consciously engaging in auto-criticism with this film when she describes one of the most problematic scenes, one involving Pasolini interviewing African college students that I will discuss presently. She remarks, "Pasolini . . . most likely used the interview with the students as a form of auto-critique" ("Voicing the Popular," 90).

23. Montuori, "Complex Thought," 4.

24. As Annovi points out, "The African students, all of whom are young, male, middle

class, and polyglot, certainly do not represent or speak for the majority of African people" (*Pier Paolo Pasolini*, 152).

25. Raizen, "Voicing the Popular," 89.

26. Bhabha, *Location of Culture*, 340.

27. Pasolini, "Written Language of Reality," 222.

28. Sartre, preface to *Wretched of the Earth*, 12.

29. Butler, "Violence, Non-violence," 8, 9 (emphasis in original).

30. Boone, *Homoerotics of Orientalism*, xxiii. In this excellent study, Boone sympathetically discusses Pasolini's *Il fiore delle mille e una notte* (416–21) but does not address his other films.

31. Said, *Orientalism*, 181.

32. Said, 103.

33. The war, which dates from July 6, 1967, to January 15, 1970, was ongoing while Pasolini was in Africa shooting the footage for *Appunti per un'Orestiade africana* but was three months concluded by the film's work-in-progress premiere on April 16, 1970, at the MIDEM trade show in Cannes. However one looks at it, it certainly represents fresh bloodshed, contemporary to the time of the film.

34. See Kojève, *Introduction to the Reading of Hegel*.

35. Quoted in Stack, *Pasolini on Pasolini*, 83.

36. Freud, "Note upon the 'Mystic Writing-Pad.'" For an extended discussion of the ramifications of Freud's ideas, see Derrida, "Freud and the Scene of Writing."

37. Raizen, "Voicing the Popular," 90.

38. After watching this segment several times, I was able to determine which student was almost surely speaking. The top of his head briefly appears from behind that of another student. He looks directly at Pasolini, nodding affirmatively as the director responds to what had just been said. Still, we never see him as he speaks, never match the voice to lips moving on the screen.

39. Oddly, Pasolini tells us we are in "Tanganyika," which was the name of the country immediately following its independence from Great Britain in 1961. It became Tanzania after merging with Zanzibar in 1964. By referencing a regional identity that characterizes a colonialist era, rather than the postcolonial era, Pasolini seems to be suggesting that the historical past is still present and that the current political identity of the land is less than permanent.

40. Usher, "An African *Oresteia*," 128.

Conclusion

1. For instance, a syndicated American critic who covered the 1967 Venice Film Festival considered *Edipo re* one of the only commercially viable films in the competition: "A beautiful and unusual telling of that powerful story. It might even make money"

(Crosby, "Beauty, Money-Making Gone"). Upon its British debut in 1969, the *London Observer*'s critic, comparing it favorably to Saville's *Oedipus* (and unfavorably to Pasolini's simultaneously released *Teorema*), proclaimed *Edipo re* an "audacious near-triumph." Allsop, "A Hit and a Miss from Pasolini."

2. The British Film Institute's Blu-ray/DVD release of the film includes "a number of contextualising slats [that] were evidently created for use in an English language version of *Medea*" (*Medea*, Blu-ray/DVD booklet, 27). These include explanatory texts such as "The people of Colchis are about to make the annual sacrifice to the Sun God, forefather of Medea, so that he render the land fertile and the harvest good" and "Ten years later, in the rich city of Corinth, where Medea and Jason are guests of the King." While it is not clear that these were ever used, the fact that they were created suggests anxiety that Pasolini's film was difficult to follow in its original version.

3. In a final indignity, the filmmaker's name is misspelled on the cover of this DVD's container. Enjoy, if you can, "*Passolini's*" film. Or consider the mistake on the cover a parapraxis and simply give it a pass. The cover suggests we might want to move on to more interesting things, perhaps a film that actually is constituted as a final product, one that does not decide against the birth of its own fully realized self in the process of its materialization. And yet the mistake I make, almost every time I look at the container, is to further misread the already misspelled name. On first glance, I think I see "*Passion*lini," connecting this modest, little film to both the director's widely acclaimed adaptation of the "Gospel According to St. Matthew" and his own painful martyrdom in 1975. It expresses its maker's self-destructive passion; nevertheless, we are clearly encouraged to pass over it and move directly from *Medea* to the *Trilogy of Life*.

4. The film is Gianni Amelio's *Bertolucci secondo il cinema* (*Bertolucci According to the Cinema*, 1976).

5. Rosenbaum, "Orson Welles as Ideological Challenge," 190, 191, 177.

6. Fusillo, "Pasolini's *Agamemnon*," 227–28.

7. Caminati, "Notes for a Revolution," 129.

8. In Pasolini's outline, he describes the Africa project as one that "will deal expressly with the relationship between 'white' culture (i.e. Western, that is rationalistic, characterized by a bourgeoisie, and altogether industrialized) and the culture 'of color,' that is, archaic, folk, pre-industrial and pre-bourgeoisie culture (with the resulting conflict and all of its dramatic ambiguities and indissoluble problems)" ("Notes for a Poem on the Third World," 201).

9. *Teorema* was almost simultaneously prepared as film and novel; *Porcile* and *Orgia* are plays that quickly became a single film.

10. Halberstam, *Queer Art of Failure*.

11. Rowiński, "From *Accattone* to 'Profezia,'" 178.

12. Rowiński, 179.

13. After he wound up making three blockbusters in short order with the films of *The Trilogy of Life*, he famously abjured the entire enterprise and followed it up with *Salò*, the earlier films' complete negation. See Pasolini, "Repudiation of the Trilogy of Life," xvii–xxv.

14. Maggi, *Resurrection of the Body*, 5, 14.

15. See Zigaina, "Pasolini and Death"; and Kammerer with Zigaina, "In the Firing Line."

16. Barth David Schwartz mentions this theory briefly, implying that it is a distraction that has kept Zigaina from supporting investigations focused on more plausible theories about Pasolini's still unsatisfactorily explained death (*Pasolini Requiem*, 649).

17. Kammerer with Zigaina, "In the Firing Line," 160.

18. Bersani, "Is There a Gay Art?," 34.

19. Bersani, 34.

20. Miller, "*Medea*," 16.

21. Bersani, "Is There a Gay Art?," 34.

BIBLIOGRAPHY

Aitken, Ian. *European Film Theory and Cinema: A Critical Introduction.* Bloomington: Indiana University Press, 2001.

Aitken, Will. "Leaving the Dance: Bertolucci's Gay Images." *Jump Cut* 16 (1977): 23–26.

Allsop, Kenneth. "A Hit and a Miss from Pasolini." *Observer* (London), April 6, 1969, 24.

Althusser, Louis. "Freud and Lacan." Translated by Ben Brewster. *New Left Review* 55 (May 1969): 51–65.

al-Tīfāshī, Aḥmad. *The Delight of the Hearts, or What You Will Not Find in Any Book* (*Nuzhat al-albāb fimā lā uūjadu fī kitāb*). Edited by Winston Leyland. Translated by Edward A. Lacey. San Francisco: Gay Sunshine, 1988.

Annovi, Gian Maria. *Pier Paolo Pasolini: Performing Authorship.* New York: Columbia University Press, 2017.

Arabian Nights, The: Tales of 1001 Nights. Vol. 1. Translated by Malcolm C. Lyons. London: Penguin Classics, 2008.

Austin, J. L. *How to Do Things with Words.* Edited by J. O. Urmson and Marina Sbisà. New York: Oxford University Press, 1962.

Baldwin, James. *Another Country.* New York: Dial, 1962.

Barthes, Roland. "The Death of the Author." In *Image, Music, Text,* translated by Stephen Heath, 142–48. New York: Hill and Wang, 1977.

————. "Leaving the Movie Theater." In *The Rustle of Language,* translated by Richard Howard, 345–49. Berkeley: University of California Press, 1989.

————. *The Pleasure of the Text.* Translated by Richard Miller. New York: Hill and Wang, 1975.

Belau, Linda. "Sublimation, Myth, and the Work of Dreams: Radical Nostalgia and Melancholic Attachment in Pier Paolo Pasolini's *Edipo Re.*" In *Dreamscapes in Italian Cinema,* edited by Francesco Pascuzzi and Bryan Cracchiolo, 89–107. Lanham, MA: Rowman and Littlefield, 2015.

Benini, Stefania. *Pasolini: The Sacred Flesh.* Toronto: University of Toronto Press, 2015.

Bersani, Leo. *Homos.* Cambridge, MA: Harvard University Press, 1995.

————. "Is There a Gay Art?" In *"Is the Rectum a Grave?" and Other Essays,* 31–35.

————. "Is the Rectum a Grave?" In *"Is the Rectum a Grave?" and Other Essays,* 3–30.

————. *"Is the Rectum a Grave?" and Other Essays.* Chicago: University of Chicago Press, 2010.

Bersani, Leo. "Sociability and Cruising." In *"Is the Rectum a Grave?" and Other Essays*, 45–62.

———. *Thoughts and Things*. Chicago: University of Chicago Press, 2015.

Bersani, Leo, and Ulysse Dutoit. "Merde Alors." *October* 13 (Summer 1980): 22–35.

Bhabha, Homi K. *The Location of Culture*. New York: Routledge Classics, 2004.

Boone, Joseph Allen. "Framing the Phallus in the *Arabian Nights*: Pansexuality, Pederasty, Pasolini." In *Translations/Transformations: Gender and Culture in Film and Literature East and West*, edited by Cornelia Moore and Valerie Wayne, 23–33. Honolulu: University of Hawaii Press, 1993.

———. *The Homoerotics of Orientalism*. New York: Columbia University Press, 2014.

———. "Rubbing Aladdin's Lamp." In *Negotiating Lesbian and Gay Subjects*, edited by Monica Dorenkamp and Richard Henke, 149–77. New York: Routledge, 1995.

Bordwell, David. *Narration in the Fiction Film*. Madison: University of Wisconsin Press, 1985.

Bruno, Giuliana. "The Body of Pasolini's Semiotics: A Sequel Twenty Years Later." In *Pier Paolo Pasolini: Contemporary Perspectives*, edited by Patrick Rumble and Bart Tesa, 88–105. Toronto: University of Toronto Press, 1994.

Bukhārī, Muhammad I. *Sahih Bukhari*. Karachi: Muhammad Sarid, 1966.

Butler, Judith. "Violence, Non-violence: Sartre on Fanon." *Graduate Faculty Philosophy Journal* 27, no. 1 (2006): 3–24.

Caminati, Luca. "Notes for a Revolution: Pasolini's Postcolonial Essay Films." In *The Essay Film: Dialogue, Politics, Utopia*, edited by Elizabeth A. Papazian, Caroline Eades, 127–44. New York: Wallflower, 2016.

———. *Orientalismo eretico: Pasolini e il cinema de Terzo Mondo*. Milan: B. Mondadori, 2007.

Canby, Vincent. "Film: Callas Stars in Pasolini's *Medea*." *New York Times*, October 29, 1971, 29.

Chan, Kenneth. "*Goodbye, Dragon Inn*: Tsai Ming-liang's Political Aesthetics of Nostalgia, Place, and Lingering." *Journal of Chinese Cinemas* 1, no. 2 (2007): 89–103.

Chow, Rey. *Sentimental Fabulations, Contemporary Chinese Films: Attachment in the Age of Global Visibility*. New York: Columbia University Press, 2007.

"Colorado Premiere Set for Fine Arts Center." *Colorado Springs Gazette Telegraph*, January 15, 1972, 27D.

Crosby, John. "Beauty, Money-Making Gone—Hooray." *Orlando Sentinel*, September 17, 1967, 8.

Daley, Frank. "At the Movies." *Ottawa Journal*, April 19, 1972, 53.

de Carolis, Luciano. *Pasolini e il cinema: Il progetto di una teoria semiotica in "Empirismo eretico."* Florence: Firenze Atheneum, 2008.

de Lauretis, Teresa. *Alice Doesn't: Feminism, Semiotics, Cinema*. Bloomington: Indiana University Press, 1984.

———. "Queer Theory: Lesbian and Gay Sexualities." *Differences: A Journal of Feminist Cultural Studies* 3, no. 2 (1991): iii–xviii.

Derrida, Jacques. "Cogito and the History of Madness." 1964. In *Writing and Difference*, 31–63.

———. "Deconstruction and Its Other." In *Dialogues with Contemporary Continental Thinkers: The Phenomenological Heritage*, edited by Richard Kearney, 115–16. Manchester: Manchester University Press, 1984.

———. "Freud and the Scene of Writing." 1966. In *Writing and Difference*, 196–231.

———. *Of Grammatology*. Translated by Gayatri Chakravorty Spivak. Baltimore: Johns Hopkins University Press, 1976.

———. *Writing and Difference*. Translated by Alan Bass. Chicago: University of Chicago Press, 1978.

Devereux, George[s]. "Why Oedipus Killed Laius: A Note on the Complementary Oedipus Complex in Greek Drama," *International Journal of Psycho-Analysis* 34 (1953): 132–41.

Dworkin, Andrea. *Intercourse*. 20th anniversary ed. New York: Basic Books, 2006.

Edelman, Lee. *Homographesis: Essays in Gay Literary and Cultural Theory*. New York: Routledge, 1994.

———. *No Future: Queer Theory and the Death Drive*. Durham, NC: Duke University Press, 2004.

Foucault, Michel. *History of Madness*. Edited by Jean Khalfa. Translated by Jonathan Murphy and Jean Khalfa. New York: Routledge, 2006.

———. *The History of Sexuality, Volume 1: An Introduction*. Translated by Robert Hurley. New York: Vintage, 1988.

———. *The History of Sexuality, Volume 2: The Use of Pleasure*. Translated by Robert Hurley. New York: Vintage, 1990.

Freud, Sigmund. *Beyond the Pleasure Principle*. 1920. Translated and edited by James Strachey. New York: Norton, 1961.

———. *Leonardo da Vinci and a Memory of His Childhood*. 1910. In *The Standard Edition*, vol. 11, 63–106.

———. "A Note upon the 'Mystic Writing-Pad.'" 1925. In *The Standard Edition*, vol. 19, 227–32.

———. "Some Neurotic Mechanisms in Jealousy, Paranoia and Homosexuality." 1922. In *The Standard Edition*, vol. 18, 223–32.

———. "A Special Type of Object Choice Made by Men." 1910. In *The Standard Edition*, vol. 11, 163–75.

———. *The Standard Edition of the Complete Psychological Works of Sigmund Freud*. Translated and edited by James Strachey. London: Hogarth, 1953–1974.

———. *Three Essays on the Theory of Sexuality*. 1905–1924. In *The Standard Edition*, vol. 7, 130–243.

Fusillo, Massimo. *La Grecia secondo Pasolini: Mito e cinema*. Florence: La Nuova Italia, 1996.

———. "Pasolini's *Agamemnon*: Translation, Screen Version and Performance." In *"Agamemnon" in Performance, 458 BC to AD 2004*, edited by Fiona Macintosh, Pantelis Michelakis, Edith Hall, and Oliver Taplin, 223–33. Oxford: Oxford University Press, 2005.

Garmendia, Joana. *Irony*. Cambridge: Cambridge University Press, 2018.

Gerstner, David A. *Queer Pollen: White Seduction, Black Male Homosexuality, and the Cinematic*. Urbana: University of Illinois Press, 2011.

Gerstner, David A., and Julien Nahmias. *Christophe Honoré: A Critical Introduction*. Detroit: Wayne State University Press, 2015.

Gibbs, Raymond W. *The Poetics of Mind: Figurative Thought, Language and Understanding*. Cambridge: Cambridge University Press, 1994.

Godard, Jean-Luc. "Bergmanorama." *Cahiers du Cinema in English* 1 (January 1966): 52–62.

Greenberg, Clement. "Modernist Painting." *Art and Literature: An International Review* 4 (Spring 1965): 193–201.

Greene, Naomi. *Pier Paolo Pasolini: Cinema as Heresy*. Princeton, NJ: Princeton University Press, 1990.

Halberstam, Judith (Jack). *The Queer Art of Failure*. Durham, NC: Duke University Press, 2011.

Heath, Stephen. "Film/Cinetext/Text." *Screen* 14, nos. 1–2 (1973): 102–27.

Holland, Glen S. *Divine Irony*. Selinsgrove, PA: Susquehanna University Press, 2000.

Hubner, Laura. *The Films of Ingmar Bergman: Illusions of Light and Darkness*. New York: Palgrave, 2007.

Humphrey, Daniel. "In and Out, or 'The Ambiguity of the Jewel.'" *Criticism* 58, no. 1 (2016): 1–33.

———. *Queer Bergman: Sexuality, Gender, and the European Art Cinema*. Austin: University of Texas Press, 2013.

Jaffe, Ira. *Slow Movies: Countering the Cinema of Action*. New York: Wallflower, 2014.

Kammerer, Peter, with Giuseppe Zigaina. "In the Firing Line." In *Pier Paolo Pasolini and Death*, edited by Bernhart Schwenk and Michael Semff, 157–71. Berlin: Hatje Cantz Verlag, 2005.

Kelly, Kevin. "Film: Maria Callas a Hypnotic *Medea*." *Boston Globe*, March 20, 1972, 23.

Kojève, Alexandre. *Introduction to the Reading of Hegel*. Edited by Allan Bloom. Translated by James H. Nichols Jr. New York: Basic Books, 1969.

Kvistad, Ivar. "Cultural Imperialism and Infanticide in Pasolini's *Medea*." In *Unbinding Medea: Interdisciplinary Approaches to a Classical Myth from Antiquity to the 21st Century*, edited by Heike Bartel and Anne Simon, 224–37. London: Legenda, 2010.

————. "Spectres of Euripidean Refusal: Pier Paolo Pasolini's *Medea.*" In *The Politics and Aesthetics of Refusal*, edited by Caroline Hamilton, Michelle, Kelly, Elaine Minor, and Will Noonan, 130–45. Newcastle, UK: Cambridge Scholars, 2007.

Lacan, Jacques. *The Four Fundamental Concepts of Psychoanalysis: The Seminar of Jacques Lacan—Book XI.* 1964. Edited by Jacques-Alan Miller. Translated by Alan Sheridan. New York: Norton, 1998.

————. *The Psychoses: The Seminar of Jacques Lacan—Book III.* 1955–56. Edited by Jacques Alain Miller. Translated by Russell Grigg. New York: Norton, 1993.

————. *The Sinthome: The Seminar of Jacques Lacan—Book XXIII.* 1975–76. Edited by Jacques-Alain Miller. Translated by A. R. Price. Malden, MA: Polity, 2016.

Lavelle, Brian M. *Archaic Greece: The Age of New Reckonings.* Hoboken, NJ: Wiley, 2020.

Lemke, Sieglinde. "Primitivist Modernism." In *Primitivism and Twentieth-Century Art: A Documentary History*, edited by Jack Flam with Miriam Deutch, 409–14. Berkeley: University of California Press, 2003.

Lewes, Kenneth. *The Psychoanalytic Theory of Male Homosexuality.* New York: New American Library, 1988.

Luzzi, Joseph. *A Cinema of Poetry: Aesthetics of the Italian Art Film.* Baltimore: Johns Hopkins University Press, 2014.

Maggi, Armando. *The Resurrection of the Body: Pier Paolo Pasolini from Saint Paul to Sade.* Chicago: University of Chicago Press, 2009.

McDonald, Marianne. *Euripides in Cinema: The Heart Made Visible.* Philadelphia: Centrum Philadelphia, 1983.

Medea. Directed by Pier Paolo Pasolini. London: British Film Institute, 2011. Blu-ray/DVD.

Metz, Christian. *Film Language: A Semiotics of the Cinema.* Translated by Michael Taylor. Chicago: University of Chicago Press, 1974.

Miller, D. A. "*Medea.*" *Film Quarterly* 16, no. 4 (2012): 12–16.

Montuori, Alfonso. "Complex Thought: An Overview of Edgar Morin's Intellectual Journey." Meta Integral Foundation Resource Paper, June 2013, 1–23.

Morford, Mark P. O., and Robert J. Lenardon. *Classical Mythology.* 5th ed. White Plains, NY: Longman, 1995.

Morin, Edgar. *Autocritique.* 1959. Reprint, Paris: Seuil, 2012.

Muecke, D. C. *Irony and the Ironic.* New York: Taylor and Francis, 2017.

Muñoz, José Esteban. *Cruising Utopia: The Then and There of Queer Futurity.* New York: NYU Press, 2009.

Nowell-Smith, Geoffrey. "Pasolini's Originality." In *Pier Paolo Pasolini*, edited by Paul Willemen, 4–20. London: BFI, 1977.

Oeler, Karla. "*Nran Guyne: The Colour of Pomegranates.*" In *The Cinema of Russia and the Former Soviet Union*, edited by Birgit Beumers, 138–48. London: Wallflower, 2007.

Osias, John. "Pasolini's *Medea*: Nature Uberalles." *Daily Californian* (UC Berkeley), August 19, 1971, 7.

Pasolini, Pier Paolo. "The 'Cinema of Poetry.'" In *Heretical Empiricism*, 167–86.

———. "Confessioni tecniche." In *Uccellacci e uccellini: Un film*, 44–56. Milano: Garzanti, 1975.

Pasolini, Pier Paolo. *Fabrication (Affabulazione)*. Translated by Jamie McKendrick. London: Oberon Books, 2010.

———. *Heretical Empiricism*. 2nd English ed. Translated by Ben Lawton and Louise K. Barnett. Washington, DC: New Academia, 2005. Originally published as *Empirismo eretico* (Milano: Garzanti, 1972).

———. "Infabulation." In *Manifesto for a New Theatre*, 31–131. Translated by Thomas Simpson. Toronto: Guernica, 2008.

———. *My Cinema*. Bologna: Edizioni Cineteca di Bologna and Luce Cinecittà, 2012.

———. "Notes for a Poem on the Third World." In *My Cinema*, 201–4.

———. *"Oedipus Rex": A Film*. Classic Film Scripts. Rev. ed. Translated by John Mathews. London: Lorrimer, 1984.

———. *Pasolini on Pasolini*. Cinema One 11 Edited by Oswald Stack. Bloomington: Indiana University Press, 1969.

———. *Pier Paolo Pasolini: A Future Life*. Rome: Associazione Fondo Pier Paolo Pasolini, 1989.

———. "Repudiation of the Trilogy of Life." In *Heretical Empiricism*, xvii–xxv.

———. "The Unpopular Cinema." In *Heretical Empiricism*, 267–75.

———. "Why That of Oedipus Is a Story." In *"Oedipus Rex": A Film*, 5–13.

———. "The Written Language of Reality.'" In *Heretical Empiricism*, 197–222.

Peretti, Luca, and Karen T. Raizen, eds. *Pier Paolo Pasolini, Framed and Unframed: A Thinker for the Twenty-First Century*. New York: Bloomsbury Academic, 2019.

Pinkerton, Nick. "Reverse Shot: Tsai Ming-liang." Museum of the Moving Image, April 17, 2015. http://reverseshot.org/interviews/entry/2043/tsaimingliang_interview_2015.

Raglan, Lord [Fitzroy Somerset]. *Jocasta's Crime: An Anthropological Study*. London: Methuen, 1933.

Raizen, Karen T. "Voicing the Popular in *Appunti per un'Orestiade africana*." In *Pier Paolo Pasolini, Framed and Unframed: A Thinker for the Twenty-First Century*, edited by Luca Peretti and Karen T. Raizen, 79–97. New York: Bloomsbury Academic, 2019.

Ramble, Patrick. *Allegories of Contamination: Pier Paolo Pasolini's "Trilogy of Life."* Toronto: University of Toronto Press, 1996.

Rank, Otto. *The Incest Theme in Literature and Legend: Fundamentals of a Psychology of Literary Creation*. Translated by Gregory C. Richter. Baltimore: Johns Hopkins University Press, 1992.

Ravetto, Kriss. "Heretical Marxism: Pasolini's Cinema Inpopolare." In *Strategies for Theory: From Marx to Madonna*, edited by R. L. Rutsky and Bradley J. Macdonald, 225–48. Albany: SUNY Press, 2003.

Reed, Rex. "Another Stanley Steamer Comes Puffing into Town." *New York Daily News*, October 29, 1971, 60.

Rhodes, John David. "*Medea*." Illustrated booklet on *Medea* Blu-ray/DVD. Directed by Pier Paolo Pasolini. London: British Film Institute, 2011.

———. "Pasolini's Exquisite Flowers: The 'Cinema of Poetry' as a Theory of Art Cinema." In *Global Art Cinema: New Theories and Histories*, edited by Rosalind Galt and Karl Schoonover, 142–63. Oxford: Oxford University Press, 2010.

———. "Watchable Bodies: *Salò*'s Young Non-actors." *Screen* 53, no. 4 (2012): 453–58.

Rich, B. Ruby. "The Gay Nineties." In *Sundance Film Festival '92 Program*, edited by Barbara Bannon, 56–66. Salt Lake City: Sundance Institute, 1992.

———. "A Walk in the Clouds: Julián Hernández." In *New Queer Cinema: The Director's Cut*, 96–99. Durham, NC: Duke University Press, 2013.

Richards, Keith. "Export Mythology: Primitivism and Paternalism in Pasolini, Hopper, Herzog." In *Remapping World Cinema: Identity, Culture and Politics in Film*, edited by Stephanie Dennison and Song Hwee Lim, 55–64. New York: Wallflower, 2006.

Rigoletto, Sergio. "Pier Paolo Pasolini's Erotic Imagery and the Significance of the Male Body." In *Masculinity and Italian Cinema: Sexual Politics, Social Conflict and Male Crisis in the 1970s*, 101–25. Edinburgh: Edinburgh University Press, 2014.

Rohdie, Sam. *The Passion of Pier Paolo Pasolini*. London: British Film Institute, 1995.

Rosenbaum, Jonathan. "Orson Welles as Ideological Challenge." In *Movie Wars: How Hollywood and the Media Limit What Films We Can See*, 175–96. Chicago: A Capella, 2000.

Rosenfeld, Megan. "*Medea*: Callas." *Washington Post–Times Herald*, February 11, 1972, B11.

Rowiński, Krzysztof. "From *Accattone* to 'Profezia': Pier Paolo Pasolini and Productive Failure." In *Pier Paolo Pasolini, Framed and Unframed: A Thinker for the Twenty-First Century*, edited by Luca Peretti and Karen T. Raizen, 177–93. New York: Bloomsbury Academic, 2019.

Rubin, Gayle S. "The Traffic in Women: Notes on the 'Political Economy' of Sex." In *Deviations: A Gayle Rubin Reader*, 66–86. Durham, NC: Duke University Press, 2011.

Rumble, Patrick. *Allegories of Contamination: Pier Paolo Pasolini's "Trilogy of Life."* Toronto: University of Toronto Press, 1996.

Russell, John. "Crowd Laughs During *Medea*." *San Bernardino (CA) Sun-Telegram*, January 12, 1972, 29.

Ruti, Mari. *The Ethics of Opting Out: Queer Theory's Defiant Subjects*. New York: Columbia University Press, 2017.

Ryan-Scheutz, Colleen. *Sex, the Self, and the Sacred: Women in the Cinema of Pier Paolo Pasolini.* Toronto: University of Toronto Press, 2007.

Said, Edward W. *Orientalism.* New York: Vintage, 1979.

Sartre, Jean-Paul. Preface to *The Wretched of the Earth,* by Frantz Fanon, 7–31. New York: Grove, 1963.

Schoonover, Karl, and Rosalind Galt. *Queer Cinema in the World.* Durham, NC: Duke University Press, 2016.

Schur, David. "Jocasta's Eye and Freud's Uncanny." In *Bound by the City: Greek Tragedy, Sexual Difference, and the Formation of the Polis,* edited by Denise Eileen McCoskey and Emily Zakin, 103–18. Albany: SUNY Press, 2009.

Schwartz, Barth David. *Pasolini Requiem.* 2nd ed. Chicago: Chicago University Press, 2017.

Schwenk, Bernhart, and Michael Semff, eds. *Pier Paolo Pasolini and Death.* Berlin: Hatje Cantz Verlag, 2005.

Sedgwick, Eve Kosofsky. *Between Men: English Literature and Male Homosocial Desire.* 30th anniversary ed. New York: Columbia University Press, 2016.

Sedgwick, Eve Kosofsky, and Andrew Parker. Introduction to *Performativity and Performance,* edited by Eve Kosofsky Sedgwick and Andrew Parker, 1–18. New York: Routledge, 1995.

Shapiro, Susan O. "Pasolini's *Medea*: A Twentieth-Century Tragedy." In *Ancient Greek Women in Film,* edited by Konstantinos P. Nikoloutsos, 95–116. Oxford: Oxford University Press, 2014.

Siciliano, Enzo. *Pasolini: A Biography.* Translated by John Shepley. New York: Random House, 1982.

Sinfield, Alan. *Out on Stage: Lesbian and Gay Theatre in the Twentieth Century.* New Haven, CT: Yale University Press, 1999.

Sisto, Antonella C. *Film Sound in Italy: Listening to the Screen.* New York: Palgrave Macmillan, 2014.

Sitney, P. Adams. *The Cinema of Poetry.* Oxford: Oxford University Press, 2015.

Smith, Paul Julian. "The Caress of the Camera in the Cinema of Julián Hernández." *Film Quarterly* 68, no. 3 (2015): 81–86.

Sophocles. *The Theban Plays.* Translated by E. F. Watling. New York: Penguin Classics, 1947.

Stack, Oswald [Jon Halliday]. *Pasolini on Pasolini.* Bloomington: Indiana University Press, 1969.

Steffen, James. *The Cinema of Sergei Parajanov.* Madison: University of Wisconsin Press, 2013.

Thomas, Kevin. "Repertory Approach Used in Presenting Unusual Films." *Los Angeles Times,* July 30, 1972, Calendar, 20.

Todini, Umberto. "Pasolini and the Afro-Greeks." *Stanford Italian Review* 5, no. 2 (1985): 219–22.

Trentin, Filippo. "Pasolini's Anti-relationality: *Porcile* and the Negative Turn in Queer Theory." *LaRivista* 4 (2015): 216–23.

Trento, Giovanna. *Pasolini e l'Africa, l'Africa di Pasolini: Panmeridionalismo e rappresentazioni dell'Africa postcoloniale*. Milan: Mimesis, 2010.

Usher, M. D. "An African *Oresteia*: Field Notes on Pasolini's *Appunti per un'Orestiade africana*." *Arion* 21, no. 3 (2014): 111–49.

Viano, Maurizio. *A Certain Realism: Making Use of Pasolini's Film Theory and Practice*. Berkeley: University of California Press, 1993.

Ward, David. *A Poetics of Resistance: Narrative and the Writings of Pier Paolo Pasolini*. Madison, NJ: Fairleigh Dickinson University Press, 1995.

White, Hayden. *The Content of the Form: Narrative Discourse and Historical Representation*. Baltimore: Johns Hopkins University Press, 1987.

Wilson, Kristi M. "Hero Trouble: Blood, Politics, and Kinship in Pasolini's *Medea*." In *Of Muscles and Men: Essays on the Sword and Sandal Film*, edited by Michael G. Cornelius, 28–39. Jefferson, NC: McFarland, 2011.

Zigaina, Giuseppe. "Pasolini and Death: A Purely Intellectual Thriller." In *Pier Paolo Pasolini and Death*, ed. Bernhart Schwenk and Michael Semff, 25–37. Berlin: Hatje Cantz Verlag, 2005.

Zimmerman, Paul D. "Life with Mother." *Newsweek*, September 13, 1971, 192.

INDEX

Unless otherwise noted, all titles refer to motion pictures.

Absyrtus (character). *See* Apsirto

Abuladze, Tengiz, 77

Accattone (1961), 1, 54, 118, 123, 141, 142, 145, 151

Aeetes (character), 65, 68–69, 71, 76, 78

Aegisthus (character), 98

Aeolus (character), 62

Aeschylus, 4–5, 97, 98, 100, 101, 109, 120

Affabulazione (play), 100, 148

Africa: 5, 97–98, 100–111, 112–15, 120, 133; art, 5; nation states, 104; tribal culture, 103–4

Agamemnon (character), 98, 110

Aitken, Ian, 3–4, 134

Aitken, Will, 135

Ajib (character), 138. *See also* Yunan

alienation, 9, 18, 51, 79

allegory, 21, 28, 68, 73, 85, 87, 100, 110

Allsop, Kenneth, 151

Althusser, Louis, 139

al-Tīfāshī, Ahmad ibn, 138

Amelio, Gianni, 151

anachronisms, 15, 53, 77

anal sex, 21, 23, 32, 37, 138

Anatolia, 53

ancient Greece, 22, 24, 25, 29, 103, 111

Andrei Rublev (1966), 59

Angelo (character), 46

annals (narrative form), 59, 61

Annovi, Gian Maria, 99, 100–101, 148, 149–50

Another Country (novel), 49, 141

anthropology, 99

Antigone (character), 43, 110

antirelationality. See negativity

antirelational school. See negativity

Antonio das Mortes. See Dragão da Maldade contra o Santo Guerreiro, O

Antonioni, Michelangelo, 9, 116, 135, 141

Apollo (character), 98

apparatus, 49, 91, 112

Appunti per un film sull'India (1968), 148

Appunti per un'Orestiade africana (1970/1973/1975), 17, 97, 98–115, 116–18, 150

Appunti per un poema sul Terzo Mondo (uncompleted film series), 118

Apsirto (character), 65, 68–72, 74–76, 78, 80, 89, 144, 145

Apsyrtus (character). *See* Apsirto

Arabia, 24, 108

Arabian Nights (1974). See *fiore delle mille e una note, Il*

archaic, the, 3–5, 17, 24, 26, 29, 59, 61, 74, 77, 93, 115, 134

archaic cinema, 29, 48, 76, 90, 93

archaic consciousness, 3–4, 52, 98

archaic culture, 75, 78

Archaic Greece, 4–5

Archaic Mesoamerica, 4

archaic modernism, 3, 6, 7, 17, 18, 24, 58–59, 75, 76, 90, 104, 114

archaic past, 95, 115

archaic queerness, 61, 80

Archaic School (film movement), 77–78

archaic worldview. *See* archaic consciousness

Argonauts, 60, 73–74, 79, 81, 84

Argos, 79

aristocratic cinema. *See* unconsumable films

art cinema, 2, 5, 8, 48, 51, 53, 117

Asti, Adriana, 9

Athamas. *See* Orchomenus

Athena, 98

Athens, 4, 37, 96, 98, 110–12

Austin, J. L., 135

authorship, 56–57

Autocritique (book). *See* Morin, Edgar

autocritique (concept), 14, 75, 102, 104–5, 108

avventura, L' (1960), 9, 116

Bacon, Francis, 5

Bafrian War. *See* Nigerian Civil War

Baldwin, James, 48–49, 141

Barbieri, Gato, 147

Barthes, Roland: "Death of the Author," 57; "Leaving the Movie Theater," 49–51, 58, 64, 76, 87, 94; "Pleasure of the Text," 64

New Historicism, 136
New Pathways. See Vie nuove
New Queer Cinema, 6, 134
Newsweek, 53
New York, 118, 134, 142
New York University, 135
Nigerian-Bafrian War. *See* Nigerian Civil War
Nigerian Civil War, 97, 109–10
Night, The (1961). See *notte, La*
Nights of Cabiria, The. See notti di Cabiria, Le
1900. See Novecento
Notes for an African Oresteia. See Appunti per un'Orestiade africana
Notes for an African Orestes. See Appunti per un'Orestiade africana
Notes for a poem on the Third World. See Appunti per un poema sul Terzo Mondo
Notes towards an African Orestes. See Appunti per un'Orestiade africana
notte, La (1961), 9, 116
notti di Cabiria, Le (1957), 141
Novecento (1976), 9, 118
Nowell-Smith, Geoffrey, 76, 145

obscenity (legal charge) 56
Odyssey, The, 98
Oedipus: character 5, 14, 23–25, 28–47, 121, 139–40; feet, 30–31; meaning of name, 30, 139; mythology, 5, 14, 19, 24, 26–28, 31–32, 36, 44, 47, 70
Oedipus at Colonus (play), 47
Oedipus complex. *See* Freud, Sigmund
Oedipus Rex (1967). See *Edipo re*
Oedipus Rex (play), 20, 23–24, 26, 28, 117, 140, 148
Oedipus the King (1968), 116, 151
Oeler, Karla, 77
Oidipodeia, The (lost poem), 139–40
120 journées de Sodome, Les (novel), 16
Orchomenus (character), 62
Oresteia, The (trilogy of plays), 97–98, 100, 133, 148
Orestes (character), 5, 14, 98, 109–10, 112, 133, 148, 149
Orgia (play), 100, 151
Orientalism (book), 108
Orientalism (concept), 14, 100, 102–6, 108–9, 133, 136
Orientalismo eretico: Pasolini e il cinema de Terzo Mondo, 133

Oscar nominations, 53
Osias, John 81
Oxford English Dictionary Online, 6–7
Ozu, Yasujirō, 25

Palmer, Lilli, 116
pansexual, 42
Parajanov, Sergei, 77, 146
Parker, Andrew, 135
Pasolini e il cinema: Il progetto di una teoria semiotica in "Empirismo eretico," 133
Pasolini e l'Africa, l'Africa di Pasolini: Panmeridionalismo e rappresentazioni dell'Africa postcoloniale, 133
Pasolini, Pier Paolo: "The 'Cinema of Poetry,'" 2–3, 8–9, 11, 48, 55, 57, 58, 90; Communism, 133–34; "Confessioni tecniche," 1–2, 3; criminal conviction, 133; "Repudiation of the Trilogy of Life," 152; self–martyrdom/suicidal impulses, 56–58, 62, 80, 119–20; sexual desire for father and brother, 28; sexuality, 34, 42, 55; "The Unpopular Cinema," 56–58; voice, 98, 99, 149; "The Written Language of Reality," 136
Pasolini, Susanna, 42
passion, En (1969), 148
Passion of Anna, The. See passion, En
Patriarchy, 94
PCF (*Parti communiste français*). *See* Communist Party (France)
Pelais (character), 73, 83, 95
Pelops (character), 28, 39–40
performative speech acts, 135
Persia, 108
Persian War (fifth century BCE), 4
Persona (1966), 148
perversion, 49
Pesaro, 2
phallocentrism, 37
phallogocentrism, 7
phonocentrism, 12
Pier Paolo Pasolini: Image, Object, Sound (conference), 135
Pilade (play), 100
Pinkerton, Nick, 141
Plato, 43
Platt-Lynes, George, 101
Plummer, Christopher, 116
polysexual, 42
popular films, 54

ABOUT THE AUTHOR

Daniel Humphrey is associate professor of film studies and women's and gender studies as well as the coordinator of the film studies program at Texas A&M University. He is the author of *Queer Bergman: Sexuality, Gender, and the European Art Cinema* and articles in *Criticism, Screen, GLQ, Post Script, Invisible Culture,* and elsewhere. His research interests include queer theory, feminist theory, European art cinema, the culture and politics of the "New Left," American independent cinema, and the horror genre.

CPSIA information can be obtained
at www.ICGtesting.com
Printed in the USA
FSHW011915230820
73203FS